THE RELIGIONS OF MANKIND

THE
RELIGIONS
OF
MANKIND

Edmund Davison Soper

Third Edition, Revised

ABINGDON-COKESBURY PRESS
New York   •   Nashville

THE RELIGIONS OF MANKIND

SET UP, PRINTED, AND BOUND BY THE PARTHENON PRESS, AT NASHVILLE, TENNESSEE, UNITED STATES OF AMERICA

TO THE MEMORY OF
MY MOTHER

PREFACE

THIS IS A NEW EDITION, SOMEWHAT REARRANGED AND TO A CONSIDERABLE extent rewritten, of a book that has been in use since 1921. Although it was thoroughly revised in 1938, since that time events have taken place which make another complete revision imperative. The most important of these have been World War II and its aftermath, which have shaken every land and its people and deeply affected every phase of their life. All the religions of the world have been compelled to adjust themselves to a new situation, and in a number of cases to reinterpret their history, teachings, and practice.

In addition it has been my high privilege to spend the past two years in India. Having retired from my professorship in Garrett Biblical Institute in 1948, I have been visiting professor of the history of religion in Leonard Theological College, a union institution training men and women for the ministry and other forms of Christian work. This experience has made it possible, by renewed study and direct contact, to view the religious situation from a favorable angle and in a new light. This has occurred just at the time when every religion is under the exhilarating spell of the newly achieved Indian independence and is asserting itself to make its position more plausible and to win the approval of Young India, eagerly in search of a satisfying philosophy of life. The result has been a deeper appreciation of the seriousness and complexity of the problem of belief and practice in a land so profoundly religious as India.

Attention could not help being directed to the shock of the war and the revolutionary political and social changes which have affected the Islamic world as well as China and Japan, not to speak of South Africa and all the countries of the West. Especial attention has been given to the reinterpretation of the life and work of Confucius, which has come

7

about through the combined work of Chinese and Western scholars. Attention may also be called to the work of a small group of scholars in bringing to light aspects of Japanese Buddhism, particularly with reference to the important Zen sect, hitherto unavailable to Western readers.

Not only has the entire text of the book been overhauled, but a certain amount of adjustment and rearrangement has been made. The two introductory chapters have been combined in one, as was the case in the first edition. Most of the contents of the former chapter on Zoroastrianism have found a place in a new chapter dealing with the religion of the Jains and the Sikhs as well as that of the Parsis. No one can be long in India without realizing the significance of these religions in the history and present life of the people.

The volume has not been enlarged despite the great amount of important new material available. From the beginning this work has done service widely as a text in colleges and seminaries, so it has been felt that it must be kept down to a size which will continue to make it available for for students who may thus have their introduction to the religions of mankind.

The work of revising and typing could not have been accomplished had it not been for the courtesy and sympathetic co-operation of Dr. Marvin H. Harper, principal of Leonard Theological College, nor without the skill and patience of his secretary, Mrs. Ivy Moulton, who unraveled the jungle of a much revised, crossed-out, and rewritten copy and did it with amazing accuracy. My unbounded gratitude is theirs.

Edmund D. Soper

CONTENTS

CHAPTER V

THE RELIGIONS OF INDIA: HINDUISM

CHAPTER VI

THE RELIGIONS OF INDIA: JAINISM, SIKHISM, PARSIISM

christian

CHAPTER VII

BUDDHISM

CHAPTER VIII

THE RELIGION OF CHINA

CONTENTS

CHAPTER IX

THE RELIGIONS OF JAPAN

CHAPTER X

JUDAISM

CHAPTER XI

MOHAMMEDANISM

CHAPTER XII

CHRISTIANITY

CHAPTER I

THE STUDY OF RELIGION

The Nature of Religion

Religion is as old as human nature and as ineradicable as the sense of right and wrong. But only after religion had passed through many stages of development did anyone attempt to define it. Cicero was one of the first, and his statement was the simple one that religion was the worship of the gods. He is also responsible for connecting the word "religion" with the Latin *relegere*, which means "to read over again," a derivation not accepted by later writers, who favor *religare*, "to bind." While the latter etymology is generally accepted today, it is still doubtful, and even if it were made certain by further investigation, it would not be of much practical assistance in reaching a satisfactory definition. The late Dr. W. Warde Fowler, of Oxford, shows at length[1] that the Latin word *religio* had a growth during the long period from the days of early Rome to the time when it was introduced into the vocabulary of the Christian Church and made to carry the full treasure of meaning which the new religion had brought into it. The particular connotation at any time of such a word as "religion" is more important than its etymological derivation.

Is a definition of religion possible? An extreme view is taken by Professor C. C. J. Webb, who declares that "a definition of religion is needless and impossible."[2] If we judge by the almost universal practice of writers on religion, very few seem to have been carried by Professor Webb's drastic statement. We would be tempted to say that a definition of religion is greatly needed and is not impossible. The purpose of such

[1] *The Religious Experience of the Roman People*, pp. 459-62.
[2] *Group Theories of Religion and the Individual*, p. 37. I am indebted for a number of the following definitions to a list of definitions of religion compiled by the late Professor Robert E. Hume, of Union Theological Seminary.

13

a definition is to provide a basis of identification. How is the student to know in the welter of impressions which comes in upon him what is religious and what is not? A definition should enable him to detect religion and disentangle it from what is not religion though very similar and closely connected with it. Religion doubtless is much more than is embodied in a definition, but it is at least that. We may be treading on safe ground and feel sure we have a dependable clue.

The assumption of everyone is likely to be that he knows what religion is, that is, until he makes the attempt to put down exactly what is in his mind. Then it becomes apparent that his ideas are hazy and ill-defined, and that too much had been taken for granted in his assumption of knowledge. One's own viewpoint so affects his outlook that the danger always is that he will take what religion means to him, put it into a statement, and call that religion. We have a religion, but so has the Zulu, and any definition worthy the name must be sufficiently inclusive to serve in any land and among any people. Religions differ greatly, but there must be some element or elements which all the religions have in common, or no definition is possible. The common element or elements must be distinctive of religion, so that we may be able to trace the development of this one thing through the maze of the forms it has assumed.

A few definitions roundly disparage religion. Salomon Reinach writes thus: "I propose to define religion as: A sum of scruples which impede the free exercise of our faculties." [3] One more may be given, that of Giuseppe Sergi: "Religion is a pathological manifestation of the protective function, a sort of deviation of the normal function, a deviation caused by ignorance of natural causes and their effects." [4] These definitions lack the fundamental requirement of a definition. They are out of sympathy with religion, however it may be defined. They do not spring from any real insight into the meaning of what they are attempting to define. Such insight can come only as a result of sympathetic investigation of religious beliefs and practices, and this is sadly lacking in the case of these scholars. A student must understand before he defines, and to understand religion he must view it from within, feeling at home amid the factors which make up the complex thing we know by that name.

Not far removed from this completely negative attitude is that which was held by the English Deists of the eighteenth century. To these skep-

[3] *Orpheus: A General History of Religions* (English trans.), p. 3.
[4] *Les Emotions*, p. 404.

14

tical writers religion had but little value in its own right. Its main object was to bolster up morality, to help keep people decent and respectable. Society is looked upon as a great police organization. All religious and civil authority springs from fear and is necessary in order to keep men subservient and within bounds. It is quite evident that these men had no adequate appreciation of religion. While they had high regard for decent living, they had never heard the thunders of Sinai. Had they done so, they might have had a more profound conception of the very morality which they professed to admire so highly. They never realized that righteousness has its source in the inmost nature of God himself. Such a view would have saved them from superficiality and would have raised religion to its rightful place of primacy. They did well to set morality and religion in the closest relationship, but by failing to appreciate the nature of the bond they placed religion where its chief work could not be accomplished and did violence to the morality which they were so concerned to maintain.

Turning now to definitions of men who have shown high regard for religion, we may expect a very different type of definition. There are those definitions which restrict religion to one function of the human mind. Such is that of Hegel, who makes religion a matter of the intellect. One of his statements is this: "Thus religion is the Divine Spirit's knowledge of itself through the mediation of finite spirit." Leaving aside the monistic implication in this definition as irrelevant to our immediate interest, it is clear that religion was to Hegel purely a matter of thought. Others in a later day have to a greater or less degree followed in the same direction. Max Müller makes religion "a mental faculty or disposition, which, independent of—nay, in spite of—sense and reason, enables man to apprehend the infinite under different names and under varying guises." [5] This was later modified: "Religion consists in the perception of the Infinite under such manifestations as are able to influence the moral character of man." [6] But in both cases the emphasis is intellectual, in spite of the necessity which caused Professor Müller in the second to incorporate the moral implication of religion as a part of his definition.

Religion has been defined in terms of the emotions. One of the most famous of all definitions is that of Schleiermacher: "The essence of the religious emotions consists in the feeling of an absolute dependence." [7]

[5] *Introduction to Science of Religion*, p. 17.
[6] *The Origin of Religion*, p. 21.
[7] *On Religion*, p. 106.

While this may be one-sided, the emphasis placed upon the emotional factor in religion has deeply influenced subsequent attempts. In the present day Professor John McTaggart has a definition with a similar emphasis: "It seems to me that religion may best be described as an emotion, resting on a conviction of a harmony between ourselves and the universe at large." [8] While it rests on a conviction, religion is "described as an emotion." The emphasis is the same as that of Schleiermacher. And finally, religion has been defined as a matter of the will, or the fulfillment of moral obligation. Kant stands first here with his declaration that "religion is the recognition of all duties as divine commands," and Matthew Arnold may be said to emphasize the same side of religion in his well-known word, "Religion is morality touched by emotion." [9]

In all of these cases we would be doing an injustice to insist that no place was given in religion to the other faculties of the human mind, but the emphasis clearly has been as indicated in the quotations. The difficulty is that the emphasis is placed so strongly on one or another of the factors that religion becomes less comprehensive than it actually is. Religion is coming more and more to be recognized as all-embracive, as functioning in every department of human life, as involving the intellect, the emotions, and the will if it is normal and true to type. So while all these definitions are true as far as they go, and have been widely influential in subsequent studies, they are nevertheless partial and incomplete.

Another set of definitions—and these are the product of recent years—divide on the question of the individual as contrasted with the social emphasis in religion. The following statements are both from psychologists. The first is from William James: "Religion, therefore, as I now ask you arbitrarily to take it, shall mean for us the feelings, acts, and experiences of individual men in their solitude, as far as they apprehend themselves to stand in relation to whatever they may consider the divine." [10] A more recent definition, coming from A. N. Whitehead, is even more sharply individualistic:

Religion is the art and the theory of the internal life of man, so far as it depends on the man himself and on what is permanent in the nature of things. This doctrine is the direct negation of the theory that religion is

[8] *Some Dogmas of Religion*, p. 3.
[9] *Literature and Dogma*, p. 46.
[10] *The Varieties of Religious Experience*, p. 31.

16

primarily a social fact. . . . But all collective emotions leave untouched the awful ultimate fact, which is the human being, consciously alone with itself, for its own sake. Religion is what the individual does with his own solitariness. . . . Thus religion is solitariness; and if you are never solitary, you are never religious.[11]

The other side is presented by Professor A. C. Watson, who defines religion as "a social attitude toward the nonhuman environment." [12] Both of these types of definition emphasize an important factor in religion, but must we not see that religion is both individual and social? The danger lies in laying such exclusive emphasis on one or the other of these factors that no standing room seems left for the other. Religion is individual in that for each man his religious experience is his own. He has a vertical relationship which is between himself and the higher powers on whom he believes, but James goes too far when he speaks of the religion of "individual men in their solitude," for a man's religion is so far determined by his lateral relationships in society that what he has is not his alone, nor did it come to him in solitude. Religion does undoubtedly conserve social values, and it is most fortunate that this feature of religious life has been emphasized. Professor J. B. Pratt suggests very happily that "the inborn nature of the individual determines what might be called the *form* of his religious life. The *matter* is chiefly the contribution of society." [13] The social aspects fill the horizon in the earlier stages of development, when man as an individual can scarcely be said to exist, but gradually, as personality develops and each man begins to stand out in his separate individuality, a consciousness of a certain uniqueness comes over him, and he realizes that while he belongs to society he is separate and detached from others in his own individuality and in his relation to the powers on whom he is dependent.

There are those who define religion in terms of worship. Professor Allan Menzies states it thus: "Religion is the worship of higher powers from a sense of need." [14] Professor A. S. Geden comes to this conclusion: "On the whole, then, it would seem that the essential quality or nature of religion is best described as consisting in worship." [15] One other, the

[11] *Religion in the Making*, pp. 16-17.
[12] Quoted by Professor W. K. Wright, *A Student's Philosophy of Religion* (rev. ed.), p. 528.
[13] *The Religious Consciousness*, p. 74.
[14] *History of Religion*, p. 13.
[15] *Studies in the Religions of the East*, p. 53.

17

striking statement of Professor Auguste Sabatier, may be given: "Prayer is religion in act—that is to say, real religion." [16] In these cases, as the context shows, worship is broadened out to become the expression of the total attitude of man, in the fullness of his life, toward his God. Yet, ordinarily speaking, religion is more than worship. The attitude of the worshiper must include more than the worship itself, or else his religion is restricted and incomplete. Yet the central act of religion is worship, and religion would die without it, so an adequate definition must provide for this relation toward the higher powers or be found wanting.

In our own day a class of definitions is being presented with no necessary reference to higher powers or to God. The classic statement, and that which has largely influenced others of the class, is that of Professor Harald Höffding: "The conservation of value is the characteristic axiom of religion." [17] Professor E. S. Ames has a definition very similar: "Religion is the consciousness of the highest social values." [18] These definitions run counter to those we have been considering in that religion is defined with no reference to any higher power. The question which is raised is this: Is the distinguishing thing in religion something subjective, or is it objective? Is the difference between religions one growing out of differences in what religion is thought to contribute to men or of differences in the object of religious worship and adoration? To put it in other words: Must a man believe in God or some higher power to be religious, or can he be religious with no reference to divine powers of any kind?

A definition has been offered by Professor W. K. Wright which combines both the subjective and objective factors: "Religion is the endeavor to secure the conservation of socially recognized values through specific actions that are believed to evoke some agency different from the ordinary ego of the individual, or from other merely human beings, and that imply a feeling of dependence upon that agency." [19] Here Professor Wright asserts that the conservation of values is essential to religion, but also just as clearly that there must also be "some agency" other than human on which man must feel his dependence.

Values always form a most important element in religion. Men want something which has value for them. If it did not have value, they would not pursue nor desire it. There are satisfactions of various kinds which are

[16] *Philosophy of Religion*, p. 27.
[17] *Philosophy of Religion*, p. 10.
[18] *Psychology of Religious Experience*, p. vii.
[19] *A Student's Philosophy of Religion* (rev. ed.), p. 47.

craved, and these desires form the dynamic of religion as of other human activities. But the question arises: Is the conservation of these values the inner core of religion? True, it is the inevitable accompaniment of religion, but is it the differentia of religion? There are certain desires which men have, desires emotional and intellectual, individual and social. Now, if religion is the conservation of values with no necessary reference to man's attempt to secure this conservation through his relationship to higher powers, religion may be defined without any reference to anything supernatural. That is incidental, even though it may be frequent and even almost inevitable. God or some other higher power remains only a means to an end, and the end which is sought is the reality in religion.

But it is possible to go further. Man is after all sorts of things—material, physical, social, moral, and spiritual. He tries every means at his disposal to find peace and satisfaction, and among them is a certain conscious relation with unseen higher powers. This relationship, purified and developed, becomes the chief glory of his life, raising him to a new dignity, bringing peace and unity to his troubled mind, and taking its place as the inspiring center of his whole life. He is suffused with a glory unknown to him before, and to know God is the supreme desire and chief end of his existence. At all stages it does conserve values, but so do many other things which could never be called religion. This one relationship is unique: it makes its contribution to life as do the other factors, but it is to be distinguished by a content which places it in a class by itself. The desire to conserve values is the soil out of which religion springs, and the conservation itself the end which religion seeks, but neither is to be confused with the thing itself, which is a relation of men to powers higher than themselves.

What, then, is religion? We have seen that religion consists of a number of elements. It makes a demand on the whole of man's life, intellect, emotion, and will; it is both individual and social; it is worship, yet it is more than worship; it conserves all the values which give worth and meaning to human life. But at its core religion is always a relationship, a conscious relation of human beings and God or higher powers, however they may be conceived. The definition which includes all these features as successfully as any is that of Léonce de Grandmaison: "Religion is the sum total of beliefs, sentiments, and practices, individual and social, which have for their object a power which man recognizes as supreme, on which he depends and with which he can enter (or has entered) into relation." [20] A very convenient form of statement is that given by Professor William Newton Clarke, "Religion is the life of man in his superhuman relations." [21]

THE ORIGIN OF RELIGION

In 1865 Sir John Lubbock, in his volume *Pre-historic Times*, attempted to show that religion was not universal, that there were tribes of men scattered fairly widely over the earth which had no religion, no worship, no belief in higher powers with whom they were related. Professor Robert Flint felt it necessary in his Baird Lecture for 1877, *Anti-Theistic Theories*, to answer Sir John Lubbock at length. The interesting thing is that the answer followed the same method as the argument it was answering. In each case reports from travelers and others were studied and criticized to determine as nearly as possible what the actual condition of the tribes under scrutiny indicated. The conclusion reached by Professor Flint was this: "An impartial examination of the relevant facts, it appears to me, shows that religion is virtually universal." [22]

Such a claim as that of Sir John Lubbock is no longer made. Not only has the more careful study of savages led to a deeper understanding of their life, but psychology has been developing as a science by leaps and bounds and has made almost unnecessary any further investigation among savages themselves to determine the fundamental question of the essential religious nature of man. But even before this development had not more than begun, Professor Flint had sensed the conclusions reached by psychology in a more recent time and declared that "the world has been so framed, and the mind so constituted, that man, even in his lowest estate, and all over the world, gives evidence of possessing religious perceptions and emotions." [23] We are dealing, then, with a normal factor in human life—religion in one form or another is universal.

It is the origin of religion that we are now to investigate. The immediate impulse is to go back in history to the beginnings and there make a study of man in the process of becoming religious. There must have been a time when man had no religion but was developing into a religious being. But we have no way of knowing when and how that took place. Go back as far as history extends, and man is religious. The same evidence

[20] *The History of Religion*, I, 5.
[21] *An Outline of Christian Theology*, p. 1.
[22] P. 288.
[23] *Ibid.*

20

is forthcoming when archaeology is called upon for its testimony. The prehistoric remains in Europe and elsewhere, as far as they prove anything, show man possessed of certain ideas and performing acts which give strong evidence of his being religious. If, then, we are to know anything about the origin of religion—for it surely must have had an origin—we are compelled to go elsewhere for the help we need.

The only other course open is the appeal to psychology, both individual and social. This means that we must seek to find what in man this thing called religion is genetically, what it is which always develops in this way no matter where man is found, and what relation it has to the social organization of the group to which he belongs. It is hard to know what to call it psychologically. Not an instinct surely, when one realizes the meaning of the instinctive life as now given by psychological analysis and experiment. According to Alexander Bain an instinct is "that untaught ability to perform actions." [24] Religion is not as simple as that; it is more complex, the reaction resulting from the combined action of the more fundamental features of the mental life. But this is not to say that religion is not deeply rooted in human nature. As G. A. Coe states it: "This way of organizing experience in terms of ideal values is a first item in the religious nature of man. It is present in all normal individuals, and is a type toward which freedom, popular education, and democracy tend." [25] We may not be able to arrive at a term more definite than that just used, "the religious nature of man," but the fact to be emphasized is that the organizing of experience into what we call religion is the normal thing in the life of a human being.

A very old theory of the origin of religion is that of Lucretius, who in a famous statement ascribed the origin of religion to a sense of fear. But it was not only in ancient times that fear was made responsible for the origin of religion. In very recent years it has been receiving a new emphasis. In a popular volume, *This Believing World*, Lewis Brown begins his first chapter thus: "In the beginning there was fear; and fear was in the heart of man; and fear controlled man." [26] He has been rightly charged with the error of oversimplification, but that should not blind us to the full recognition of the influence of fear in religion. It has been tremendous. Not only in times past but even today and in the most advanced religions it wields its sway and destroys the peace

[24] Quoted by James Ward, *Psychological Principles*, p. 53.
[25] *Psychology of Religion*, p. 324.
[26] P. 27.

21

and distorts the vision of men and women who should have the experience which casts out fear. A far more scholarly and profound discussion is to be found in Paul Radin's volume *Primitive Religion: Its Nature and Origin*. He makes the strong statement, "With fear man was born." [27] This fear, however, was not just a vague "being afraid in the dark"; "rather it was the fear inspired by a specific economic situation." Much emphasis is laid by this writer on the economic insecurity of primitive man. We cannot account for the rise and early development of religion without making fear a significant ingredient in the complex process. But to make fear and fear alone responsible for religion is to exclude other factors which must not be left out. No single cause can be assigned as the originating principle of so all-embracing an experience as religion. Professor George Foot Moore goes a step further and makes the statement: "If we seek a motive, universal, supreme, perpetual, it will be found in the impulse to self-preservation." [28] This helps to answer the quetsion, Why do men fear? They are afraid of being harmed or destroyed, and they desire self-preservation more than anything else.

Until the time of the English Deists in the eighteenth century, Christians, Jews, and Mohammedans alike assumed a primitive divine revelation, and that settled the whole question. They conceived that in the beginning—that means when the first man was created and placed in the Garden of Eden—God revealed to him in some manner the essential truths of religion, such as the existence of one God, the obligation to obey him, and the hope of immortality. Thus furnished, he began his career; but when sin emerged, the revelation became hazy and indistinct and finally was well-nigh obliterated. The difficulty with this picture of the origin of religion is that it rests on no solid foundation of fact. The Bible makes no clear statement which would lead to this conclusion. When man began to play his part in the biblical narrative, he performed religious acts and felt that he stood in the presence of God his Creator—so much is evident, but nothing is said as to origins. The easy way in which Christian thinkers accounted for the non-Christian religions was to refer them to the devil as their author. This was a simple solution of a difficult problem, and it carried the Christian Church until within the last century or two, but it is too simple to be convincing and betrays an ignorance so profound that it is hard to be patient with it today.

[27] P. 7.
[28] *The Birth and Growth of Religion*, pp. 3-4.

22

Toward the end of the last century Professor Andrew Lang wrote a volume entitled *The Making of Religion*, whose third edition was published in 1909. His purpose was to bring out into clear light the presence among primitive peoples of the belief in All-fathers or "High Gods." Every volume now coming from the press finds it necessary to devote attention to this theory. It has gained momentum in recent years by the elaborate researches of Father Wilhelm Schmidt, of the University of Vienna, and others. What is his claim? Very simply it is that these All-fathers, or "High Gods," not only are to be found very widely distributed but are the remnant of an original primitive revelation made by God to the progenitors of the race and handed down without break since that day. It is "the original belief of the human race as a whole." All other lesser conceptions of higher powers are evidences of degeneracy, of a fall from sublime heights to low and unworthy beliefs. It is a simple theory; can it be accepted? That there is no longer a question of the existence of these high deities in primitive religion is now admitted by every writer on the subject. Nor is the attempt any longer made to explain the presence of this conception in the minds of primitive peoples by missionary influence. The idea is too widespread and too deeply rooted in the thinking of these peoples to be accounted for in this way.

Scholars have not generally been carried by Father Schmidt's argument. Such an anthropologist as Professor Paul Radin has no hesitation in accepting these divine beings in primitive religion. His theory is that here are to be found in primitive society exceptional men who are leaders in thought and are quite capable of conceiving the idea of great gods as well as of little, insignificant spirits. But that is very far from leaping to the conclusion that these divine beings were in the minds of men at the very beginning and that they were the result of a special divine revelation. Professor E. O. James says that this theory "raises more problems for the theologians than it solves, and it is certainly to go beyond the legitimate limits of anthropological evidence." [29]

The Deists had their own notion of the rise of religion. They were willing not only to allow that man might have had an original endowment of religious ideas, but they had the matter quite thoroughly worked out. One of their number, Herbert of Cherbury, claimed that this original endowment consisted of five things: (1) belief in the existence of God, (2) the duty of man to worship God, (3) virtue and piety as the chief

---

[29] Quoted by Oesterly and Robinson in *Hebrew Religion: Its Origin and Development*, 2nd ed., p. 5.

elements in worship, (4) the necessity of repentance and amendment, and (5) a future world of rewards and punishments. Man would have been all right had he retained the simplicity of his original belief, but this was not to be. A class of men arose who came to be known as priests. They found they could work upon the fears and credulity of men and by so doing gain advantage for themselves. In order to fasten their grip upon men they devised beliefs and ritual practices which worked upon their superstitious fears and gave the priesthood a hold like bands of iron. This, then, explains the origin of the religions which have grown up among men. No one would be foolhardy enough now to propound such a theory. It is too superficial and shows ignorance of the true nature of religion and its deep foundations in human life.

We may approach more recent theories by way of that enunciated by Professor E. B. Tylor in his epoch-making volumes on *Primitive Culture*. It is called the animistic theory, that is, early man attributed life to nature and the objects around him. He looked upon the world around him as animated, as possessing a spirit like his own. He did this by the only instrument of reason he had to explain what he saw and heard and felt. It was the principle of analogy, according to which all he saw was explained by reference to his own experience. If he saw a tree bend under the wind, he could explain it only by thinking that he too could blow, and thus in a lesser but similar fashion do what he saw happening in nature. He could blow, and so there must be some invisible but very big somebody out there who was blowing very hard and causing the trees of the forest to bend and groan in the gale. To him somebody more or less like himself was accountable for everything that happened. He carried this idea to such lengths that the very existence of a separate thing, even a dead thing like a stone, might be explained on the basis of an inner spirit which was its life. Thus all nature became alive, filled with innumerable spirits everywhere and in everything. There was to early man and there is to the savage today no such thing as inanimate nature. It was all alive and throbbing with a life like his own.

Coming to the point which concerns us immediately, Professor Tylor held that religion had its origin in the relationship which man established with certain of the spirits of his animism. This theory has been criticized by Professor R. R. Marett in his book *The Threshold of Religion*. He agrees with Professor Tylor in his general decision that primitive man came finally to an animistic conclusion, but he feels that the finished animism of Professor Tylor gives evidence of considerable de-

24

velopment in early man. According to Professor Tylor's theory, man attributed a definite, distinct spirit to the objects of nature, to each tree and mountain and spring in his vicinity. But, says Professor Marett, how could man thus attribute a spirit to what he saw when his own spirit life was so uncertain? Early man's thinking was confused and indistinct because, in the nature of the case, he was not capable of anything more. In this condition it takes far too much for granted to believe the savage capable of distinguishing distinct spirits in the nature which surrounded him. What Professor Marett feels is that to primitive man nature was characterized by a kind of aliveness just as he was conscious of a certain aliveness in himself. Now, even in this early stage religion had its beginnings; man did not have to wait until he could attribute a separate spirit to each object of nature in order to have a religion. So we have what may be called preanimistic religion, or "animatism," thus leaving the designation "animism" for the developed belief in spirits. So this general aliveness later developed into the definite personification of the objects of nature, but the process has been completed long since; no savages are now to be found in the preanimistic stage.

A further development of the theory just stated is that of Herbert Spencer. He accepted the animistic explanation of primitive thinking but emphasized that aspect which deals with the spirits of the dead. As far back as we can penetrate, man is seen offering sacrifices to the spirits of his departed ancestors, and this Herbert Spencer believed was the earliest form of religion. Ancestors, then, were the first beings worshiped. Even the more inclusive worship of the objects of nature around him came after the worship offered to those who had died and as ghosts continued their existence not very far away. The criticism to be made here is that one aspect of primitive religion can scarcely be made to account for the origin of religion any more than some other aspects which have been mentioned.

It will be apparent that man has a certain capacity for religion which is his normally, simply because he is a man. Man has a bent in the direction of religion which needs only the proper stimulus to become religion in one of its many recognizable forms. An inner response to an influence from without is the only way to account for religion in the life of man; and both factors, the subjective and the objective, are necessary to account for the final product. What is that influence from without to which the mind of man responds? We are aware that man is affected by many influences from outside himself: the total impress of

25

nature, his environment, the outside world, the society of which he is a part, and the unseen, mysterious world which surrounds him. The points of contact are without number, and through every one come pouring in all kinds of stimuli. Most of these contacts have no particular religious significance, but some affect him as so strange, so mysterious, so awesome that he trembles when he is in their presence. This sense of mystery and awe in the presence of what he conceives as higher powers coupled with a deep dissatisfaction with his condition, which urged him on to secure what he did not have—this must be the beginning of religion.

When one believes that God has been revealing himself to man in many forms and at all periods in the long story of life, it is possible to take one further step. We are told that there is a light which lighteth every man coming into the world, and that there is an inner law in the breasts of men which acts as a monitor over their thoughts and deeds. We may not believe in a primitive revelation in the sense that it consisted of a number of religious ideas placed in the mind of primitive man, but it is a very different matter to believe that man's religious nature, his religious proclivity, is the gift of God, a part of his original endowment, without which, whatever nature or society might have done, religion would never have become a feature of his life.

The Development of Religion

Two results of our study are doubtless already apparent. One is that religion is always a relationship between man and higher powers. The other is that all religions hark back to primitive forms and are developments from these simple beginnings. This introduces us at once to our present subject, the development of religion.

The first question is, What is the key to this development? Or, What causes a religion to develop into something more complex and sublime? The clue to this question has already been found in the discussion of the origin of religion, where it was seen that without a conscious sense of need man would never have possessed a religion at all. The same causes which led to the first beginnings of religion undoubtedly are the explanation of its development. We may say, then, that the development of religion follows and is determined by a sense of need. When needs are simple and crude, the religion partakes of the same simplicity and crudity; when needs become more extensive and refined, religion changes to meet the new and enlarging needs. We may be sure of this because no savage people have ever been found with a highly developed religion. The religion they possess is suited to their needs and is on the level of their advancement in culture. Intelligent people demand a religion suited to their outlook on life, or else the religion will be discarded. If it is not able by reinterpretation or the assimilation of new elements, borrowed or discovered by some farsighted prophet, to meet the newer needs, it is laid aside for other forms or for another religion which promises to fit in better with the advance in civilization. In every period of transition from an old order which has become outworn to a new order as yet untried this process has gone on. Some religions have ceased to exist and have been replaced by new religions which interpret better than the old the aspirations of the people as they look forward with hope to a better day. In other cases religions have shown a remarkable capacity of adaptation and have continued to live and thrive until our own time.

There is no more significant or interesting feature of the study of the religions of the world than this ability to adapt. Certain well-marked periods of crisis are to be discovered in the story of every civilized or even semicivilized people, and it is just at these crucial turning points when, after religion has remained stationary, sometimes for a long period, a new life can be discovered stirring among men, and the result is the ushering in of a new age. Just at the present time the religions of the world are passing through such a crisis. The invasion of the Orient by ideas entirely strange, the well-nigh complete acceptance of Western education, and the contact with the moral and religious ideas of Christendom have created an unprecedented situation involving a crisis in the moral ideals and religious beliefs of all the peoples who have come under their influence.

One of the questions raised by such considerations concerns the strange inequality in development. While no people have been discovered who have failed to show some evidence of advance, that advance in many cases is so slight that, compared with the great religious systems of the world, it is very sluggish and almost stagnant. The question arises, Why should one religion have advanced and others remained almost in their primitive stage? Why should one people have developed needs and others not? Again, Why should a people remain savage for untold ages, then suddenly begin the march forward? What makes the difference between peoples? Is it racial precocity? Is it outward stimulus? Is it economic, or

27

social, or political? No final answer has been found to these and similar questions.[30]

We may say at once that the growth of anything so complex as religion cannot be accounted for by any single cause. Religion must develop through the interaction of many elements, each complex in itself. In the first place, while the general trend is toward progress, there come periods of retrogression, of degeneracy, when the advance made seems in danger of being lost. This phenomenon is to be found in many places and makes it very difficult to speak of the whole movement as an evolution— if by that term is meant steady advance out of lower forms into higher. Development for man, individual and social, is, as Professor George Galloway points out, a vocation.[31] He may not be able to secure what he wants, and his choices may be circumscribed by his outlook and his environment, but—and this is the important point—he must assert himself or nothing happens.

There is, however, another side to this problem of religious development which is even more significant. Does the whole burden of development rest on man alone? Is he the only one concerned in his advance toward a more satisfying life? All the religions have a very definite answer to this question—a decided negative. All believe that in one way or another God has been seeking to make his will known to man. Thus the course of the history of religion is from this standpoint the progressive revelation of God to men, a revelation disclosed as rapidly as men were able to receive it. There is, then, a divine pedagogy, God in his gracious purpose meeting man with his needs and giving him that which leads him into fuller life. It is a gradual process, but man is not alone in its realization. God himself is seen giving himself in ever fuller measure until, in the Christian revelation, we see him as he is in the face of Jesus Christ.

If the development of religion proceeds along with and is demanded by the enlarging needs of man, it must be at once evident that the stages in religious growth are co-ordinate with the stages of civilization and culture. Religious development cannot be understood apart from that of culture in general. The steps of the cultural movement are roughly parallel with the steps in the development in religion. We may follow the

[30] See Arnold J. Toynbee, A Study of History, Vol. I, or in the one-volume abridgment of D. S. Somervell.

[31] Philosophy of Religion, chap. V.

three stages as given by Professor Galloway, namely, the tribal, the national, and the universal.[32]

1) *The Tribal.* We do not know how man was organized socially in the beginnings of his life. There are theories according to which he lived promiscuously with his fellows, with no family life, but there is an influential body of opinion today which holds that a monogamous relation between a man and his one wife was the earliest form of relationship in society. This view is gaining in influence; the theory of the horde with no family life is losing its hold. But whatever may have been the fact in prehistoric times, we know of no simpler form of communal organization than the tribe. It is spoken of as the "rudimentary form" of social union, and is the form in which all primitive or savage peoples live today. In this stage the individual is of little consequence, and the group as a group is the end-all. There is little or no reflection on life and its meaning, and material interests force themselves on the attention so exclusively that little opportunity is offered for anything higher. In this stage law is custom, the members of the tribe being united by the blood-bond, and each member doing, as a matter of course, what is expected of him. What affects one affects all, and the blame for what one does is shared by all. Piety—if the word can be used at all—consists in being loyal to the tribe and obeying its mandates and those of the tribal deities. On this level man's interests are determined by the constant necessity of securing enough to eat, and by watchfulness against the dangers of nature and the attacks of his enemies. Under these conditions the savage never rises above his material wants and desires, and his religion remains on that same low level.

2) *The National.* Man could never get away from the lower stage by pure reflection. Some change induced from the outside was necessary to produce a new stage culturally and religiously. A new set of needs must be created, and this growth is accompanied by the disappearance of the tribe and the rise of the nation. We do not know exactly how this change was brought about, but conjecture has been able to make quite a satisfying picture. Wars must have had much to do with it, when one tribe established its rule over weaker ones, and tribes were brought together and cemented in defense against common enemies from without. Migrations caused by overpopulation and the failure of sufficient subsistence cannot be left out as an important factor. But out of it came at long last and in a number of significant cases the state, with a capital city which

[32] *Ibid.*, chap. II.

exercised authority over the country lying about. In such a state, conditions of life differ greatly from those in a tribe. There is now division of labor, the soldier and the priest, the artisan and the farmer, emerging and taking their places in the social organism. Reading and writing are now to be found among human accomplishments, and out of them grow chronology and the writing of annals.

Such a civilization demands gods far different from those of the tribe. They must be stronger and wiser and more distinct. A certain division of labor is found among the divinities, and we come to have what are known as "departmental gods." With more complexity in society came gods with more attributes and a richer life. One of the great developments at this stage is a new kind of social morality, and this had the important effect of moralizing the idea of divinity. The deities begin to be associated with moral ideals in a manner unknown before. With great officials in the nation, from the king himself to the lesser men who are in more immediate contact with the masses of the people we find the "monarchian idea" worked out among the gods, supreme gods lording it over the lesser divinities, and so on down to gods which scarcely deserve the name. At the same time much that belonged to the tribal past is dragged along and helps to make more confused the picture of a people's life and religion.

3) *The Universal.* The universal is the outgrowth of a deepening and individualizing of religion. As religion ceases to be merely the possession of a group as such and is seen to involve an individual relationship between the soul and his God, it becomes, potentially at least, universal. What is good for a man as an individual is good for another man until by implication and in the ideal this good begins its journey to claim the allegiance of all men everywhere. Only a few of the religions have thus burst the nationalistic bonds and sought to become international or universal. Most of the great religions have remained through the ages attached to one people or nation. It is a distinct advance when they deepen and develop to such an extent that the very hope of their continued existence seems to lie in propagating them to the ends of the earth.

SUGGESTIONS FOR FURTHER STUDY

Farnell, L. R. *The Evolution of Religion.* New York: G. P. Putnam's Son, 1905.

Galloway, George. *The Philosophy of Religion.* New York: Charles Scribner's Sons, 1914. The nature and development of religion.

30

James, E. O. *The Beginnings of Religion.* London: Hutchinson and Company, 1948.

————. *The Concept of Deity.* London: Hutchinson and Company, 1950. A survey of the whole development of the idea of God.

Le Roy, Alexandre. *The Religion of the Primitives.* New York: The Macmillan Company, 1922.

Lowie, Robert H. *Primitive Religion.* New York: Boni and Liveright, 1924.

Marett, R. R. *The Threshold of Religion.* 2nd ed. New York: 1914. An epoch-making volume, as valuable today as when first written.

Pratt, J. B. *The Religious Consciousness.* New York: The Macmillan Company, 1920. One of the best of the many discussions of the psychology of religion.

Radin, Paul. *Primitive Religion: Its Nature and Origin.* New York: Viking Press, 1937.

Schmidt, Wilhelm. *The Origin and Growth of Religion.* New York: Dial Press, 1931. Presenting an extreme view, much discussed in recent books.

Söderblom, Nathan. *The Living God.* New York: Oxford University Press, 1933. Especially Lecture I.

Waterhouse, Eric S. *The Dawn of Religion.* London: Epworth Press, 1936.

CHAPTER II

ANIMISTIC RELIGION

ANIMISTIC PEOPLES AND THEIR HABITAT

No NAME FOR THE RELIGION WE ARE ABOUT TO CONSIDER IS ENTIRELY satisfactory. The designation "tribal religion" has been used because all the people who have this form of religion are in the tribal stage of organization, but the term does not penetrate into the inner meaning of the beliefs and practices of these groups. Probably the most widely used designation at the present time is "primitive religion." The difficulty is that what we are dealing with is not really primitive. The religion of the most backward peoples in the world gives undeniable evidences of development out of something more simple and crude. At best it only approximates the primitive and is far removed from what might be described correctly by that word. There is objection also to the word "animistic" because that attitude of mind is not left behind when higher forms of religion are attained, and so is not peculiar to those who are at the religious stage which is designated by that name. But it is used here because it is the animistic outlook or interpretation of their world which dominates all the thoughts and actions of the backward peoples. Their religion is the relationship which these peoples have established between themselves and certain of the spirits of their animism.

There is good reason why this form of religion should be most carefully investigated, and why it should be studied first. As has already been pointed out, all the more fully developed religions of the world have emerged out of these more primitive forms. Even among the most civilized and cultured peoples many remnants or vestiges of this early stage are still to be found. Superstitions of all kinds abound, many of them innocent and others far more serious in their effect. The good fortune to be expected from an old horseshoe and the ill luck which flows from the number thirteen will suggest a score of other superstitions known and more or less believed in among our own friends and relations.

What is the meaning of these strange "survivals"? No adequate explanation can be given without an understanding of the animistic outlook. These furtive beliefs have been handed down only because in each generation receptive minds have responded eagerly to such stimuli, minds which have failed to rise to the stage from which these puerile notions should have been banished.

No census has been taken of the animistic peoples as a whole. We know how many there are in the United States, in India, and in some other countries, but for the most part they have lived until so recently outside the pale of civilization that any exact enumeration has never been attempted. At the present time we must depend upon estimates. One writer gives a hundred and fifty-seven millions[1] and another a hundred and seventy-three millions.[2] In no place is the population dense, the very conditions of their life making anything approaching overcrowding impossible.

They are scattered more or less over both hemispheres. No continent, not even Europe, is without some representatives of these uncultured tribes. We have on this side of the Atlantic the Eskimos and the many tribes of aboriginal Indians, in both North and South America. The largest single group is in Africa where the various Negro and Bantu tribes occupy the central and southern parts of the continent. On the mainland of Asia are various aboriginal tribes, such as the Ainu in Japan, the Lolos and other tribes in the mountain and desert fastnesses of west China, the hill tribes of India, such as the Bhils, the Gonds, and many others. In many cases the more primitive peoples have been displaced by the coming of those who, emigrating from a previous abode, have taken possession of the country and driven the former occupants back into the more inaccessible and undesirable sections of the country. There they have remained much as they were centuries ago. Again, in the island world of the southern Pacific conditions are much as they are in Africa. A large population of animistic tribesmen, out of touch through ages with peoples of a higher civilization, live a life which has taken its form with no outside influence to turn it from its natural development. The great islands of Sumatra, Java, Borneo, and New Guinea, the Philippines, and many hundreds of lesser islands off the coast of Asia are inhabited by countless tribes of people in various stages of development. Attention must also be called to the aboriginal tribes in

[1] "Missions," Encyclopaedia Britannica, 11 ed.
[2] Zeller, as quoted in Warneck's History of Protestant Missions, 10th German edition.

33

Australia, very low in the cultural scale, and in New Zealand, where the Maori have advanced farther than most of these primitive peoples. Besides these are the people of the hundreds of small islands, some little better than coral reefs, scattered over the face of the broad Pacific. Coming now very rapidly under the influence of Western nations, these people are showing many signs of change. They are still for the most part in the animistic stage, but this condition must soon be exchanged for another as they come into more intimate contact with the commerce and education and religion of the Western world.

The great variety of animistic peoples scattered over the world is an embarrassment when their religious life is to be studied. Each tribe has religious practices and beliefs which differ from those of others. It would seem that the only way in which the religion of these people could be adequately presented would be to take each tribe or group of similar tribes separately and give an account of its religious rites and beliefs. This is the only way in which the great national religions can be treated, so individual are they and so different in their history and outlook. But while the religion of one tribe is not the same as that of another, the differences are not so great as those between the more developed faiths. As soon as certain differences are noted a marked sameness is to be discovered. The thought-life of these people is weak and covers a very limited range. Its reactions are spontaneous and naïve, and hence more or less alike even among peoples separated by half the circumference of the globe.

Before taking up the various aspects of savage belief and life it may be well to call attention to several of its more general characteristics. It has been suggested that the religion of peoples living in the tribal form of organization exhibits three marked peculiarities, that it is traditional, natural, and spontaneous.

1) *Traditional.* These forms of religion, like the culture out of which they spring, have no written language and no literature. This means no history and no possibility of any significant and conscious progress. No advance can be made until the existing social order has been changed into something higher. Religion may do this, but it must be religion brought in from the outside. Other causes, economic, political, and social, will do their part, but they too must be of foreign, not native origin. A traditional civilization is always stationary; it rises to higher levels only when its acts can be recorded and transmitted to posterity in forms which are permanent.

34

2) *Natural.* By which is meant that the satisfaction of the natural physical needs and desires of life is about as far as the savage goes in his outreach. He is of necessity so occupied with the material and physical that no other needs are felt. Shelter and enough to eat, provisions for his animals, protection against his enemies, the satisfaction of his primary impulses—these are about all he thinks about. He is not awake to himself and the latent possibilities of his deeper nature. Spiritual attainment is denied him because he has never felt any aspiration after higher things. This condition is not accidental; it is inevitable so long as people remain on this level. We are dealing, then, with man undeveloped and curtailed and cramped and dwarfed. He is a man, to be sure, but a man without the touch which lifts him out of the purely natural into the sphere of the moral and spiritual reality.

3) *Spontaneous.* That is, such religion springs from no founder, nor have there been any crucial turning points which have determined the direction it should take. It has grown spontaneously as a feature of the life and culture of the tribe, and as unconsciously as any other feature. Like everything else in the life about him the animistic savage takes religion for granted, as he does the chief of the tribe and the hill which stands opposite his village. Everything to his mind has always been as it is now and needs no further justification or explanation. Religion is perfectly normal and as much a part of his life as sleeping at night or going to battle when an enemy approaches. Spontaneity, together with the other two characteristics just mentioned, shows us religion at its lowest level and almost at a standstill. Variations are to be found, but they are variations within the limits given by these three descriptive terms.

ANIMISM AND THE MYSTERIOUS POWER

All people believe in spirits. No people have been discovered without such a belief. These spirits are everywhere—in the sky above, on the earth beneath, in the depths of the waters, and in dark caverns and recesses of the mysterious mountains. All nature is tenanted by an invisible host of spiritual beings not far away from man and likely at any moment to make their presence felt in any one of a hundred ways. It is easy to understand why the savage should think that animals are possessed of spirits like ourselves but it is not at first sight evident why inanimate objects should be thought of as so possessed. But we must always remember that the animist can interpret everything only in terms of his own life and powers, on the principle of analogy. He has no other recourse. Rivers and lakes,

35

mountains and hills, trees and shrubs, sticks and stones, are the dwelling places of spirits. The clouds, the stars, the sun, and the moon likewise are what they are because of indwelling life. Savage man lives in a densely populated world. Not only are these spirits the invisible souls of the objects around him, but there are legions of free spirits flitting around in the air, homeless wanderers, not belonging in any one place but at liberty to travel and range over a wide area. His life is obsessed by a sense of helplessness and uncertainty. He cannot tell when and where a mischievous imp may trip him as he walks or some devilish ogre pull him under the surface of the water and cause him to drown. And then there is the smallpox demon who may attack his village, or the blight which may destroy his meager crop. Whatever happens is caused by spirit agency. "What spirit killed my cow?" asks the savage, or "Who caused the awful flood last spring?" The savage, in other words, is an animist; he lives in a world that is alive and throbbing with vitality.

But while he believes in spirits, primitive man is not spiritual in the true sense. He has not learned to distinguish between a material and a spiritual world. To him there is no essential difference between the visible and the invisible. He may not be able to see the spirit, but it might be seen, he thinks. He looks upon it as a more or less thin, vapory substance which has qualities not possessed by the heavier, tangible things he sees, but is of the same general character. Very naturally he identifies the soul with the breath, for when a man ceases to breathe, his spirit or soul has left. This breath cannot usually be seen, but it can be felt, and on occasion when condensation takes place, it has visible form and can be seen flowing from a man's mouth and nostrils. He identifies this with the soul of the man himself; he has not risen above the purely physical in his explanation of the unseen world around him. The soul is also identified with the blood. Does not life flow out with the blood as it leaves an inert corpse?

That dreams have played an important part in making the realm of the spirit real there can be little doubt. A dream is just as real an experience to people living on this plane as the experience of their waking moments. They or their spirits actually do the things they dream about. While they dream, their bodies may remain in the place where they lay down, but their spirits have traveled far and have passed through strange and wonderful experiences. There is no doubt about it at all. The difference between a dream and death is that when one dreams, his spirit has departed for a season only, while when a man dies his spirit does not come back. Flowing naturally from this is his unfailing belief in a life after death. His ideas may differ according to natural conditions and social environment, but the belief is there, unquenchable and strong.

There also exists in the mind of primitive peoples the conception of a mysterious pervasive power present in the universe and recognized in many forms of activity. The familiar name by which it is known is taken from Polynesia, where it is called *mana*. But it is known by other names, *manito* by the Algonquian family of Indians, *orenda* by the Iroquoian family, and *wakan* by the Sioux, and by still other names elsewhere. The word *mana* came into our vocabulary through the classic statement of Bishop R. H. Codrington, in his volume *The Melanesians:* "It is a power or influence, not physical, and in a way supernatural; but it shows itself in physical force, or in a kind of power or excellence which a man possesses. This *mana* is not fixed in anything, and can be conveyed in almost anything; but spirits, whether disembodied souls or supernatural beings, have it and can impart it; and it essentially belongs to personal beings to originate it, though it may act through the medium of water, or a stone, or a bone." [3] Professor C. H. Toy sums up its meaning in this short sentence: "It is, in a word, a term for the force residing in any object." [4]

This conception of *mana* is not to be found among the most degraded savages—some development seems to be necessary before men rise to the thought. It is true also that as civilization advances the idea is laid aside and ceases to function as a definite belief. But among animistic peoples as they are found the world over the idea of this quasi-personal force is present and very influential as an explanation of about all that happens. Men are alive and do things, chiefs have authority, a tree puts out fruit and leaves, an animal secures its prey, a fisherman is successful with his catch, and a thousand other things are what they are and accomplish what they do—all because of this mysterious power.

THE HIGHER POWERS OF ANIMISTIC RELIGION

Primitive animism is not religion but the raw material out of which religion is made. It has been called the "Seed of Religion." There is, then, a distinction between animism, which is a philosophy or interpretation of life, and animistic religion, which is based on it. Of the more definite

---

[3] P. 119.
[4] *Introduction to the History of Religions*, p. 101.

question of the objects of worship, the first thing to be said is that they are the spirits of their animism, impregnated, one might say, with the mysterious power mana. Not all of them are worshiped, but the more primitive peoples know of no other objects of worship. Let us beware just here of concluding that these people do much thinking in our sense of the word. Their religion is far more a matter of the emotions than of the intellect. Their minds are greatly confused, and what they do depends to a much greater extent on the impulse of the moment and the excitement born of a dance or a period of fasting or an impressive ceremonial than on sober thought. The instability of savage nerves is mentioned frequently by writers on the life of primitive people. Their reactions are largely of the high-strung, emotional type and they cannot be understood without taking this into consideration. As a result their choice of divinities and the worship accorded them is a choice determined by the emotional reaction of the savage to his environment. He is aware of scores and hundreds of spirits around him; he turns to some of them in worship, and this becomes his religion.

We do not know what spirits he worshiped first. All we know is that man is found worshiping a great variety of beings and doing it rather indiscriminately. The question of interest, however, is to determine why certain objects were chosen instead of others, for although the savage may not know why, there must be some reason for his choice. One thing is sure: the only being he would worship must be one which for one reason or another appears to him as possessed of power superior to his own. For this reason the gods and spirits are frequently called "powers." That is the necessary and almost the only necessary qualification. In wisdom, skill, cunning, as well as in physical prowess he must exceed the might of man. These qualifications are determined in ways which to us appear naïve and utterly inadequate. Mere physical force may not seem to us to be indicative of superiority, but it does to a savage. But besides this he is struck by what is strange, uncanny, mysterious, or even grotesque and queer. All these aspects of the things he finds go beyond his comprehension and suggest power, and often for no other reason than their mysteriousness. And in this way the pantheon, if it can be dignified by that name, of savage people is not consistent and the same. New objects are constantly attracting the attention of the animist and taking the place of other powers now shrunk down to more ordinary dimensions.

Inanimate objects are worshiped wherever animists are found. Trees are alive and provide shade and food—should they not be worshiped?

38

Although the tree is rooted to one spot, it responds to every influence without. Swayed by the breeze, or smitten by the storm, it is never at rest. Murmurs are heard in its leaves, or its branches creak and writhe as in agony; sounds are emitted from the gaunt stem or hollow trunk—voices, the savage doubts not, of the indwelling spirit whose life seems permanently associated with the fixed tree.[5]

Stones are also widely worshiped. To a savage a stone may be very much alive despite its immobility. It is so hard and sometimes so strange in color and shape that he is deeply fascinated and turns in real admiration to it and asks for some boon. Added to this is the fact that some of these stones fell from heaven and hence must surely be divine. Meteorites have been the objects of adoration in many countries. But besides these, plants and mountains and fire and winds and waters are objects of worship, and in each case there is some reason for the choice.

The greater objects of nature—the overarching sky, the dazzling sun, the resplendent moon, the distant stars—all come in for their share of attention in the cult. But it must be said that the lesser objects of nature, more nearly connected with their daily wants and work, occupy the attention of these simple people far more than the grand, awe-inspiring heavenly bodies. At a later time, when religion had achieved a higher level, these greater objects came to their own. The last form assumed by paganism before it went down before Christianity in the fourth century was the worship of Sol Invictus, the "Invincible Sun."

If objects inanimate serve as divinities for the savage, how much more animals, full of life and movement and cunning. The majesty of the lion, the ferocity of the tiger, the wisdom of the elephant, the cunning of the fox, the mysteriousness of the snake, led in each case to an attitude approaching worship. They inspired fear and needed propitiation. Savages attribute to animals a wisdom and cunning far beyond their due which lifts the animals up to a plane as high, if not higher, than man himself and makes worship seem quite natural. And even where actual worship is not paid to animals, they are held sacred, and marks of respect and veneration are shown them.

The worship of human beings is widely spread, though it is too much to say that it is universal. Living men—chiefs, kings, emperors, and saints—have been deified and worshiped in the course of human history. A great man is possessed of power of the same kind as causes one to

[5] Edward Clodd, *Animism*, p. 72.

39

tremble in the presence of a strong animal or a rushing torrent, and hence may be worshiped. The cult of the dead is highly important. Historical personages, legendary or mythical ancestors, among many peoples have been looked upon as legitimate objects of worship. Among savages, however, as well as among peoples more civilized, a man's own ancestors are raised to a high place among his gods. A careful distinction should probably be made between reverence and worship. In many cases the attitude is not that of a worshiper at all, but there is no question that such adoration often rises to the height of veritable worship. As early as the fourth century B.C. the Sicilian Euhemerus promulgated the theory that all the gods were deified men who had passed over into the spirit world.

Death makes a difference. A man cannot be the same after he dies that he was when alive. Not hampered by his body, he is free to roam at large. He has powers which were not his before. He has not, however, become a spiritual being, in our sense of the word, even though his is invisible. He has the same desires and wants. Food and drink, clothing and weapons, and in the case of the great man, servants and attendants are as necessary as before. He has not passed beyond the pale of his former relationships and knows quite well what is going on. It is even thought that his condition in the other world is determined at least in part by the treatment he continues to receive from his family. Should he fail to receive what he believes to be his due, his anger is aroused, and he may inflict sore chastisement on his relatives here below. It is chiefly those of the past two or three generations who are worshiped. Even in China, where ancestor worship has been carried along through all the stages of its development, after the second or third generation the ancestral tablets are removed to the clan hall. When memory becomes weak or fails, the ancestor fades out of the life of the living and his place is taken by those more recently lost.

What of the motives which actuate men when they worship their departed dead? Undoubtedly regard and reverence and the desire to provide for their comfort have had influence wherever this worship is found, but the general testimony is that fear is the most powerful motive. No one can tell what might happen if the sacrifices were neglected. As spirits, resentful of the neglect and unfaithfulness of their descendants, they would undoubtedly bring ill luck and catastrophe upon the living family. This form of worship is distinctively social and tends to keep the family together and gives its members common interests and a common sanction for their ethical standards.

One of the most singular and baffling features of the religion of savages is fetishism. The term comes from the Portuguese *feitiço* (Latin, *facere*, "to make"), a word applied by Portuguese sailors to the little objects held sacred by West African natives, which were regarded by the Europeans as charms or talismans. What does it mean in modern religious nomenclature? There is much confusion, so much so that a number of careful students have in recent years excluded the word from their discussions. Yet even Dr. Geoffrey Parrinder, a very vigorous opponent of the use of the term, realizes that it may be used for the worship of "charms, amulets, and talismans which form a subordinate part of the religions' complex." [6] The trouble has been caused by the uses to which the word has been put. The philosopher Comte makes it mean what is commonly called by the general name of animism. Dr. Nassau and Miss Kingsley have given the name to all the religious practices of the West African Negroes. It is not in either of these senses that the term may be used legitimately.

A fetish may be defined as (a) any object whatsoever, which (b) is thought to be inhabited by a spirit, and which (c) its possessor may make use of for his own benefit. There must be some reason why the native selects a particular object, something about it which appeals to him and shows that it possesses supernatural power. Some object strikes him as being out of the ordinary, and that is enough; he will take it as his fetish. "So the fetish consists of a queer-shaped stone, a bright bead, a stick, parrots' feathers, a root, claw, seed, bone or any curious or conspicuous object." Professor E. B. Tylor relates the story of how a man chose a stone about as big as a hen's egg for his fetish. "He was going out on important business, but crossing the threshold he trod on this stone and hurt himself. 'Ha, ha!' thought he, 'Art thou here?' So he took the stone, and it helped him through his undertaking for days." [7] In West Africa a fetish is not so much found as made or concocted by the witch doctor or medicine man.

Now, the fetish is very much like a human being. It possesses personality and will; it can feel and knows the meaning of anger and resentment as well as gratitude and kindness. It is also semihuman in that while the particular spirit which belongs to the natural object can belong to no other, it can be and is sometimes separated from the object and seems to disappear. Then the natural object ceases to be of any value; that is, it ceases to be a fetish. Everything depends on the presence of the spirit to

[6] *West African Religion*, see Index under "Fetishism."
[7] Haddon, *Magic and Fetishism*, p. 73.

make the fetish object a source of benefit to its possessor. When the spirit leaves, it is no longer a fetish; it is only an inert, useless stick or stone, or whatever it may be.

The fetish is treated as an object of worship, has offerings made to it, and is addressed in prayer. But this is only a part of the procedure. If the ends sought are not gained in this way the attitude changes, and the fetish is coaxed and even commanded to bring about the desired result. If this does not succeed, the little thing is scolded for its disobedience, and it is on record that a fetish has been punished. And finally if this vigorous treatment proves unsuccessful, the conclusion is reached that the spirit has departed, or at any rate that some more powerful spirit is interfering with the operation of the fetish. About all there is to do after such a discovery is to lay it aside or throw it away altogether. The savage doesn't lose faith in his theory or practice; he has only come to the conclusion that the particular fetish he had is of no use. He must proceed to find another.

In our discussion of the origin of religion attention was directed to the presence among primitive peoples of a belief in All-fathers or "High Gods." Dr. Paul Radin states, "As far as our present actual knowledge goes, it can be said that the most typical instances of an aboriginal belief in a Supreme Deity are to be found among the simplest and among the most complex of primitive civilizations." His list includes "the southeastern Australians, the Andaman Islanders, the Negritos of the Philippine Islands, and the Selknam of Tierra del Fuego"—all representative of simple cultures. Of those representing complex cultures the list includes "the Polynesians, the major civilizations of West, East, and South Africa, and the Caddoan, the Dakota, and the Winnebago Indians of the United States." [8] These gods have definite names. Among the Australian aborigines they are known as Daramulun, Baiame, Bunjil, Nurelii, and in America as Ahone, Pachacamac, Tui Laga, and other names. But very much more important is it to know what they stand for in the savage mind. Bishop Alexandre Le Roy tells of four classes of names which he believes are descriptive of their character and activities. There are expressions which carry with them (a) the idea of the creator or organizer, (b) the thought of greatness and power, (c) the conception of these beings as the soul of the universe, and others (d) which connect them with the light, the sky, or the sun. [9]

---

[8] *Primitive Religion*, p. 257.
[9] Alexandre Le Roy, *The Religion of Primitives*, pp. 115-19.

How did the conception of these beings arise? We simply do not know. Andrew Lang's opinion is that supreme beings were conceived by savages attempting to answer the question, Why do we perform these religious rites? They constructed etiological myths, stories intended to explain origins. It is held by others that these high gods are idealized chiefs or dead heroes elevated in later generations to a superhuman plane.

How does this conception of high gods function in the actual life of these people? That is a far more important question, and it is surprising to learn that all the authorities agree that it plays an insignificant part. Daramulun (or any other of these beings) does not enter into their life. He is off at a distance, paying little attention to men. He has no local habitation or temple; no offerings are made to him. He is looked upon in a hazy way as a creator and as the controller of nature, but has nothing to do with the individual man. These gods are "away on the fringe of their consciousness." [10] They may at one time have been more important but now other deities occupy the attention of these primitive peoples and are worshiped by them.[11]

Are the gods or higher powers of animistic religion good gods? What, in other words, is their character? We already have a clue. The beings worshiped partake of the character of the nature from which they are taken, and the simple fact is that nature has no moral character. It is not moral or immoral, but simply nonmoral; it is neutral ethically. But there is another side to the question: nature may not be good or evil in a moral sense, but she does not treat people in the same way on all occasions. Sometimes she is like a tender mother or a beautiful summer afternoon, when peace reigns everywhere and no sign of disturbance appears on the horizon. But nature has other moods and may become as fierce and ravenous as a wild beast, "red in tooth and claw." A West Indian hurricane, a tornado, an earthquake, a tidal wave, a volcanic eruption—all represent that other side, which is very different from the calm and quiet of an autumnal sunset. Yet all come from the same source. What can the savage think of nature and the spirits who are so kind and also so destructive? In his mind they may have a common origin, but he distinguishes between the spirits which are beneficent and kind and the demons which are constantly seeking to do him harm.

The mind of the savage, however, is occupied far more with the demons whose influence he is seeking to escape than the good spirits which might

[10] E. W. Smith, The Religion of Lower Races, p. 55.
[11] For the latest, most authoritative treatment, see E. W. Smith, ed., African Ideas of God.

be depended on to take his side and accomplish his desire. It is exceeding doubtful whether, before man had begun to till the soil and thus formulate the conception of the gods and goddesses of fertility and agriculture, his mind was not so occupied with the malignant spirits which were constantly on the watch to do him injury that little opportunity was offered for thought about the good spirits whom he might have discovered. But when the age of agriculture is reached, unmistakable signs indicate that the soil which furnishes food for man and beast is looked upon as kindly. But even then the fear of the evil spirits which bring blight and drought and the grasshopper is not absent. The savage has confidence in certain spirits, but he lives a life of fear nevertheless, a life not to be envied as idyllic by those who live under more favorable conditions. So long as man remains in the tribal form of organization he seems unable to rise above the purely natural into the realm of ethical good. He has his standards of action, and the moral does enter in and determine to some extent his conduct, but, to use Professor Galloway's words, "there are no instances of the evolution of an ethical religion by a tribal group." [12]

Totemism and Taboo

Closely connected with the religion of animistic peoples are customs and practices without which their life—and consequently their religion—would be very different. One of these is totemism. A totem is an animal (or sometimes a plant or even an inanimate object) very closely related to a group which because of that relation holds it as something sacred. The group is sometimes named after the totem, from which it is often thought to be descended. The word "totem" comes from the language of the Ojibway Indians (Chippewa) and signifies "a group." This relation of the group to its totem separates it from other groups, each with its own totem. The totem clan became a form of social organization determining many features of the life of the tribe. It is found developed most fully among the American Indians and the aboriginal tribes of Australia, but clear indications of its presence are to be discovered in many other regions.

Totemism is so complex and multiform that no attempt can be made to describe it here. Its connection with religion, however, must be pointed out. The totem animal, to which the totem clan believes itself related, is frequently regarded as the ancestor of the group. There is no difficulty

[12] *Philosophy of Religion*, p. 108.

among the savages in believing in a relationship between men and animals. They are so much alike that passage from one species to another is not strange nor unheard of in tribal traditions. As the ancestor of a group of men and women the animal may even be worshiped. It must not be killed or maltreated. The only exception to this rule is that among some peoples the totem animal is killed on certain important occasions and eaten sacramentally by all who belong to that totem clan. They look upon it as the re-establishment of the bond between the group and its totem, thus insuring friendly relations during the time to come. But even where this custom does not prevail and no worship is offered, the people are bound together closely and feel a sense of sacred obligation which is not far distant from religion. A common obligation holds them together and leads them to feel a sense of mutual obligation and responsibility.

Closely connected with totemism are several other customs most important in the life of the savage. There is, in the first place, exogamy, or marriage outside the totem clan. This custom is very widespread and is one of the most beneficial provisions in savage life. It effectually prevents intermarriage between close relatives—effectually, for the savage does not break over these unwritten but absolutely binding customs. The origin of exogamy is unknown.

Another custom calls for notice. Among savage peoples rites of initiation are practiced upon young men and women. When at the time of puberty they pass out of childhood into manhood and womanhood, they are initiated into the secret lore of their people. Then is disclosed to them the meaning of customs and practices previously withheld, and they are admitted fully into the adult life of the tribe. The ceremonies are long and complicated, and subject the initiates to great pain and weird and disgusting and even indecent ordeals. Accompanied by noise and dances which are crude and often unseemly, the ritual is performed in strict adherence to the traditions handed down from generation to generation. These ceremonies are largely social, but some of the secrets divulged are of a religious nature, having to do with sacred objects and the cult connected with them.

Tabu (taboo) comes from the Polynesian tapu, which means "sacred" or "prohibited." Thus a tabu is a prohibition placed upon contact with or use of certain things set aside as peculiarly sacred. The totem is tabu to the members of that totem clan, but tabu has a far wider application. It is a widespread idea, and all over the world the practice is in full force, affecting the acts and plans of men in almost all their relations. An illus-

45

tration may be taken from the Todas, a backward people in South India, whose religion centers around a dairy ritual.

Many, though not all, of their buffaloes are sacred, and their milk may not be drunk. The reason why it may not be drunk anthropologists may cast about to discover, but the Todas themselves do not know. All that they know, and are concerned to know, is that things would somehow all go wrong if anyone were foolish enough to commit a sin. So in the Toda temple, which is a dairy, the Toda priest, who is the dairyman, sets about rendering the sacred products harmless. Thus the ritual is essentially precautionary. A taboo is the hinge of the whole affair.[13]

The number of tabus is almost endless. Tabus against coming into contact with rulers and chiefs, against having social intercourse with strangers, against contact with persons at certain times and under certain conditions, such as mourners, women, warriors, hunters, and fishers. There are tabued articles such as iron, sharp weapons, the head, the hair, and the nails. The use of names under certain conditions is also prohibited —personal names, names of relatives, of the dead, of kings and other sacred persons, and the name of Deity. In the Old Testament the ark of the covenant was tabu (I Chronicles 13:7-10), and the Sabbath (the Fourth Commandment). The Hebrews would not use the name of God, which was probably *Yahweh*, but in its place substituted the word *Adonai*, which means "Lord."

The question may be asked relative to tabu, Why is the prohibition placed upon an object, thus rendering it sacred and inviolable? Professor Marett would account for tabu by the presence of *mana*, the pervasive force which vitalizes and in this case renders dangerous the things which possess it. The object or the person which is tabu is believed to possess an especially large amount of that mysterious power which if released by contact will cause calamity, pain, ill luck, and even death. That we must have prohibitions to keep us from harm is most evident. A baby must not be allowed to touch a hot stove—that suggests a hundred other salutary "Thou shalt nots." The main difficulty with the whole theory as held by savage people is that it is devoid of reasonable regulation. The practice runs wild, and no discrimination is made between a prohibition which is wise and preventive of harm and a prohibition which can only hamper normal life and activity.

[13] R. R. Marett, *Anthropology*, pp 217-18.

Animistic Worship

Up to the present we have been dealing largely with belief—what the savage believes about the world in which he lives, the spirits which are everywhere, and about himself and his fellows. He has his theories, and they effectively control his life and its relationships. But he acts as well as thinks; he doubtless acts before he thinks; to him an act is more important than the thought he has about it. Professor W. Robertson Smith pointed out that ritual precedes belief, that the reaction of a savage to his environment is first of all emotional, an act, a dance, a ceremonial, and only latterly an intellectual thing, a belief or a conception. It is far more a matter of his feet and hands than of his head. So in discussing the worship of the animistic peoples we are entering into the very citadel of their religious life, into that which to them is religion itself.

The motive which actuates his worship—is it fear or faith? Does he have confidence in the spirits with which he deals, or is he afraid that they may do him injury unless he does something to propitiate them or ward them off? We have already seen that the savage knows of beneficent spirits who bring him good things, but this is a very little part of the story. His mind is more fully occupied with the thousand evil-minded spirits, the imps and demons, who would crush him if they could and are constantly seeking opportunity to do so. Many witnesses are forthcoming to tell of their experience among savage peoples, an experience of deep pity as they have witnessed the dread and terror which fill their minds. J. H. Weeks, who spent fifteen years among the Boloki of the Upper Congo, writes:

Their system of belief has its basis in their fear of those numerous invisible spirits—invisible to the ordinary man, but not to the medicine man—which are constantly trying to compass their sickness, misfortune, and death; and the Boloki's sole object—and the same may be written of his near and distant neighbors on the Congo—is to cajole or appease, to cheat or conquer, and even destroy the troublesome spirits; hence their witch doctors with their fetishes, their rites, and ceremonies. If there were no spirits to be circumvented, there would be no need for medicine men or middle-men, and no need of fetishes or mediums for getting into touch with the spirits.[14]

It is no beautiful picture which confronts us when we penetrate into the inner life of the savage, and only distance makes possible a certain

[14] *Among Congo Cannibals*, p. 259.

enchantment as the "simple, rustic life" of a primitive tribe as described by the traveler who fails to penetrate the dark recesses "at the back of the black man's mind." One further quotation is needed to complete the picture and relieve the strain: "It would be no doubt a great mistake to imagine that the minds of the Bantu, or, indeed, of any savages, are perpetually occupied by a dread of evil spirits; the savage and, indeed, the civilized man is incapable, at least in his normal state, of such excessive preoccupation with a single idea, which, if prolonged, could hardly fail to end in insanity." [15] We undoubtedly have in this attitude of fear on the part of the savage the best explanation of his backward state. Nobility of character and the development of society never spring from the disorganizing motive of fear. To develop the possibilities in man and to organize his life in ever higher forms of social intercourse require a basis of trust and confidence—trust and confidence of men in one another, and even more fundamentally in the spirits and powers on whom they are dependent. And these things cannot be found in savage life and religion— only the beginnings are there.

In early religion, sacrifice and worship are almost synonymous. To come directly to the objects which are offered in sacrifice, the general statement may be made that they are the things which man himself needs or desires for his nourishment and comfort and pleasure. Here is analogy at work again; the spirits are sufficiently like men to need what they need and like what they like. So food and drink, clothing and utensils, constitute the body of sacrifice the world over. A certain value must always attach to the object offered, or it is not efficacious. Life is the most precious thing in the world, and this recognition has led to the taking of life in sacrifice and offering it to the higher powers. This led very early and widely to the offering of human life, and the custom continued until the sensibilities of men turned against such inhumanity with horror and animals were substituted for human beings. But even today the practice prevails here and there, and is with difficulty rooted out by civilized governments which have made themselves responsible for the conduct of savage tribes.

The forms of sacrifice are many.

The head of the animal or man may be cut off (and custom often requires that a single blow shall suffice), its spine broken or its heart torn out; it may be stoned, beaten to death, or shot, torn in pieces, drowned or buried, burned to death or hung, thrown down a precipice, strangled or squeezed to death.

[15] *Folklore*, chap. 20, pp. 51-52.

The sacrifices may aim at causing a speedy death or a slow one. The corpse may be burned, in part or as a whole; portions may be assigned to the priest, the sacrificer, and the gods; the skull, bones, etc., may receive special treatment; the fat or blood may be set aside, and they or the ashes may be singled out as the share of the god, to be offered upon the altar; the skin of the victim may be employed as a covering for idol or material respresentative of the god, either permanently or till the next animal sacrifice. The blood of the victim may be drunk by the priest as a means of inducing inspiration, its entrails may be employed in divination, its flesh consumed in a common meal, exposed to the birds and beasts of prey, or buried in the earth.[16]

So varied are the usages in the practice of sacrifice in different parts of the world.

To placate an angry god is one idea lying back of sacrifice. It is not the only purpose, but it prevails as widely as sacrifice is found. He may be rendered propitious by gifts or bought off by the bounty which is spread before him. In the dire straits to which he is often reduced the savage is willing to do anything to secure immunity from disease or security from any one of a hundred dangers which surround him. But he has another purpose in many of his sacrifices. He is conscious that the god is displeased because of something wrong that has been done. A tabu has been broken or a custom has been infringed, and the god must be rendered friendly again. Again a sacrifice is offered by way of atoning for the wrong done. An animal may be killed or burned; the sins may be laid on a scapegoat and the animal sent out into the wilderness bearing away the guilt of the people.[17] The guilt is acknowledged and the right of the god to punish is recognized. The god is willing to accept a substitute in an animal slain, and thus the idea of the vicariousness of suffering and punishment is established. These conceptions come to their fruition only in the higher religions where the sense of sin has become clear and poignant, but the ideas themselves root back into the earlier forms when men began to feel a sense of responsibility to higher powers.

Closely connected with sacrifice is prayer. It may be that the earliest prayer was a call to the spirits to come and partake of the sacrifice which was offered. It is always the expression of a desire, the making of a request that this or that may or may not take place. It is the instinctive utterance

---

[16] N. W. Thomas, "Sacrifice," *Encyclopaedia Britannica*, 11th ed.
[17] *Leviticus* 16:5-10, 20-22.

of the human heart when in distress or threatened by some danger. The prayer of savages never rises higher than purely material needs and desires. This being true, savage prayer never reaches up to the level where prayer is looked upon as communion with God, and where this is considered the very essence of the exercise. The chief danger in prayer is that it may revert to a spell or incantation, the value of which lies in the mere repetition of the words. Whether we understand their meaning or not makes no difference; there is potency in the words, and they will bring the desired end by being uttered. So far is this carried that "spell-narratives" about the gods are told, the belief being that even talking about a thing makes it happen. Should the worshiper know the name of his god, he has in his possession a powerful lever to bring to pass what he desires. The name is looked upon as a part of the personality, and to be able to use the name to reinforce a request is to be far more sure of receiving the boon than would otherwise be true.

Widely extended is the belief in the necessity of cleanliness in approaching the spirits to be propitiated. The purifications are often really cleansing so far as the body is concerned. The hands, the feet, the mouth, and frequently the whole body must be clean to come acceptably into the presence of the higher powers. But as in so many other features in savage life reason does not give direction where it is seriously needed. Uncleanness is connected closely with the idea of tabu and is incurred by contact with ceremonially dangerous and sacred things, like corpses, newborn infants, blood, and a hundred other things. To us the so-called purification seems in many cases as defiling as the uncleanness itself. The chemical purity of the cleansing agent has nothing to do with its efficacy. The most disgusting things are considered highly purifying and are believed in implicitly, even in religions advanced far beyond that of the people we are studying. Only at a comparatively late stage did the idea of moral defilement arise and seem more terrible than ceremonial uncleanness. Then the outward act of purification became a symbol of the inner cleansing from the defilement of sin.

Early in the history of religion a class of men arose known as priests, medicine men, witch doctors, shamans, exorcists, and mediums. They are the members of the community through whom communication is had with the supernatural. The essential and distinguishing characteristic of the priest in the entire history of religion is that of mediator between men and the powers on whom they are dependent. Not just anyone can be a priest. He must demonstrate his ability to hold intercourse with the gods.

50

This he does by intoxication or ecstasy or epileptic seizures real or induced and in other ways which to the savage clearly indicate that the priest is in the possession of some spirit other than his own. The ejaculations and groans and incoherent utterances of the priest or medium are to him full of meaning, needing only the interpretation of the priest himself to be seen in their true light as a divine message. Women also act as priests and sorcerers, performing all the functions which men perform. They too are endowed with strange, mysterious powers, often to a far greater degree than men. The office frequently becomes hereditary in certain families; and when that point is reached, the priesthood becomes a rigid institution and tends to secure an ever stronger hold upon the people.

What has been said might imply that the effect of the services of these go-betweens is beneficial, and so it often is. But there is another, a dark and terrible, side to the shield. Particularly as witch doctors prey upon the community and spread dreadful woe and terror. It is they who "smell out" the men and women who are supposed to have caused trouble to the tribe or to have brought death into a family. Thousands of innocent people have been done to death because an evil deed was fixed upon them by the witch doctor or the medicine man. So abject is their belief in and subservience to these harpies that there is no protestation; the accused go to their death with no thought of resistance even when entirely innocent.

Another and very different function is that of being the wise man and seer. In many cases these men who are set apart and thus lead a different life from others are responsible for the thought life—such as it is—in primitive society. It is they who are the thinkers, the developers of the ritual, the repositories of the sacred lore, the men who peer out and see what the ordinary man does not see at all. Even at these low levels they hear more than their fellows and see farther, so they claim, and the people believe in them implicitly.

Magic and Religion

Magic has already been referred to and necessarily so when dealing with the religion of animists. But we must remember that magic is one thing to us and another to the savage. We look back upon it after it has shown itself to be what it really is, after the distinction between magic and religion has become clear. Religion for us expresses itself in worship of higher powers. The attitude is one of dependence, coming into the presence of

God in humility to thank him for his goodness and to make request for certain good things after which we crave. Magic, on the other hand, comes out of a very different attitude. Instead of seeking our desires by humble entreaty, the attitude in magic is that of self-sufficiency, as though there were another method of securing our ends without recourse to petition. We ourselves possess the good luck talisman; we know what will charm away the sickness; we can by doing this or that, by "knowing the trick," bring good fortune and accomplish our desire. The attitude is entirely different from that of true religion. In one case we trust God; in the other we trust some contrivance or spell or charm. In one case we secure our aims by making a request; in the other we secure them by coercion. In religion we seek; in magic we demand. The two attitudes are not always kept apart. Even among Christians there is the constant danger that prayer, to use one illustration only, may be looked upon as meritorious in itself and as efficacious by its very performance, as though we might secure the desired object because we go through the act of praying—and that is magic pure and simple.

But to the savage in the darkness of his soul such a distinction is out of the question. He is in trouble and confusion in the presence of the dangers and uncertainties of life. At his wits' end, he is willing to do anything to get relief and secure what he so much desires. Animism is the background of all his thinking about the universe. Some kind of *mana*, or spiritual influence, is everywhere, and whatever he does or gets must be done through spirit agency. In the use of these agencies he is led into one or the other or both of two methods. He is in fear of the spirits who can do him injury; he must placate them by offerings and make request of them by prayer; and this is religion, crude as it may be. But this is not all he can do. He has discovered that if he does certain things results follow which are what he wants. He can hit two stones together and produce a spark. He believes that helpful influences can be evoked by what he may do, and around this belief and the coincidences which he has noted he has built up what might almost be called a science of cause and effect, but of course the savage has no conception of the meaning of a law of nature. All that is effected is to him the result of the activity of living spirits. This being the case, we cannot expect him to see the difference between what he does when he sacrifices and prays and what he does when he uses some magical device. He does not think much about it at all; he finds that it works; he knows that the all-pervasive *mana* or some spirit is accountable for it, and that is enough for him.

This discovery that by doing one thing another happens leads him into an elaborate system of acts which are based on several simple and to him most obvious axioms. He believes implicitly that things which were once connected continue to have some relationship even though they may be separated by a long distance. A coat which was once owned by a man still has some connection with him even though he has discarded it or given it away to another. If, then, you desire to do something to the original owner you may find the coat a convenient medium. By tearing or burning it a most uncomfortable experience may be caused the man to whom it belonged. Especially is this true of the hair and nails, which are so much closer to him than his coat. Great care is exercised in many places by savages to bury all these cuttings and parings so that an enemy may not do them injury by taking advantage of the possession of a part of them, which still is considered as intimately connected with their body and its welfare. This is called contagious magic, and finds a thousand applications in the world of the animist.

Then, again, the savage is unable to get away from the feeling that like produces like. If this be true, a result can be attained by imitating it. A rain-maker in one of the islands in Torres Straits painted the front of his body white and the back black. The explanation was that "all along same as clouds—black behind, white he go first." [18] This is called mimetic or homeopathic magic. Then, too, names and certain words have magical power, and the same is true of talismans and amulets, which can bring to pass what may be desired or ward off impending dangers.

When in fetishism the savage gives himself to coaxing and compelling his fetish to do his bidding, the debasing character of the practice is evident. Only because he may be able to look on some other of his spirits, not as "gods at his disposal," but as powers to be feared and supplicated, is there any possibility of advance into higher forms of religious faith. Unknown to him the struggle between magic and religion has begun, and only by the gradual ascendancy of the true spirit of religion has man attained the higher reaches of religious experience. And today we find ourselves in the same conflict, the difference being that, knowing its danger, we may set ourselves consciously and deliberately to trample magic underfoot and raise religion to its exclusive place in our lives as we come into the presence of God.

[18] Quoted by A. C. Haddon, *Magic and Fetishism*, p. 17.

SUGGESTIONS FOR FURTHER STUDY

Clodd, Edward. *Animism*. Chicago: Open Court Publishing Company, 1905.

Frazer, J. G. *The Golden Bough*. New York: 1922. A monumental work now available in convenient form.

Haddon, Alfred C. *Magic and Fetishism*. Chicago: Open Court Publishing Company, 1910.

Hartland, Edwin Sidney. *Ritual and Belief*. New York: 1914. A very thorough treatment of religion and magic.

Le Roy, Alexandre. *The Religion of the Primitives*. New York: The Macmillan Company, 1922. Written by a Roman Catholic bishop, a deep student of African religion.

Lowie, Robert H. *Primitive Religion*. New York: Boni and Liveright, 1924. The work of an American anthropologist.

Marett, R. R. *The Threshold of Religion*. New York: 1914.

Radin, Paul. *Primitive Man as Philosopher*. New York: D. Appleton and Company, 1927.

———. *Primitive Religion*. New York: Viking Press, 1937. A brilliant volume, to be read with caution.

Smith, Edwin W. *African Ideas of God*. London: Edinburgh House Press, 1950. A series of studies by competent scholars in direct contact with the African.

CHAPTER III

THE RELIGIONS OF EGYPT AND MESOPOTAMIA

EGYPT AND ITS PANTHEON

E GYPT IS A GIFT OF THE NILE." SAID HERODOTUS IN THE FIFTH CENTURY before Christ. It is the truest thing that could be said of this narrow ribbon of a country, which is little more than the banks of this wonderful river. Egypt is so isolated from other countries by deserts and the sea that her religious development took place for long centuries without contact with other peoples and cultures. The Egyptian has always been intensely religious. His religion was of a unique type, as we shall see, but it was genuine and deep. He was conservative beyond most people who have ever lived. Somehow he never felt he could lay aside anything he had ever picked up or discovered. Thus at the end we may study not only what the Egyptian thought then but all he had ever believed in the millenniums of his history—in fact, it all continues to be his belief still. Professor George Foot Moore sums it all up in a pregnant sentence: "The Egyptians of later ages could learn but not forget—the most fatal of all disqualifications for progress." [1]

These people were singularly lacking in philosophic power. They seemed incapable of abstract thinking—it was all in the realm of the concrete, of visible symbols. The priests of Heliopolis and Thebes did work out a kind of theology, as we shall see, but it was not in conformity with any well-knit philosophy. The Egyptians seemed always to be able to hold the most contradictory views at the same time with no sense of incongruity. What would have been abhorrent to the Greek seemed perfectly natural to the Egyptian. He wanted to see things clearly; he was not willing to leave much to the imagination. His art consisted of clear line-drawings without perspective, depth, or mystic hazy background. His writing consisted of pictures and with difficulty could be made to

[1] *History of Religions*, I, 148.

express the abstract conceptions which even he must sometimes employ. So his religion was practical and lacked philosophical and mystical depth.

Professor Henri Frankfort called attention to what he believes is the "single basic conviction" which lay back of and determined the entire thought life of the ancient Egyptians. This conviction is that "the universe is essentially static." The Egyptian held that he lived in a changeless world. While such a view is untenable to us, "what matters is that Egyptians held it, and that it informed not only his theology but also his moral and political philosophy. . . . The peculiar character of Egyptian religion appeared to be derived precisely from an implicit assumption that only the changeless is ultimately significant." [2]

The nomes, or little principalities, of Egypt, each with its central town and its prince, had each a chief god of its own. These gods may all in the beginning have been without names, but names must very soon have been attached. The gods were originally confined to one locality, but very early the same name was to be found in several places. This arose, it may be, as one name was carried by war to another nome, for these little principalities were frequently in conflict with one another. Or, perhaps, the god of one nome appeared even beyond his own borders to be specially powerful and able to bring good to his people, so he was adopted by another nome, and his name was added to the name of the god or gods there. Another early tendency is also to be noted; the gods of some of the nomes began to take on a deeper significance. Amen, the god of Thebes, came to be regarded not only as a local divinity but in a more general way as the god of fertility and generation. This would lead naturally to an expansion of the sphere of influence of this god, and so it was with others.

The various heavenly bodies, the Nile, their kings, trees, and even piles of stones were looked upon as divine and received worship. But by far the most numerous objects of worship in Egypt were animals. This was one of the peculiarities of the religion, and struck the people of Greece and Rome as being strange as it does us. The pagan Celsus is quoted by Origen as saying:

If a stranger reaches Egypt, he is struck by the splendid temples and sacred groves that he sees, great and magnificent courts, marvelous temples with pleasant walks about them, imposing and occult ceremonies; but when he had

---

[2] *Ancient Egyptian Religion*, pp. vii-viii.

entered into the innermost sanctuary, he finds the god worshiped in these buildings to be a cat, or an ape, or a crocodile, or a he-goat, or a dog.[3]

In the period when these words were written Egyptian religion was decadent and exhibited this tendency toward animal worship even more exuberantly than in an earlier and more healthy period of its history. When the Romans were masters of the country, one of the legionnaires "who had accidentally killed a cat was torn to pieces by the mob. . . . For the majority of the people the cat was an incarnate god." [4] Thoth, the god of Hermopolis, was either a baboon or an ibis; the god of the district of the first cataract, Khnum, was a he-goat; and Apis, the god of Memphis, a bull. There was no bird or animal or creeping thing or beetle or fish or frog which did not take its place in the pantheon of the Egyptians. Animal worship is to be found in many other places, but nowhere did it assume such proportions and dominate the thinking of the people as in Egypt.

Many of their gods came to be humanized and at so early a date that we do not know them in any other guise. The worship of an animal as an animal did not seem to be satisfactory; a god must be more like a man to be worthy of worship. It has been asserted that even when they were in animal form they were thought of more as human beings than as animals. Certain gods are represented with human bodies but with animal heads. Khnum is represented as a man with a ram's head; Hekt as a woman with the head of a frog; Sekhmet, the wife of Ptah, is the lioness-headed woman, over whose head is placed the solar disk, crowned with the poisonous uraeus-serpent. This headpiece is also to be found in connection with other divinities. Then there are gods represented as complete human beings, head and all, but the man or woman god was often given some symbol to indicate a connection with the animal which maybe it originally was. Hathor, for example, is a full-fledged woman with a crown of cow's horns on her head. Amen-Ra is a man holding in one hand a scepter and in the other the keylike symbol of life and having his head crowned in several ways in different places, either with the sun's disk and two long feathers or with a pair of ram's horns. It was after Christianity had begun to do its work in Egypt that the condition described by Celsus obtained in all parts of the country. The Egyptian could not get away from his old crude conceptions despite his advance

[3] See Wiedemann, *Religion of the Ancient Egyptians*, p. 181.
[4] Sayce, *The Religion of Ancient Egypt*, p. 101.

in culture and refinement. We must be reminded that he lived in a static universe.

At Heliopolis in the days of the Middle Kingdom (about 2000 to 1790 B.C.) the priestly thinkers constructed a theology in which their god, the sun god Ra, was placed in a position of supremacy above all the gods of the land. So powerful was the influence of this priesthood and so highly favored by the rulers that their theology spread far and wide until for the first time all Egypt, officially at least, came to recognize Ra as the chief god of the whole country. It was a movement toward monotheism, but it did not reach that goal; it was not sufficiently exclusive to rule out the presence and influence of other gods who were looked upon as helpers of the one supreme god Ra. One of the results of the exaltation of Ra was that many other gods were assimilated to him—that is, they were fused or identified with him in name and in attribute—and thus a new conception of a god came into existence. The other priesthoods naturally did not want their gods to be eclipsed, so they joined their gods' names with that of Ra and declared that Ra was their god too, only it was the Ra who had been united with the original god of their temple. So we find such hyphenates as Ra-Horus, Ra-Amen, and many others. Only a few of the old gods, like Osiris, Ptah, and Thoth, were able to preserve their identity, so strong was the influence exerted by the priests of Heliopolis and their theology.

Here is the work of priests seeking to register in theory what practically had come to be the position of their god in the unified empire. But priests in other cities took another direction. They constructed triads of gods, grouping them as father, mother, and son. At Thebes we find Amen the father, Mut the mother, and Montu the son; at Memphis it was Ptah, Sekhmet, and Imhetep; and again at Abydos, Osiris, Isis, and Horus. In the stories told of these trios the son inherits his father's authority and becomes his mother's husband. The mother does not die, not being connected with the sun as the husband and son are. Like the sun, which after the day's work sinks to rest beyond the western horizon, all the divine beings connected with him have the same kind of mortality and must look forward to an eclipse or death at the end of their journey.

Other artificial combinations were worked out. We come upon enneads, or groups of nine gods. The idea of a group of three was still present, but now it was a multiple of three and not the original simple triad. At Heliopolis and in a few other places two enneads were gathered together, a greater and a lesser. These combinations would seem to be the work of men who were not content to see their pantheon in confusion with no order or classification of the deities. They wanted to explain the origin and relationship of the gods, and did so by placing their great god at the apex of the ennead and the others as derived from him in a descending series. It was a clumsy and artificial construction on the part of priests, who were not able to drop any gods from their list, and who tried thus to bring some kind of unity out of the disorder. Another development grew out of the subordination of many gods to the sun-god Ra. It was a kind of solar pantheism. The sun, and only the sun, exists and constitutes the universe. All else is appearance, the manifestation of the supreme and all-embracing sun. This too was a priestly formulation. It represents rather a tendency than a finished and widely accepted belief. All the while the people went on in their own way worshiping their local gods, animals, and trees, and other spirits, little influenced by the colleges of priests in the great centers of official religion.

Of all the many gods and goddesses of Egypt several stand out as especially important. We have already mentioned Ra, the sun-god of Heliopolis. He is represented as a man with the head of a falcon over which is seen the sun disk and the uraeus-serpent. He "represents the sun in the fullness of his strength." [5] This is the most frequent form of the sun-god. From the beginning to the end of the history of Egyptian religion Ra is powerful and even dominant. His only rival is Osiris, who is represented as a man with a beard, bound around with the clothes used in mummification but with his two hands sufficiently free to hold a shepherd's crook and a whip, both of them symbols of authority. Osiris is the ruler of the dead, the supreme god of all that concerns the hereafter. At first he seems to have been looked upon as the personification of natural phenomena, notably the Nile. "His continually repeated death and resurrection were manifested by the Nile as it yearly dwindled and swelled again to inundation, spreading over the fields its fertilizing mud. From this soil sprang the luxuriant crops and vegetation, and these too typified the dying and reviving god." [6] His influence grew, and other deities passed under his influence. He came to be regarded as a prehistoric king of Egypt. But, strange to say, he was murdered by his brother Set. Even so Osiris grew in influence until he held a dominant place in Egypt, fitting in perfectly with the ineradicable bent of the

[5] A. W. Shorter, The Egyptian Gods, p. 138.
[6] Ibid., p. 37.

Egyptian mind to think of death and the hereafter. Another god of the first importance is Amen, the presiding divinity at Thebes, far up the Nile from Heliopolis, where Ra was all-powerful. He is represented either as a he-goat or as a bearded man having a cap to which are attached two tall plumes. As Amen-Ra, he is the great national god of Egypt from the eighteenth dynasty onward.

In the New Kingdom the capital was Thebes, and Amen was its great god. He was so dominant that only one or two gods, like Ptah of Memphis and Ra of Heliopolis, could retain a measure of their old prestige. Then came Amenhotep IV, king of Egypt from 1375 to 1358 B.C. Educated with the priests of Heliopolis, this young prince was deeply religious. He reached the conviction that the sun-god possessed the right to universal worship, and he sought to convert his conviction into practice. He attempted to discredit all the other gods and put the sun-god in their place. It was a movement toward monotheism and, in the estimation of many of the best authorities, actually reached that goal. It was Aten, the sun disk, closely related to Ra, which was to be the object of devotion. Aten "had not, like Ra, been fused with terrestrial gods of various beastly shapes nor represented in human form, and by its freedom from such associations his name was a fit symbol for god in a purer solar monotheism." [7] Aten was declared by royal proclamation to be the one national deity; all were required to worship this god alone. The images of the other gods were to be destroyed and their names forgotten. Nothing was left undone to obliterate every vestige of their memory. The king changed his name from Amenhotep ("Amen is content") to Ikhnaten ("Spirit of Aten") and moved his capital away from Thebes. He founded a new city nearly three hundred miles to the north and called it Akhetaten ("Horizon of Aten"). Here he built wonderful temples and public buildings. He ordered that temples to Aten be erected in various parts of his far-flung empire, which extended from the Euphrates in the north to Nubia far to the south. These temples were different from other Egyptian temples. There was no image of the god as in the others. Aten was pictured as a disk, representing the sun in the sky, from which long rays extended, at the end of each of which was a human hand, hands of blessing offering to men the bounty of the beneficent sun. Nothing like it had ever been known in Egypt. In the mind of the king Aten was a very jealous god; the attempt was made to wipe out every other form of worship. Especially was the reforming

[7] G. F. Moore, *History of Religions*, I, 182.

zeal of the king directed against Amen, who as the recognized national god was more of a rival than any other.

Amenhotep IV was a very young man. His reign covered about seventeen years, and he probably died before he was thirty. He has been called the "great idealist," the "great reformer," the "world's first revolutionist," the "first individual in human history." There is, of course, some reason for this, but there is another side. The summary which Dr. Ernest Budge furnishes must be quoted: "The facts known about the life and reign of Aakhunaten seem to me to prove that from first to last he was a religious fanatic, intolerant, arrogant, and obstinate, but earnest and sincere in his seeking after God and in his attempts to make Aten the national god of Egypt." [8] Dr. Elliott Smith examined the skeleton supposed to be that of the young king and said of it, "The cranium, however, exhibits in an unmistakable manner the distortion characteristic of a condition of hydrocephalus." [9] He was never a vigorous king politically, and his great kingdom developed serious weakness during his reign. He gave himself to religion and let other things take care of themselves. A distinct disintegration from which Egypt never recovered began to take place. This strange king was succeeded by the husband of his eldest daughter. He in turn was succeeded by another son-in-law, the Tutankhamen widely known in our day by the recent discovery of his sumptuous tomb in the Valley of the Kings. This king took the capital back to Thebes and did all he could to restore the worship of Amen. The restoration was continued by his successor, who attempted to obliterate the name and worship of Aten from the land. So Amen-Ra was avenged; the reform had failed. How could it be otherwise? The powerful priesthoods of Amen and Ra were against it, and the common people did not and could not know what the upstart innovator was attempting to do.

In the thousand and more years which followed this attempted reform Egyptian religion failed to show any signs of originality or significant development. The temples became more wealthy and powerful, but the life had departed. It was a state cult, and the common people found little there for them. The old local gods were about all they had to give comfort to the heart and confidence in facing the trials of life. The worship of animals seemed to eat even more deeply into their life. Not only the one animal in a temple was worshiped but the whole species

[8] *The Gods of the Egyptians*, I, 106.
[9] Quoted by Budge, *op. cit.*, p. 75.

was reverenced and held in high honor. It would seem that the people were reverting to prehistoric conditions and losing a part of what they had gained during the long course of their history. The influence of Greece was strongly felt under the reign of the successors of Alexander the Great, the Ptolemies, who ruled from 323 to 30 B.C. A new god, Serapis, derived from the ancient Osiris-Apis, with Greek ingredients, became prominent during this period. His worship spread rapidly until he became the national god. But he could not revive the dying paganism. Accompanied by his wife, the old Egyptian goddess Isis, this new Greco-Egyptian deity took his journey to make new conquests out across the Mediterranean, and we shall meet him again in Rome in the day when that city was reaching out after a more satisfying religion.

THE INDIVIDUAL HERE AND HEREAFTER

Two unique features distinguish Egyptian religion from all others—the extent to which the worship of animals was carried and the belief in individual immortality. Only a few cynical pessimists were skeptical of a hereafter, and they ordered their lives according to the familiar philosophy, "Eat, drink, and be merry, for tomorrow we die." The form taken by the belief was determined partly by conditions in Egypt. "The dry and microbe-free climate," [10] where nothing decays but merely dries up, seemed to suggest the possibility of a kind of physical immortality in which the body might be rendered everlasting and partake of the immortality of the more immaterial parts. Egyptian architecture is above everything else massive, built to stand the ravages of time. The gigantic pyramid tombs of the kings, the ponderous sarcophagi found in all the cemeteries, as well as the temples themselves, suggest permanence. Built out of the hard rock to be found in inexhaustible quantities so near at hand, the ancient monuments have come down to us with little damage through four or five thousand years. The practice of mummification provides additional evidence of the keen interest of the Egyptian in a continued existence. The idea was that the body must be preserved as necessary to immortality. Theories of the life beyond were held which might be considered inconsistent with the necessity of the preservation of the body, but inconsistencies were of little consequence to an Egyptian, and he kept right on making mummies of the bodies of his dead in sublime indifference to any untoward theories which might stand in his way.

[10] "Death (Egyptian)," Hastings' *Encyclopaedia of Religion and Ethics.*

The Egyptian looked forward to death and the judgment with fear and trembling. Not only so, but with his fundamental conviction that changelessness was of the essence of the universe in which he lived he was puzzled by the fact that death seemed not to be an evidence of changelessness but of real movement and transformation. How did he react to the glaring fact that all must die? "We meet, then, once again a paradox. The Egyptians, who conceived the world as static, conceived their future condition as perennial movement. But it was the recurring movement that was part of the established and unchanging order of the world." [11]

When a man died, professional embalmers would remove the entrails and place them in jars, which were buried. This would prevent the jackals from devouring them and clear the body of the parts which would prevent successful preservation. "The body itself was laid in salt water and treated with bitumen; it was then rolled in bandages and cloths, while the abdominal cavity was also plugged up with linen rolls and cushions." [12] In all cases the mummy was laid in a coffin of wood or stone. The chests were frequently decorated

with a number of doors intended to afford exit and entrance to the dead man. At the head-end, where the face lay, it was not uncommon to insert a pair of eyes; by the aid of these the deceased was expected to look forth from the coffin and behold the rising sun. The inner surfaces were at a later time inscribed with texts relating to the life after death, chapters from the Pyramid-Texts and from the Book of the Dead; in addition there were pictorial representations of all possible things which the dead man could need in the hereafter.[13]

And then the embalmed body was laid away for safekeeping, for poor people very simply, for the wealthy in elaborate tombs, and for kings in such buildings as the pyramids, which are still standing, the most permanent buildings ever erected by man. The dead needed the care of their living relatives, so offerings were made at the tomb. In order to secure rest and service in the next world those who had been accustomed to servants were provided with ushabti-figures, "answerers," which were little porcelain doll-like images in mummy form, very doubtful in origin and meaning, but provided to serve the dead person.

[11] Frankfort, op. cit., p. 107.
[12] Steindorff, *The Religion of the Ancient Egyptians*, p. 149.
[13] *Ibid.*, pp. 150-51.

The Egyptians had worked out an elaborate psychology. To us it seems fantastic, naïve, and very confusing, as it attempts to name and give a distinct character to various phases of the personal life. Besides his body man had an immortal soul, which was composite. There was the Ka, whose exact significance is still under discussion. It is described either as a man's double or as his guardian spirit with which he was furnished at birth and which was liberated from the body at death. "The Ka, which had been the companion of the body in life, at death attained to independent existence. It was to the Ka that funerary prayers and offerings were made; to the mummy alone they were useless." [14] The Ka and the mummy could be reunited, it was believed, the mummy reanimated and a new life lived, but in all cases food and drink must be offered at the tomb. Besides the Ka there was the Ba (or Bai), which may best be described as the soul of the departed man. It is pictured as a bird with human head, which would visit the mummy in the tomb. But this too must be fed and provided with the necessities of life, as though the next life were not essentially different from this.

The abode of the dead was variously pictured by the Egyptians. They were not careful to work out a consistent picture but, true to themselves, were quite willing to accumulate all the ideas which arose and take their pick and make combinations as they might choose. There was the early belief that the dead continued to live in the tomb a life not very different from the life they had lived before. They must eat and drink, and this was provided for by the relatives. What was not provided in this way was to be secured by magical incantations and prayers, these being painted on the coffin or mummy chest as an aid to the memory of the dead. He might at times leave the tomb and wander around, but in doing so it was necessary for him to be on his guard against ghostly enemies. He might interfere in the affairs of his living relatives, who dreaded his approach and influence. He was not as happy as they and was looked upon as restless and anxious, able by the aid of magic to assume different shapes and thus be a source of terror.

Then, again, there was a belief that men—at first it was only kings, but later extended to all—might live a life of bliss among the gods in heaven, accompanying them on their journey and enjoying their fellowship. To accomplish this a ladder was believed to exist somewhere in the west, and up this ladder the dead might climb if, peradventure, they knew the necessary magical formulas. But even this abode was not en-

[14] Wiedemann, op. cit., p. 241.

64

tirely unlike the world in which they had previously lived. Still another conception places the dead in the lower world. Beneath this earth there is another called Twet, through which runs a river like the Nile. Here in long passages and in deep caverns the dead dwell. By night they have the light of the sun, for through the twelve sections into which this subterranean river course is divided the sun makes his progress, ready to appear at sunrise the next morning in the eastern sky of the real Egypt overhead. The gates separating the twelve sections are guarded by serpents and demons, and the sun-god in his magnificent barge must know these monsters' names to secure passage. It was believed at a later time that dead men might share this nightly voyage of the sun, that is, if they were acquainted with the appropriate incantations and magical formulas.

We come lastly to the most important of these conceptions—that connected with Osiris. And here it becomes necessary to refer to the myth, told in several forms, about Osiris and his relation with the dead. Osiris was one of the ancient divinities of Egypt. He was murdered by Set, who dismembered his body and scattered it over the delta. The mourning wife, Isis, wandered over the land seeking the body of her husband, while Horus, their son, vowed vengeance. In the end Osiris was restored to life and became the "King of the Western Folk," presiding over the realm of the dead. This god had died and was alive again; here lay the significance of the myth and the belief connected with it. Like him, men who knew that death was sure and could not be evaded might hope to rise again to a new life. The belief expanded and deepened until the idea of the life beyond was that men might become like Osiris; even more than this, that they might become Osiris himself, losing in a real sense their own personal identity. Dead men were identified with him until they were thought of as Osiris so-an-so. This has been given as a reason why the Egyptians never became ancestor-worshipers. The dead relative ceased to be bound to them now that he had become Osiris; no motive now remained to offer worship to him as a separate being.

As Osiris in the myth had been declared "just" by the judge before whom he was tried, so every man before entering his realm must come before a similar court. The judge now is Osiris himself, and at his side are forty-two terrible creatures before whom confession must be made. The confession is for the most part a statement of the sins one has not committed, though some positive good things are mentioned. "I have not done what the gods abominate," "I have not allowed anyone to be hungry," "I have done no murder," "I oppressed no man in possession

65

of his property"—so run the items of this confession. But this personal confession is not sufficient; his heart must be "weighed on a great balance against the symbol of justice." The heart of the man found wanting is devoured by a hippopotamus which stands close by and ready. This is about all we know of the fate of the wicked. The good are rewarded by life in the realm of Osiris. Thus, particularly in the later day, the moral sanction becomes an important feature in the thought of the hereafter, though it must be said that the unfortunate prevalence of magic in all that was connected with death and the condition of the dead was so powerful that the conception of the future was only partially moralized.

THE GODS OF BABYLONIA AND ASSYRIA

Three thousand years before Christ a civilization had been developed in the lower Euphrates Valley. Like that of Egypt it was a river civilization. In each case the control of the water supply had made necessary concerted action and political organization. Economic necessity was responsible for the formation of a number of small city states, each with its prince or king and its chief god. In these respects the civilization in Babylonia was like that of Egypt, but there was a wide divergence whose cause is at once evident by a glance at the map. Egypt was isolated and developed her culture separated from foreign influence. Babylonia, on the other hand, was open on all sides to the incursion of ideas as well as of armies. These invasions might come from the mountains of Elam on the east, the desert on the south and west, and down the long Mesopotamian Valley which reached off toward the northwest. In fact, her history was given direction many times by forces which found their way to Babylonia from each of these sources.

The religion of the Euphrates Valley had passed out of the animistic stage when the little city states appeared upon the scene. Yet there is plenty of evidence that everything was built upon an animistic foundation. The people continued to believe in the Zi, or spirits, in whom they had believed in the days before any advance had been made in civilization. As the states were in process of formation, certain of the spirits of their former belief grew in importance and became gods with personality and distinct attributes. This process was hastened by the political relationships which became more complex as time passed. The god of one city came to exercise influence as far as his city was able to carry its conquests. But even at the end of the process, when the gods had become far more than nature powers, evidences could be found which pointed back to their more humble origin. According to Professor Morris Jastrow, the gods were personifications of the sun and the moon, the power manifesting itself in vegetation, and that of the waters and the storm. Larsa and Sippar had Shamash, the sun-god; Ur and Harran worshiped Sin, the moon-god; Uruk had Ishtar, the mother-goddess; while Eridu had Ea, the water-deity, as its patron; and Enlil, of Nippur, was the "lord of the storm." Professor Robert W. Rogers listed over sixty gods and goddesses gathered together on one tablet, though many of these are duplications.

Nearly every place in early times would have a sun-god or a moon-god or both, and in the political development of the country the moon-god of the conquering city displaced or absorbed the moon-god of the conquered. When we have eliminated these gods, who have practically disappeared, there remains a comparatively small number of gods who outrank all the others.[15]

In an early day the priests in the greater temples began to form triads. The earliest of these was that of Anu, Enlil, and Ea. Anu was the patron divinity of Uruk and was associated with the overarching heavens, Enlil with the earth and the atmosphere immediately above, and Ea with the waters, those on the earth and those below. Thus this triad is inclusive of the universe as conceived by the thinkers of the time. A second series of three consists of Sin, Shamash, and Ishtar, gods of Babylonia, who did not differ essentially from the Sumerian gods of the first triad mentioned. Under Hammurapi, Babylon became the capital of an empire and Marduk, the patron divinity of the city, the god par excellence of the empire. But even this position could be maintained only by a process which transferred to him the power and attributes of Enlil of Nippur and Ea of Eridu. Particularly was this true of Enlil, doubtless because he was looked upon as the venerable patron of the oldest seat of civilization and hence worthy of respect and honor, even when another city was now the seat of far wider authority and influence.

Only one other god could ever vie with Marduk in power, and that was Ashur. He was the god of the Assyrian empire and, as the recognized head of the pantheon, marched at the head of the armies as they traveled far from the capital carrying destruction and terror all over western Asia and even as far as Egypt. He differed from all the other gods mentioned in that his worship was imageless. He was represented as the disk of the sun from which rays or wings proceeded in all directions. He was of a more

[15] *The Religion of Babylonia and Assyria*, p. 79.

spiritual type than the other gods, but this does not seem to have pre-vented him from being associated with all the cruelty and bloodshed which accompanied the destructive march of the armies of Assyria as they ruthlessly destroyed one city after another.

The gods were given consorts or wives, but all we know of many of them is their names. For the most part they were of little or no signifi-cance. But one among them stands out as a power of the first magnitude. It is Ishtar, the goddess of generation and fertility, the goddess of love and sexual relationships. Starting no doubt in the perfectly justifiable veneration of fertility in field and animal and man, and being looked upon as presiding over the increase upon which all life depends, this goddess became the patroness of practices connected with her worship which could only be debasing and demoralizing.

An extensive mythology has come down to us from Babylonia. The conflict of Bel or Marduk with the monster Tiamat tells the story of creation in such a manner that Marduk is honored and his city, Babylon, is placed before all others, so that it has been called "a great political treatise." But the myth was religious as well and exercised an undeniable influence upon the biblical account of the creation. In the Bible, how-ever, the gross polytheism has been laid aside, and the wonderful prose-poem is made to give honor to the one God Almighty, maker of heaven and earth. There is also the epic of Gilgamesh, the great hero with many exploits to his name, to whom is told the deluge story with features so nearly akin to the story in Genesis that it is impossible not to see a close connection, but here also the Babylonian version revels in gods and their relations with men, thus representing a level far below that occupied by the parallel narrative in Genesis.

MAN'S APPROACH TO THE DIVINE POWERS

Egypt's worship of animals and views concerning immortality were noted as unique. Neither of these had any place to speak of in Babylonia and Assyria. Here the approach to the gods by divination stands out so prominently that it cannot be avoided in any account, however brief, of the religion. Divination was practiced to learn or "divine" the will of the gods sufficiently in advance to be able to prepare for what was com-ing; in no sense was it to turn the gods from their purpose. Many methods of divination were known. One of them was to drop oil into a basin of water and determine from the manner in which the oil scattered what the future might be. But of all the methods the favorite was

68

examination of a sheep's liver, called hepatoscopy. The theory on which hepatoscopy was based was that the gods identified themselves with the animal which was about to be sacrificed. By observing the part of the animal which was considered the seat of life the will of the gods could be ascertained. Among the Babylonians the liver was believed to be the seat of life, probably because so large an amount of blood was to be found in that organ. The function of the heart was not clearly recognized. At a later date, as among the Romans, when the heart had taken the place of the liver as the seat of life, the heart together with the liver was examined in the practice of divination. The liver of the sheep, which has a very diversified surface, was most commonly used. This offered scope for an almost infinite number of combinations of signs, which were worked out into an elaborate system.

Another form of divination was by astrology, the observation of the heavenly bodies. A co-ordination was supposed to exist between the happenings on earth and the movements of the stars and planets and the sun and moon. The basis on which this theory rested was the belief that the gods and the heavenly bodies were one and the same, so that if the heavens might be correctly read the will of the gods was thereby determined. The first place in astral lore was taken by Sin, the moon-god, the "lord of wisdom." Astrology in Babylonia did not trouble itself with the petty affairs of the individual but only with important matters of state, and here we must note that the concept of the state stood for the solidarity of people, king, and god. So while the common people had some impersonal share in the transactions of the state with the great gods, they had no alternative in their own affairs than to go to the spirits and demons, which they believed surrounded them and deal with them directly or through sorcerers and witches. The people as well as the priests became adepts in interpreting dreams, omens, portents, monstrosities, and prodigies. In the words of Professor Morris Jastrow, "the significance attached to omens was the most conspicuous outward manifestation of the religious spirit of the people taken as a whole." [16]

But there was more to their religion than that. The elaborate ceremonials in the temples, while shot through with the vitiating influences of magic, contained elements of religious aspiration and fervor. The Incantation Rituals were in the hands of a special class of priests who had worked out a gorgeous ceremonial calculated to impress the worshipers deeply. Unfortunately, however, the gist of the whole exercise was

[16] *Civilization of Babylonia and Assyria*, p. 266.

to avert the anger of the deities which might be done only through a series of incantations. The magical has penetrated the religion so deeply that it is impossible to escape it. The fear of the gods makes almost impossible an approach based on trust and confidence in the good will of the divine beings. A higher stage is reached in the Penitential Psalms. The worshiper feels and confesses that he has done wrong. He appeals to this god and that for forgiveness and cleansing. The sins confessed run all the way from moral evil to merely ceremonial offenses, discrimination between the two not being carefully made. Even at this stage, the highest reached by the Babylonians, there is much to be desired.

In strange and almost complete contrast with Egypt the Babylonians faced an utterly cheerless prospect as they faced life beyond death. The lot of the dead is not to be envied. There is nothing to do and no pleasures to enjoy in the dusty, cold, and dark prison where the dead, huddled together indiscriminately, live out their miserable existence. There is no chance of a return to the clear upper air, except maybe for a short time. There is no retribution for the wicked, no reward for the good, and no hope of anything better. The only thing to make their condition worse would be for the corpse to remain unburied or be mutilated. Then even a harder fate is his, to roam over the world and feed upon offal in company with other miserable ghosts. And yet, like the early Hebrews who held a somewhat similar belief relative to the future life, these people developed an ethical system which does them high honor. The old religion ceased to be as an organized faith when the Assyrian and Babylonian empires passed from the scene, but their influence did not perish. Babylonian astrology and divination and other features of their occult lore traveled westward and exerted a potent influence in the latter days of the paganism of Greece and Rome, and even today the gypsy astrologer and fortuneteller remind us of the days when these and other forms of hocus-pocus were in their glory in the Euphrates Valley.

SUGGESTIONS FOR FURTHER STUDY

Egypt

Breasted, J. H. Ancient Times. 2nd ed. Boston: Ginn and Company, 1935. Chs. III, IV.

———. Development of Religion and Thought in Ancient Egypt. New York: Charles Scribner's Sons, 1912.

Frankfort, Henri. *Ancient Egyptian Religion.* New York: Columbia University Press, 1948.

Moore, George Foot. *History of Religions.* Rev. ed. New York: Charles Scribner's Sons, 1922. Vol. I, chs. VIII, IX.

Petrie, W. M. Flinders. *Religious Life in Ancient Egypt.* Boston: Houghton Mifflin Company, 1924.

Shorter, Alan W. *An Introduction to Egyptian Religion.* London: George Routledge and Sons, 1931.

Steindorff, Georg. *The Religion of the Ancient Egyptians.* New York: G. P. Putnam's Sons, 1905.

Babylonia and Assyria

Breasted, J. H. *Ancient Times.* Chs. V, VI.

Jastrow, Jr., Morris. *Aspects of Religious Beliefs and Practice in Babylonia and Assyria.* New York: G. P. Putnam's Sons, 1911.

————. *The Civilization of Babylonia and Assyria.* Philadelphia: J. B. Lippincott Company, 1915. Chs. IV, V.

Moore, George Foot. *History of Religions.* Vol. I, ch. X.

Rogers, Robert William. *The Religion of Babylonia and Assyria.* New York: Methodist Book Concern, 1908.

71

CHAPTER IV

THE RELIGIONS OF
GREECE AND ROME

RELIGION BEFORE HOMER

WE KNOW LITTLE ABOUT THE RELIGION OF THE GREEKS BEFORE THE time of Homer. What is known is not by direct evidence so much as by inference. Hints of all kinds are given which seem to point back to practice and beliefs of an age long since past. Putting these various clues together and interpreting them on the basis of analogous situations in the development in other countries, we may form tentative conclusions, more or less convincing. It may be inferred that the early Greek was an animist, and thus in the same line of development with other peoples whose origins are known. Evidences are not lacking that their deities were nature gods, and that they reverenced and even worshiped their ancestors. It is probable that at an early time the gods were sufficiently differentiated to be considered in charge of this or that interest. They had in some sense become departmental gods, especially connected with the great functions of nature and human life. The reason why so much indefiniteness should exist at this point is that the Greek mind so soon conceived of its gods as being like men and so completely separated them from the objects in nature with which they had been connected that the relation became indistinct and can now scarcely be discovered—they had become complete personalities like the Greeks themselves.

We know that the coming of the seasons was the signal for the holding of religious festivals, that these early Greeks believed in a future life, and looked upon their departed ancestors as able to confer blessing upon their faithful descendants. There is no reason to think that images were worshiped in this period, nor that the references to animals and their connection with the gods pointed back to a totemic organization of society. In all probability each community had its god of the heavens who sent the light and the rain, the great god we know later as Zeus.

Athena, the maiden goddess of Athens, was emerging through several transformations and can begin to be identified. There was a goddess representing "Mother-Earth," the kindly giver of life. There is evidence that they worshiped the patron of the chase, the shepherd god, a god of fire, and the spirits of the sea.

The physical configuration of Greece had much to do in determining certain aspects of their culture and religion. Their religion was parochial and different in the various tiny states into which Greece was divided by the sea and mountains. Their independence and love of local initiative, however, had as much to do with the divisiveness which was the bane of Greek political life as their geographical situation. From the beginning to the end the Greek polis, or city, and its surrounding territory was the unit which determined the characteristic form of Greek political life. In like manner Greek religion was a religion of city states, each cult differing in some particulars from that of its neighbors, with its own divinities and its own worship. In spite of the degree of unity attained in a later time the local forms were so tenacious that they never ceased to mark off the cult of one state from that of another.

These factors are highly important in the study of Greek religion. The best known and greatest of the gods of Greece was Zeus. Connected with the overarching sky, the giver of the bounties which come with the light of the sun and the rain, Zeus was early acknowledged as a god by all the Greek states, but in each case the Zeus worshiped had a secondary title. This title was local and represented the god peculiar to each state, whose name at least had been retained when he had been identified with the great Zeus. The small local community also made possible one of the forms of worship, the communal meal, in which all the citizens took part. At this meal the close connection between the city and its gods was sacramentally celebrated. The god was looked upon as kindly disposed toward his own people, not an angry god in need of propitiation. Greek religion had its somber, more tragic phase but in general, particularly in the earlier period, was marked by an airy cheerfulness and delight in beauty which were characteristic of the race.

THE HOMERIC CONTRIBUTION

The Iliad and The Odyssey of Homer reflect the life and religion of about 1000 B.C. The epics fulfilled the twofold function of depicting the gods as they were conceived by the people at an early day and crystallizing for hundreds of years the religious ideas of the growing communi-

ties of Greece. The chief religious characteristics of the epics is anthropomorphism. The gods were personalities like men and women. They were
superhuman, to be sure, but for all that they were only human beings
built large. Their power was manifested in nature and in the life of the
states. The world was ruled from Mount Olympus, the residence of
King Zeus and his celestial court. He, as the chief ruler of the universe,
guided the events of human history and determined the destiny of men.
While every conception of the gods was cast in a human mold, the epic
always insisted on a difference between men and gods. The gods were
not confronted with the trials and sufferings of men; they were immortal
and lived on heavenly nectar and ambrosia, far removed from death and
decay. Yet they were not omniscient, and in their passions and feelings
were just like ordinary men. It is almost an indignity to man to say this
because in their intercourse on Olympus the gods were guilty of such
unworthy conduct as to bring a blush to the cheek of high-minded men.
So we feel, and so the thinkers and writers of the classical age in Greece
felt. They condemned such conduct in gods as well as in men, refusing
to believe that any god worthy of their reverence should show such
weaknesses. It may be said that while in the epic the gods appeared at a
disadvantage, living in the company of one another on the celestial
heights, yet in the cults of the Greek states as individuals and in their
relation to men and human affairs they were seen in a very different
light, thus emphasizing the difference between the Homeric mythology
and the religion of the Greek states. In the local cults the gods appeared
as objects more worthy of reverence and worship.

Zeus was the greatest of the gods. He accompanied the Greeks as far
as their colonies were planted and became more than any other the
national god. He was "the protector of political and social groups from
the state to the household. He also took under especial cognizance moral
relations among men." [1] Artemis was the goddess of wild nature and
destroyed life, but, strange to say, was the protector of all life as well.
After a long evolution she appeared as a chaste huntress, punishing those
who did not remain pure and clean. Apollo, the model of manly beauty
and perfection, was a shepherd and the deity of shepherds. At the same
time he became the god of revelation and at Delphi rendered decisions
on perplexing practical questions. Here all Greece came and offered him

[1] G. F. Moore, *History of Religions*, I, 416.

74

homage, thus quickening the latent sense of unity which Greece so much needed. Hermes was another shepherd god closely associated with Apollo. He was so swift of foot that he came to be recognized as the messenger of the gods.

Besides these there were Poseidon, the god of the sea; Athena, second only to Zeus, the patroness of civilization, the inventive genius, skilled in arts and industries; Aphrodite, the beautiful goddess of fertility and of love; Hera, the wife of Zeus, presiding over husbandry and industry, the patroness of married women; Hephaistos, the skillful artificer, patron of craftsman, god of fire and forge; Ares, the warrior, the fickle god, husband of Aphrodite; Demeter, "Mother-Earth," the goddess of the fertile soil and of tillage, who at a later date emerged into great prominence in the Eleusinian mysteries. There were many other divinities, each preserving his individuality despite the number of the gods in the pantheon. There was no worship of gods bent on doing injury to humanity. If at any time ill fortune came, it was because the gods, capricious like men, were temporarily angry. There was nothing vague nor mystical about the Greek idea of divinity. The outlines were clear, the form perfect, and everything connected with the worship of the gods was beautiful and harmonious. Unfortunately "they were not far enough off or holy enough to make religion so potent a factor as it might be in Greek life." [2]

While in general the relation between gods and men was sympathetic and familiar, there was another side. Death was present, and was only baleful and horrid. There was some sense of wrongdoing and the need of sacrifice because of sin. There was a lower world, the abode of the Chthonian gods, whose shadow fell at times over the path of man even in sunny Greece. Worship, however, was more of a companionship, doing reverence to a great king in the heavenly realm, without any of the cringing fear and abject servility so common in other religions. Combined with an artistic temperament of the finest quality, religion expressed itself in outward forms of exquisite beauty. All that the Greeks did was beautiful and harmonious, and in no feature of their life was the result more telling or more influential than in the temples of their gods. By the time of the epic poems all the coarse and cruel features of the early cult had been laid aside, and every expression of the religious sentiment was in accord with the finest taste, a fitting counterpart to the beauties of nature and art to be seen in every direction.

[2] Arthur Fairbanks, A Handbook of Greek Religion, p. 148.

THE MYSTERIES

Not for centuries after the rise of the epic did the worship find its full development. Temples grew in beauty and elegance; images were gradually introduced; and the ceremonial became more ornate and finished in form and content. But in all I have described there was little chance for the individual as an individual to express his religious emotions. Everything was performed by the family or clan or city; it was corporate worship with little reference to the individual. But by the seventh century before our era the individual had come to a place of importance as a citizen, and with this new attainment were born new deeds and aspirations which could not be satisfied by the formal, though beautiful and decorous, worship of the corporate body of citizens. He needed and demanded what was more personal and individual and vital. The seventh century before Christ saw a great change; there occurred what has been called "a great religious revival."

Far to the north in Thrace lived a strange god named Dionysus. He was "the old spirit of vegetable life, incarnate in the bull, incarnate in the wine." [3]

His worship was of a distinctly orgiastic character. Groups of his worshipers, mainly women, found their way at night with torches into wild glens on the mountains; the music of drums and cymbals and flutes stirred sensitive spirits till their whirling dances and wild summons to the god induced a religious frenzy; serpents were fondled, the young of wild animals were now suckled by human mothers, now torn in pieces and eaten raw. The fawn-skin garment, the wand tipped with a fir cone and wreathed in ivy, sometimes horns attached to the head, recalled the god to whose service they were devoted. [4]

The idea in all this wild worship was "the identification of the worshipers and the god. The wilder the frenzy, the more the worshiper felt himself free from the restraints of the material world." All this was incongruous with the orderly and beautiful worship of the Olympian gods and could find its way into Greek life only because of a deep need unsatisfied by the regulated forms of the established religion. It is true that the crudeness of the frenzied practices was toned down as they traveled south and became a permanent feature of Greek religious life, but we are dealing in Dionysius worship with something foreign, which could have been

[3] *Ibid.*, p. 241.
[4] *Ibid.*

admitted only because of strong new desires which were stirring in the hearts of the people. A longing for purification, the hope of immortality, and a desire to experience religion in the inner life and to be stirred emotionally were abroad in the land and could not be repressed.

Another expression of the same spirit was the increasing importance attached to the worship of Demeter, already referred to as goddess of the soil and crops. According to the myth, Persephone, the daughter of Demeter, was seized by Hades and carried away to the lower world. Demeter, controlling the growth of the grain, brought men and gods to the point of famine by failing in her grief to perform her wonted function. Zeus was compelled to intervene, and succeeded in bringing Persephone back to earth and her mother. Having tasted the food of Hades, she had to return and spend a third of the year with him, but she came again with the blooming flowers and rejoiced the hearts of all. The touching story took renewed hold on the imagination of the Greeks and as a feature in the mysteries of Eleusis became especially prominent in the classical age at Athens. The rescue of Persephone from the land of the shades became the earnest of their expectation that men too might look for a real immortality on the other side of the grave. "It is another instance of the resuscitation of plant life after the winter's death taken as the promise and proof that man too may rise to newness of life." [5]

The great Eleusinian mysteries, which were expressions of the new spirit, were performed at Athens and the adjacent Eleusis in the fall of the year and became a part of the established religion. The procession of the initiated and the neophytes as it wended its way slowly to the sacred precincts of Eleusis was in itself impressive. There the ceremonies, of which we have exceedingly scant information, lasted two or three days. The important thing was not the doctrine which was imparted but the impression made. The myth of Demeter and Persephone was doubtless enacted, vividly picturing the return of the soul from the realm of Hades. The purpose of the rites and ceremonies was to satisfy the longing for immortality by the assurance which comes through an emotional reaction. The rites eventually became a scandal, through the inevitable tendency to allow a formal ceremony and an emotional reaction to take the place of righteousness and amendment of life.

There were still other manifestations of the same reaching out after a religion which was calculated to stir the inner life. The Orphic brotherhoods, wandering evangelists of a new life, were to be met all over

[5] Moore, *op cit.*, pp. 450-51.

Greece. For a time in the fifth and fourth centuries B.C. they exerted a more wide-reaching influence than any other religious agency. They came into Greece in connection with one of the waves of the worship of Dionysus which swept over the country. They received their name from Orpheus, the sweet singer, who charmed the wild beasts and fierce men by his strains, and was even said to be able to move trees and stones. Grieving over his wife, whom he had failed to rescue from Hades, he betook himself to the mountain fastnesses, where he was killed by the frenzied nymphs who tore him limb from limb. Here were tragedy and pathos sufficient to appeal to the deepest feelings. More than any of the newer cults Orphic religion was concerned with the next life. It preached its gospel to the individual, calling upon men to put away evil, to accept a new way of salvation, and to enter into mystic and sacramental union with their god. This cult demanded personal faith, called for purifications, had its initiations, sacraments, and mystic rites. What theology it had was pantheistic; it taught transmigration of the soul, but held out a dreadful fate for those who were not initiated. The body is the prison house of man's soul, so that he can attain life and freedom only by separation from the body. The votaries grouped themselves into societies called Theasoi, like modern dissenters. They were to a certain extent ascetics, believing they were already divine and seeking for reunion with the gods.[6] Unlike the Eleusinian mysteries, which were incorporated into the established religion, the Orphic faith was a kind of vagrant, outside the regular channels of religious life. This very fact serves, however, to emphasize the inadequacy of the old formal cults and the need of the kind of gospel which the Orphic preachers proclaimed.

The Eleusinia were almost exclusively Greek, Roman citizens being the only outsiders to be admitted to the mystic rites. The Orphic brotherhoods, on the contrary, had a message for all men, "Greek and barbarian, bond and free." Man, they said, belongs to "the kindred of God." He may in this life have communion with the Deity and in the next, after being purified from all his stains, may have fellowship with him forever, this fellowship reaching the point of practical identification. Here we reach the high-water mark of Greek religion.

THE PHILOSOPHERS

At the same time the gospel of personal religion was receiving a wide hearing in Greece, another movement was coming to its own and making

[6] See James Adam, *The Religious Teachers of Greece*, p. 113.

its contribution to Greek culture. It was the rise of the philosopher and the philosophic poet. They, rather than the priests, dominated the thought life of the Greeks and gave to the people the most worthy ideas of God and the soul which have come to us out of antiquity. There thinkers and seers were not hampered by the restraints of ecclesiastical authority. The priesthoods never assumed controlling authority over the opinions and actions of men. The Greeks had no sacred scriptures to which they could appeal as authoritative and which might serve as a touchstone of orthodoxy. Nowhere in the ancient world had such liberty of thought prevailed as in Greece. It was the very atmosphere which they breathed. The human mind was loosed to venture the hardest problems and to master the world of intellect and of nature. Well was it that this opportunity came to men of such consummate ability. The Greeks have taught us how to think, and we sit at their feet today. Their minds ranged over the whole field of human learning and were irresistibly drawn to look into the human heart and interpret the thoughts and desires which religion had implanted.

The Odes of Pindar show dissatisfaction with the epic account of the gods and their actions. This poet was born in 522 B.C. near Thebes, but his appeal was to all the Greeks. He was devoted to the gods and was deeply influenced by the Homeric conception. But with all his love for the old stories he did not hesitate to reject what was crude and immoral. He would not believe that the gods were guilty of any such conduct and considered it blasphemy to impute wrong deeds to them. They must be just and truthful and were completely wise. Man, on the other hand, was a sinner, and he was frequently presumptuous in not recognizing the distinction between the gods and weak, fallible human nature.

The great dramatic poets made a most significant contribution. To them there was unity in the moral order of the universe. Zeus was raised to a lofty position as the governor of the world. His righteous rule extended over all men and held them to the exacting standards of justice and honor. Each in his own way, the three great tragedians—Aeschylus, Sophocles, and Euripides—showed little patience with the stories of the gods in the epics and exhibited the nemesis of wrongdoing and the tragic consequences of hate. They were on the side of righteousness and the higher conception of man as well as of God.

Similarly, the great philosophers of the classical period—Socrates, Plato, and Aristotle—were leaders in moral as well as intellectual development. Particularly was this true of the first two. Socrates was intent on

pricking the bubble of conceit in men who were self-satisfied and complacent in their theories, but, more than that, he was constantly seeking to
build up men in virtue. For Socrates virtue is knowledge and knowledge
is virtue, so that to know things as they are and to see clearly is to be good.
A truer conception of morality has taken us beyond this, but the deep
feeling that there was a spiritual presence in the world working for righteousness and the unconquerable hope of immortality, which made him
calm and even cheerful in the presence of a tragic death, marked Socrates
as one of the great souls in the history of ethics and religion.

Plato was the pupil of Socrates. He believed that the gods were good,
that they would never stoop to evil in any form. Thus, being righteous
themselves, they demanded the same morality in men. Receiving from
his great master an ethical and spiritual outlook on life, Plato went much
further and elaborated his philosophy into a system whose influence is in
many respects as powerful today as in past ages. According to this system
we live in a spiritual world in which ideas are the most real and important
ingredient. The great idea is God and he is one. Thus Plato was laying the
foundation for a theistic interpretation of the universe. In fact he has been
called "the founder of theistic philosophy." [7] Aristotle, "the master of
those who know," was far more interested in the world of nature around
him. His God is farther away from men than the god of Plato. Man is
midway between God and the physical universe and so has a nature both
spiritual and earthly. He had no conception of immortality as a personal
experience, as was taught by Plato and Socrates. But with many differences in outlook upon life and its problems Aristotle takes his place with
his great predecessors in the insistence of his moral demands and in his
belief in a unified universe controlled and created by a single spiritual
being over all.

In the later period as we approach the Christian Era several philosophies emerge which seek to interpret life to a changing, dissatisfied age,
an age which, according to Professor Gilbert Murray, had "lost its nerve."
Epicureanism was not guilty of recommending a life of indulgence, as
has been charged, but it had no religious message. Believing that a life
of contentment can be lived only if fear of the gods and dread foreboding
concerning the future are eliminated, Epicurus proceeded to construct a
philosophy with no reference to the spiritual world either now or
hereafter.

A very different viewpoint was that occupied by the Stoics, stern and

[7] Moore, op. cit., p. 499.

forbidding as was their outlook on life. They held that there is a God, a living God, who is present in every atom of the universe, and this God is a spirit. But when "spirit" is defined, it is seen not to be really spiritual at all. It is matter like everything else, though matter in the more ethereal form of fire and vapor. But it was in respect of morality that the Stoics had a message which reached many of the finest spirits of the age. Good and evil exist side by side, and it is man's part to choose between them. He is to do so solely for virtue's sake, not for any reward that may come by so doing—that would defeat the very end he has in view. Sternly he must suppress his impulses and live untouched by any emotional appeal. It was no milk for babes, this Stoic creed. Small wonder it found lodgment in the hearts of many of the noblest men, in Rome as well as in Greece.

But another idea was abroad in the land, the idea that matter was intrinsically evil. Basing their teaching on Plato and Pythagoras, the Neo-Pythagoreans placed God, the principle of good, in contrast and in conflict with matter, which is evil and only evil. Men are partakers of the divine nature, but are ever being drawn down into the vileness of their natural environment. This can be prevented only by overcoming their fleshly desires through a strict regimen, which included becoming vegetarians and celibates.

The last phase of the development of the Greek intellect was Neo-Platonism, whose great teacher was Plotinus. It based its teaching on the idealistic philosophy of Plato but added an element to which the great philosopher was a stranger. It was philosophy touched with emotion. It also partook of the prevailing thought of the day that matter was evil. God was separated from man by a great chasm, even though man originally came from God. But man had forgotten his origin and his birthright and went about unmindful of his heritage. He might, however, get back. This was to be done by stages, step by step regaining what had been lost, until in the end he lost himself in the God from whom he originally came.

Only enough has been said about Neo-Platonism and the other philosophies to indicate that they were religious; that they dealt not only with conduct but with salvation; that they attempted to meet the needs of men and women who in an age of confusion were seeking the light; and that they were very evidently preparing the way for the coming of the gospel of Jesus Christ, which gathered up into itself all the elements of worthy appeal to be found in the philosophies which had preceded it and

81

which in addition could embody in a personality the very essence of its living power—and this the Greek philosophies could not do.

EARLY ROMAN RELIGION

The mistake has often been made of thinking that Roman religion was about the same as Greek religion. It could easily be made because Greek religion was transported to Rome and became the possession of the Roman people. But before the Greek influence began to be felt, Rome had a religion of its own, and the character of this religion must be known before the later mixture of Greek and Roman ideas can be understood. Then it will be seen how distinctive the Roman contribution was and how its influence was a powerful factor in the later faith of the city and empire of Rome.

The early religion of the people of Rome was above everything else practical. They were an agricultural people, and their religion was suited to the simple needs of countrymen. Already we begin to see the distinctive character of whatever is Roman. These people, unlike the Greeks, were not thinkers. They had no mythology and no philosophic theories of the origins of things. They were men who did not ask questions beyond the pragmatic queries, Is it useful? Does it work? They were men of law and order and authority with capacity to conquer and to rule. They made little contribution to the intellectual life of the world, but they developed one of the most important gifts of the ancient to the modern world, Roman law. Our laws bear the impress of the various Roman codes, particularly that of the Emperor Justinian, and in the Roman Catholic Church we have in every country of the world the inheritor of the organizing genius of the ancient Romans, which exercises over its adherents today the same authority and demands the same implicit obedience as did Rome under both the republic and the empire.

The gods of the Romans were powers who were expected to do the things they were capable of doing. They were powers, numina, with scarcely enough personality to be called gods. With no image, each of these powers had its own function and was not known in any other way than in its performance. This caused a division of labor among the powers which tended to reduce the gods to very small dimensions. To illustrate:

Seia has to do with the corn before it sprouts, Segetia with corn when shot up. Tutilina with corn stored in the granary, Nodotus has for his care the knots in the straw. There is a god Door, a goddess Hinge, a god Threshold.

Each act in opening infancy has its god or goddess. . . . Pilumnus, god of the pestle, and Diverra, goddess of the broom, may close our small sample of limitless crowd.[8]

So this religion is very close to animism, but with the personal element reduced to a minimum. Such was the condition in the earliest day, but later certain of the divinities assumed an importance unknown before and became the greatest gods of the state religion. Jupiter held the first place, also called Optimus Maximus, and next came Mars, who (with Quirinus) was the god of war. Janus, after whom the first month of our year was named, was the god of opening, the old Roman god of the door at the entrance of the house. The last of these greater gods of the early days was Vesta, originally the goddess of the family hearth and latterly the guardian of the state.

The religion of the family, as has been intimated, was the earliest form of Roman religion. The only priest in that day was the father of the family, the paterfamilias. He offered the sacrifices and led the family in its religious duties. Certain of the earliest deities were distinctively family gods. Vesta, goddess of the fire and hearth, came first. The duty of caring for the fire and keeping the hearth clean fell to the mistress of the house, who thus had her part in the family worship. In a later day, when Vesta became a goddess of the state, the place of the mistress of the house was taken by six vestal virgins, charged with keeping the fire and other duties specially assigned to them. The lares watched over the household, and the penates proctected the storerooms on which the sustenance of the family depended. The manes, or ancestral spirits, were looked upon as well disposed to the living, as their name indicates. Besides these each individual had his own protecting divinity; in the case of the man it was his Genius, of a woman her Juno. These "good angels," which seem often to be little more than one's other self, have watch care through life over one's fortunes and at death go out into the great unknown with him.

As the old family religion was enlarged into the state religion, it became in a very definite sense an affair of the state. The ministers of religion were state officials, appointed and performing their duties like other officials. True to their genius, the Romans organized this religion as thoroughly as the government, of which in reality it was a part. The cult was purely a formal performance of the ritual and ceremonial with no vestige of sentiment about it. Great care was exercised to secure correctness and

[8] Allan Menzies, *History of Religion*, p. 307.

precision in the conduct of the worship, for the efficacy of the rite depended upon just these things. Like a stern earthly potentate who demanded that he be approached with circumspection and that he be addressed with the proper titles, so the gods were looked upon as making the same demands. The gods could be counted upon to prevent evils from befalling the people if they on their part performed their religious duties punctiliously and thus gave the gods the honor which was their due.

The number of festival days was large. This made necessary the organization of the religious officials, that all the duties might be properly performed. The flamens were priests assigned to this or that god, on whom the conduct of the worship rested. The augurs were the official diviners, set to the task of ascertaining the will of the god by various forms of divination, notably observation of the flight of birds and examination of the livers of sheep. Other groups might also be named, like the Arval brothers, who officiated before the goddess who provided the needed crops, and the Luperci, or wolf-men, who sacrificed goats and dogs to a rustic god on the occasion of his annual festival. In charge of the affairs of religion was the pontifex—of whom there were at first five, later fifteen —whose duties were varied, for being state officials, they were charged with duties now looked upon as purely secular. With their conception of the gods as powers, scarcely personal, there was little likelihood that any attempt would be made to represent them by images in human form, and with no images there would be no temples where the gods might dwell. This development was not reached until a later day, when Rome came under the influence of foreign faiths.

The Contact with Greece

With all the changes introduced into Roman religion by contact with outside cults what has already been described continued through the period of the republic, that is, from 509 to 27 B.C. But even before that, Roman religion had been modified by contact with a people close at hand. The Etruscans lived in Italy just north of the Tiber and were thus early brought into contact with the Romans as they began to settle, say about 750 B.C., on the hills south of that stream. It was Etruscan influence which was responsible for the pomerium or furrow plowed around the city within which no foreign deity might be allowed to come. The Etruscans also introduced the temple, or templum, which in that day did not mean a building but a rectangular area marked off on the ground, which was supposed to be a counterpart of a heavenly rectangle, and from which the flight of birds for purposes of divination could be observed. As Professor Jesse Benedict Carter suggests,[9] the earliest religion of the Roman people, untouched by outside influences, appealed to the social instinct—it was the religion of the family and family interests. Under the influence of the Etruscans the religion made its appeal to national instinct—Rome was now a city, self-conscious and strong and able to make a name for itself in the world.

The current of Greek influence began about the time the republic was established. The story of the beginnings of contact with Greece is shrouded in legend, but the fact is that Rome came early into contact with the Greek colonies of southern Italy and at some time about the beginning of the republic came into possession of the fateful Sibylline Books. These so-called books were treasured by the Romans as a sacred possession; they were kept secret and under the control of the senate which determined when the volumes might be consulted. The important thing about them was that whenever they were consulted, the answer always came that certain deities, Greek deities in every case, should be introducted and worshiped. So important is this remarkable movement that Professor Carter says of it, "The study of the outward and the inward effects of the Sibylline Books is therefore the real history of religion in the first half of the republic." [10]

In the year 496 B.C. Rome was in difficulty; her crops had failed, and this rendered her position insecure in the war with other near-by tribes then being waged. Recourse was had to the Sibylline Books, and the result was the introduction into Rome of the worship of Dionysus, Demeter, and Persephone, Greek deities familiar to our ears. These foreign divinities were not allowed within the pomerium, so continued to be looked upon as outsiders. They dropped their Greek names and were given Roman names, those of already existing Roman gods and goddesses. Thus these new Greek divinities crowded the Roman gods out of their place until all that was left which was Roman was the name. Demeter became known as Ceres, an old fertility goddess about whom little is known. But now Demeter with the old name Ceres became an important goddess with a splendid temple and games to her honor. Dionysus was identified with the Roman Liber, the patron of the vine, and so completely absorbed what individuality Liber had developed that little was left of the Roman god save the name.

[9] *The Religious Life of Ancient Rome*, p. 63.
[10] Carter, *op. cit.*, p. 71.

After this Greek gods and goddesses came into Rome one after another until they were all there. Rome had enlarged her pantheon until it seemed literally to include all the gods of the countries with whom she was in contact. They did not come in deliberately to take the place of the old Roman gods but to perform some function for which no Roman god seemed prepared. The very idea of deity was changed in the process, the Romans coming in the end to look upon their Greek gods with Latin names just as the Greeks looked upon them, personalities like men and women, with images and temples in which they lived. It was a veritable conquest, Rome the Conqueror vanquished in the things of the mind and the spirit by the clever and versatile Greek. The Greek Zeus was identified with the Roman Jupiter, Hera with Juno, Poseidon with Neptune, Athena with Minerva, Ares with Mars, Aphrodite with Venus, Artemis with Diana, Hermes with Mercury, but in the identification the Greek god lived on in power and influence despite the Latin name which it had assumed. In the end these new deities were admitted within the pomerium and thus were looked upon as thoroughly Roman. From the time of the Second Punic War, about the year 200 B.C., no differences can be detected between the Roman and the Greek elements in the cult; it was a new religion in fact, the Greco-Roman, and such it remained until the day when it disappeared with the oncoming of Christianity.

THE INFLUENCE OF THE EAST

During the period of the republic Rome became mistress of the world. But Rome had changed; she was not as religious as she had been in the simpler days of the past. Greek philosophers had come in with their criticism of the old religious beliefs and added to the disintegration which had set in. The deterioration was not only religious but moral. Few people can stand such rapid increase in wealth and influence, and the Romans were no exception to the rule. The offices of religion in connection with the state cult fell into disuse, and men could not be found to fill positions which were vacant. Such ceremonies as were performed were carried through only in the most perfunctory manner, like any other state function. The very knowledge of some old religious ceremonies perished, and others were neglected, so that they lost all meaning. It was a desperate situation which prevailed at the time when Julius Caesar passed off the scene and his nephew Octavius, known later as Augustus Caesar, took the reins of government and began to rule. The days of the Roman Empire had come, and Augustus proved to be the man of the hour.

One of the events which mark his reign was the revival of religion. It was largely his own work. Augustus recognized that without religion a country is lost. He revived old ceremonies, filled offices which had been unoccupied for years, rebuilt temples, and in every way sought to restore religion to its old place of power in the life of the people. He brought in some new features, the most remarkable of which was Caesar worship. At first it was worship of the dead rulers of the past, then of the living emperor sitting in the seat of authority in Rome. It was not called emperor worship at first; the Romans would have resented such a bald statement as too much of an innovation. The proposal was to worship the "Genius" of the emperor, the shadowy counterpart of the living man which was more or less spiritual and otherworldly. This was not quite so much a shock to their sensibilities, but it was only a step removed from the actual worship of the emperor himself which followed in a few generations. This became the one universal form of religion and the touchstone of loyalty to the empire. By their refusal to perform the rites connected with this worship the early Christians were declared treasonous and were thrown to the lions.

The important fact to keep in mind is that emperor worship was an importation. The old Roman might hesitate at such a step, but it was natural and easy for the Asiatic, and the introduction of the strange idea is an evidence of the strength of the influence which had set in from the eastern sections of the empire. The old religion had ceased to satisfy the desires of even the stern old Romans, and its place was being taken by religions which came trooping in from Asia and Africa. Cybele, the great mother of the gods, was introduced from the wild mountains of central Asia Minor. King Attalus presented the god to the deputation which had come from the Roman senate, and this was taken to Rome and received with due ceremony. But who was Cybele, the mother of the gods, thus brought to Rome, so far from her original home? She was the wife of Attis, who had been violently killed. She mourned him with tumultuous sorrow. He was finally raised to life again amid the wildest rejoicing. Such in the briefest space is the myth brought with the goddess to Rome in 205 B.C. Her worship in Asia Minor was in imitation of the acts depicted in the myth and, as might be expected, was made up of wild and uncontrolled orgies. The staid Romans were shocked at these displays, and the cult had a checkered career in the capital, but in the days of the empire it won its way into popular favor and received the sanction of the government. There was a procession, which was followed by exercises in the

87

temple, where the old myth was retold and reacted, producing "a state of rapturous ecstasy" which swept the worshiper off his feet and lifted him into union with the deity. As Attis died and was raised to life again, so would the worshiper be sure of another life. Union with the god could be achieved by these ecstasies and also by such a sacrament as the bloody taurobolium. A man would stand in a deep trench under a grating on which a bull was killed, and the blood would pour through the grating over the head and body of the worshiper. In this bath he believed he had entered into a new life by physical contact with the life-giving blood. Later the whole process was spiritualized and interpreted as the new birth of the soul.

Already the reason that such practices, so strange to old Roman religion, could exercise so strong an influence is evident. There was an emotional appeal which was irresistible. The ancient faith had no message when men began to be alive to new desires and aspirations; it was cold and prosaic. These religions which came out of the East made an appeal to the senses, were full of mystery, and were really human and warm in sympathy. That they descended to the level of the sensual at times did not militate against their success, for there was so much more which the old religion did not possess that defects, even when seen as such, did not prevent them from being acceptable. They were religions of salvation, of rewards and punishment, of immortality, and, last but not least, they demanded personal allegiance based on belief in the goodness of the divinity.

The religion of Isis and Osiris came from Egypt and gathered a large popular following, despite persecution during its earlier days. But it too became domesticated and was considered a legitimate faith by the state as well as the people. Here, again, the appeal did not lie in its system of thought, nor in its morality, which was exceedingly questionable, nor even in its doctrine of cleansing, but in the intoxicating seduction of the ritual and the promise of immortality. Again, in this religion there is the old story, familiar in the religion of Egypt, of Isis and her husband Osiris, who was killed by the evil-minded Typhon or Set, as he was known in ancient Egypt. Horus, their son, sought to wreak vengenance on his father's murderer, but in the end Osiris was raised to a new life and Typhon was forgiven. There is here the appeal to the elemental passions of love, hate, vengeance, and forgiveness. It is warm with human interest and sympathy, and comes close to the daily life of men and women, and this the old religion could never do.

88

A variety of beliefs and practices came in from Syria. The most famous of the deities was Atargatis, the Dea Syria, whose worship was associated with dreadful sensuality. It could not help working harm, yet in the ancient world there was real confusion between the impure and the sacred, and hence greater difficulty in seeing clearly what had in it the seeds of evil. Especially was this true in religious worship, in which the elemental emotions play so important a part. From Syria, too, came astrology, which had its home in Babylon, as we have seen, and which now took on new life among the peoples of the West.

But of all these religions that of Mithras is the most interesting and the most important. Coming originally out of Persia, Mithraism was found about the beginning of our era in the mountains of Asia Minor. From there it came into Rome about 70 B.C., the last of these Oriental faiths to reach the West. But while it was slow in starting on its career of conquest, it extended farther than all the others when its message began to be known. It was carried by merchants and slaves, but especially by soldiers, and the Mithraea, or underground chapels, have been discovered wherever in the wide expanses of the empire the Roman legions were stationed. There was again the myth of how Mithras by slaying the bull brought life and plenty to the world. This scene is depicted on all the bas-reliefs in every place of worship. It was a religion for men only and made surprising moral demands upon its followers. This at once raises it to a level higher than that of other Eastern cults. Mithras was the god of light and in the later time became identified with the sun, and as Sol Invictus, the invincible sun, was the last embodiment of the pagan idea of deity before it went down forever in the brighter light of another religion from the East which was to supersede them all.

Christianity, then, was one of these Eastern faiths which found a welcome in the West and in the end became the religion of the empire. It too had a story to tell. It too touched the emotions and held out the promise of immortality. A religion from the East, and in some respects like the others, Christianity, however, rose to a level of moral sublimity and self-forgetful service unattainable by Mithraism or the religions of Isis and the Great Mother. And as compared with the other deities the Saviour of Christianity has the advantage of being a real historical character and of exemplifying in his own person all the moral excellencies of his doctrine.

SUGGESTIONS FOR FURTHER STUDY

Greece

Breasted, J. H. *Ancient Times*. Boston: Ginn and Company, 1935. Part III.

Fairbanks, Arthur. *A Handbook of Greek Religion*. New York: American Book Company, 1910. A compact but complete survey.

Farnell, L. R. *The Higher Aspects of Greek Religion*. New York: Charles Scribner's Sons, 1912.

Livingstone, R. H., ed. *The Legacy of Greece*. New York: Oxford University Press, 1921.

Moore, George Foot. *History of Religions*. Rev. ed. New York: Charles Scribner's Sons, 1922. Vol. I, chs. XVII-XX.

Murray, Gilbert. *Five Stages of Greek Religion*. New York: Columbia University Press, 1925.

Nilsson, Martin P. *A History of Greek Religion*. New York: Oxford University Press, 1925.

Rose, H. J. *Ancient Greek Religion*. London: Hutchinson and Company, 1946.

Rome

Bailey, Cyril, ed. *The Legacy of Rome*. New York: Oxford University Press, 1923.

Breasted, J. H. *Ancient Times*. Parts IV and V, dealing with Rome and the Roman Empire.

Carter, J. B. *The Religion of Numa*. New York: The Macmillan Company, 1906. A short but helpful survey of the ancient religion.

Cumont, Franz. *The Oriental Religions in Roman Paganism*. Chicago: Open Court Publishing Company, 1911. The best account of the influence of the East.

Fowler, W. Warde. *The Religious Experience of the Roman People*. New York: The Macmillan Company, 1911. An extended survey of the religion to the time of Augustus.

Halliday, W. R. *Lectures on the History of Roman Religion from Numa to Augustus*. Boston: Small, Maynard and Company, 1923.

Moore, George Foot. *History of Religions*. Vol. I, chs. XXI, XXII.

Rose, H. J. *Ancient Roman Religion*. London: Hutchinson and Company, 1949.

CHAPTER V

THE RELIGIONS OF INDIA: HINDUISM

THE RELIGION OF THE VEDAS

AT A PERIOD AT LEAST TWO OR THREE THOUSAND YEARS BEFORE CHRIST there roamed on the grassy plateaus and steppes of Central or Eastern Europe or Western Asia—it is really not known where—tribes of nomadic peoples seeking pasturage for their flocks and herds. They were white men, speaking a common language, with vivid imagination and boundless energy. For some reason—it may have been the natural increase of population which tended to overcrowd the regions already occupied—groups of these restless nomads would start off to find a more congenial home, until in the end these Indo-Europeans were scattered far to the east and south and west, all the distance from Ireland and Scotland, in the cold and misty west, to the plains of India, under a blazing tropical sun. The Aryan branch of these widely scattered peoples came into Persia (Iran, the Persian for Aryan) and India. Those who came to India must have settled first on the banks of the Indus, which means "river," or "flood," so they spoke of their new home as "the land of the Indus," from which comes the name "India." In all probability they did not come at any one time but straggled into the new country in smaller or larger groups during hundreds of years. Some would say that they were still arriving about 1500 B.C. Coming down into northern India, these Aryans spread out fanlike over the Punjab, or region of the "five rivers," and then, as the years passed, slowly extended their settlements to the south and east, taking possession of the rich Ganges Valley as they advanced.

A picture of these "tall, fair people" is given by J. N. Farquhar:

They were then soldier-farmers, equally used to the plow and the sword. They were constantly at war with the aborigines around them; and they looked eagerly for sunshine and rain to mature their crops and give them fodder for their cattle and herds. They were still a primitive people, living in simple villages, with but few of the arts of civilization, and untrammeled by the bonds of caste. They had no writing and no coinage. They ate beef and drank intoxicating drink. The tribes lived each under its own chieftain, and now and then quarrels led to war among them. The family was still in a healthy condition. Their women had a great deal of freedom throughout their lives. There was no child-marriage among them, no seclusion in the zenana, no widow-burning, and no law against the remarriage of widows. Like most primitive peoples, they practiced the exposure of girl children and old people.[1]

India has a great literature, very largely religious. But the absence of works on history is a very great drawback in attempting to trace the course of events. During the last half century archaeology has stepped in and has made a surprising revelation. It had long been thought that civilization in India began with the coming of the Aryan. Now, however, archaeological research has revealed a culture which existed in the Indus Valley at least fifteen hundred years before the arrival of the Aryan. At Mohenjo-daro and at Harappa the remains of a civilization as far advanced as that in Mesopotamia have been exposed to view. We do not know much about their religion. For the most part it was very different from that of the Aryans, and yet it is believed to "contain the germs of much that was to play a great part in the life of the people of India." [2]

These discoveries and other studies on the part of both Indian and Western scholars have made necessary a very significant change in viewpoint as to the sources of the religion we know as Hinduism. Until recently it was the accepted belief that Hinduism had its origin in the faith which was brought into India and developed by the Aryan invaders who imposed on the dark-skinned aborigines whom they encountered a new and strange religion. "This view can no longer be maintained," is the conclusion of Professor J. H. Hutton. His own position is stated thus: "Though derived no doubt from multiple sources, the Hindu religion may fairly be said to have taken its final form as the result of the impact of the social ascendancy of the Indo-European [Aryan] invaders of the second millennium B.C. on pre-existing religious institutions." [3]

[1] A Primer of Hinduism, pp. 21-22.
[2] See The Cambridge Shorter History of India, Chap. I.
[3] Caste in India, pp. 196-97.

While this conclusion cannot be escaped, the difficulty which is at once faced is that the religion of the aboriginal Dravidians, as they were called by the Aryans, cannot be ascertained with any definiteness. On the other hand, the religion of the Aryans is clearly defined and can be studied with little difficulty.

The Aryans brought with them a religion in many features similar to that of the Persians, to whom they were closely related. But soon they began to develop features quite different and very much their own. Our knowledge of their beliefs and practices is based in a collection of hymns known as the Rig-Veda. These hymns, or "praises," were composed during a long period and were committed to memory for use at the sacrifices. There were over a thousand of them, which were finally written down in Sanskrit and preserved as a single collection. All the gods whose praises are sung are nature deities, divided into three groups with eleven gods in each group. They are the gods of the celestial regions, those of the earth, and those of the atmosphere between earth and sky.

Of the gods of the high heavens three may be mentioned: Mitra, who as Mithras was well known in Persia and also in the Roman Empire, as we have seen; Vishnu, who in a later day assumed an importance in Indian religion which he had not known in the earlier period; and finally the great god Varuna. According to A. Barth, "Varuna is the god of the vast luminous heavens, viewed as embracing all things, and as the primary source of all life and every blessing." [4] The possibilities lying in the conception of this god might have raised Hinduism to a far nobler level than has been attained. Varuna was not only sublime in his majesty and power, but was the judge of men's hearts and the exemplar of nobility and truth and uprightness, who expected the same of the beings under his sway. But, most unfortunately, these possibilities were not realized, and Hinduism suffers today because Varuna and what he stood for have been discarded and other gods, representative of far different ideals, fill the minds and dominate the lives of their adherents.

There were three important gods of the earth, namely, Agni, Soma, and Yama. Agni was fire, that of lightning, the sun, and the sacrificial flame, as well as the fire of which we make use every day. As the flame ascends and seems to be traveling toward the purified abode of the gods, fire was early looked upon as a priest conveying sacrifices to the other deities. Many high functions in human life and even in creation have devolved upon this god, but in all his various forms Agni has always re-

[4] *The Religions of India*, p. 16.

mained just the material fire with which we are familiar. Soma was the name of an Indian plant, still unidentified, and the fermented juice which was extracted from it. It was intoxicating and therefore divine, thought these early Aryans. They were possessed of a spirit not their own when they were intoxicated, and their only explanation was that it must come from the gods. Here is suggested the origin of our term "ardent spirits," which literally take possession of the man who has imbibed freely. But Soma also had a celestial reference and was supposed to flow in the invisible world as well as on earth. The gods themselves attained immortality by drinking the Soma, and so would men when they drank the life-giving potion with Yama in the land of the blessed. Again here, as in the case of Agni, the physical character of the god was never lost. Soma remained until the end, and in spite of the idealizing process, the juice of the soma plant. Yama might have lived an immortal, but he chose to die. He thus was the first to cross the dreaded flood from which none return. The dead who lived nobly went to him. Not much was said about the wicked who perished or continued to exist "in dark and dismal pits" with demons and other evil spirits.

Of all the gods of the Rig-Veda, Indra took first place as the national god of the Aryans. He was the greatest of the atmospheric gods, the "king of heaven," the warrior who gave victory to his people, and at the same time was the giver of good and the author and preserver of life. Indra not only fought with the people when they were engaged in war, but fought for them with his faithful companions, the Maruts, the "bright ones," the gods of storm and lightning. Intoxicated with Soma, he rode among the clouds, striking his enemies with thunderbolts. When it is remembered that it is to the atmosphere the people of India must look not only for prosperity but for life itself, it can be seen quite readily how Indra, the god who defeated the enemies who would have prevented the breaking of the monsoon with its copious rains, would be lifted up and idealized until he became their great champion and protector.

When one reads the hymns of the Rig-Veda, he is confused by the manner in which the qualities of one god are ascribed to another and still another god so that the lines of demarcation between them become hazy and indistinct. This tendency to fuse and assimilate the gods and their functions was the beginning of a long process which continued until it led into the monism which is so characteristic a feature of later Indian thought. The Indian mind even at this early date was beginning to feel out after a unity in which there should be no distinctions, and, though the fully developed theory was not completed for many centuries, the tendency began to make itself evident very early.

One is also struck in these hymns by the ascriptions of praise to one and then another of these divine beings, just as if each god were for the time being the sole god of the universe. Many gods were worshiped, but each at times in a more or less exclusive manner. The theology oscillates between polytheism and an approach toward monotheism. It is one form of henotheism (also called monolatry), the worship of one god without rejecting other gods who may be worshiped at other times as needs and occasions may require. Professor Max Müller gave to this attitude a special name, kathenotheism, the worship of "one god at a time." The worshiper seemed a bit uneasy. He had inherited many gods, with various functions, to provide him with needed care and protection, but he was not satisfied. The desire for unity was beginning to assert itself, making the worship of a variety of gods seem incongruous. With this beginning and by a very natural process among so thoughtful a people as these Aryans, the conception changed and developed until in final outcome all the gods came to be looked upon as manifestations only, manifestations of a primal essence behind and inclusive of them all.

The worship of the gods was largely sacrificial. Animals were offered in increasing numbers as the centuries passed, until the land ran red with blood by the sixth and fifth centuries before our era. There were also elaborate rites connected with the offering of the soma and of ghi, or clarified butter. There were no temples and no images in the earliest day, the worship being conducted in the open air. Priests were in evidence very early, and as the sacrifices became more elaborate they increased their hold until in the end their grip on the people of India was complete. The theory was very simple. Sacrifice was looked upon as absolutely necessary; life could not be preserved or prosperity looked for without it. The efficacy of the sacrifice depended, not upon the moral fitness, nor upon the sincerity of the worshiper and his need, nor even upon the will of the gods, but upon the correctness with which the ritual of the sacrifice was performed. This was believed implicitly by all the people, high and low. In the earliest day the father was the priest of his family, but as the theory of sacrifice developed, it became increasingly difficult for him to master the ritual on which the fortunes of the family depended. Professional priests took his place and performed the ceremonies for him. They made themselves experts in religion, masters of ceremony and ritual, and thus became indispensable to the people. Nothing could be done without them. They dominated life and exercised their sway with ever-increasing severity./These priestly Brahmins,/ as they were called, came to occupy a unique position, wielding the mightiest power in the land. Jealous of their position, they separated themselves more and more from the other classes and were looked upon and treated as superior beings, veritable gods on earth.

The theory of the efficacy of sacrifice was carried so far that sacrifice was looked upon as irresistible. Thus the whole system became impregnated with magic. The carrying out of the ritual with minute exactness would bring about the desired end with little reference to the will of the god who was addressed. This, of course, did not tend to exalt the gods, but it did result in further enhancing the authority of the divine priesthood which could perform such wonders. It was even said that the gods themselves had attained their present position by sacrifice, and so it followed that it was not beyond the range of possibility for mortal man to reach the same goal.

I have referred to the Rig-Veda as the earliest literary product of the Indian mind, but it was only the beginning. There are in fact four Vedas, of which the Rig-Veda was by far the most important. In 1859 Max Müller suggested that 1200 or 1000 B.C. was the latest period he could allow for the composition of the original hymns in the Rig-Veda and that the various collections were formed within the next two hundred years. Scholars now are tending to re-establish these dates, rejecting theories that the development took a much longer period.[5] The writings which have been briefly listed comprise the Vedas, but there is a Vedic literature much more extensive and very influential in the development of the Hindu religion. All of the four Vedas had attached to them one or more Brahmanas. These were voluminous priestly writings which explained the sacrifices and gave directions to the various schools of priests concerning the conduct of the ritual.

Closely connected with the individual Brahmanas was another series of writings called Aranyakas, which means "Forest Treatises." That is, certain thoughtful men seem not to have been satisfied by the monotonous succession of sacrifices—though they did not repudiate them—and went off alone in the forest to think more deeply on the meaning of

[5] J. N. Farquhar, *Outline of the Religious Literature of India*, p. 17.

life and religion, and these writings are the result of their musings. But of greater importance than the Aranyakas themselves was another group of writings which were embedded in the Aranyakas and are a little difficult to distinguish from them. These are the famous Upanishads, one of the chief foundation-heads of Hindu philosophy. All these writings which have been mentioned are called sruti, which means "hearing," the things which were heard by the inspired Rishis of a day long past as they listened to the divine revelation. All other writings, no matter how important and sacred, are called smriti, "what is remembered," traditional knowledge but not inspired as are the Vedas.

The Philosophic Development

When the Aryans came into India, they possessed no belief in the doctrine of transmigration, yet it is one of the basic doctrines among Hindus today. Where did they get it? The subject is obscure, but probably the idea was suggested by contact with the aboriginal population into the midst of which they were thrown. While the Aryans came more and more to dominate the religious life of the country of their adoption, they unconciously absorbed many of the ideas of the primitive Dravidians. One of these may have been transmigration. The theory is that when a man dies his soul leaves the dying body and enters the body of some animal or human being as it comes into the world to begin its career. And the process is repeated generation after generation times without number.

While the theory doubtless came to the Aryan invaders in a very crude form, the keen minds of the thinkers among them would not allow it to rest but worked it out to its logical conclusion and made it a part of their growing philosophical system. The law or the force which determined the operation of transmigration was karma. Karma means "action" or "deed," actions or deeds in one life which work out their results in the next life, and the next, and so on through unlimited time. According to our karma we are born into a new life well or strong, good or bad, rich or poor. It is a kind of reward or retribution as the case may be, working itself out automatically and inevitably in existence after existence. There is absolutely no escape from the clutches of this inexorable law. All we can hope for is not to add to our karma, so that when what we have inherited is finally exhausted there will be no more fuel to keep the fire burning. The fuel consists of deeds—any deeds, good or bad—which stimulate life. To live, then—just to live, whether

97

nobly or dishonorably, it makes little difference—is an evil with a most unfortunate entail for the future.

The importance of the doctrine of transmigration cannot be overestimated. In the words of the Hindu Professor Govinda Das, "This is the famous doctrine of transmigration on which all our philosophy of life is based." [6] He also says, "This law of Karma, as a man sows so he reaps, is the keystone of the arch over which has been built up, through the course of ages, the vast edifice of Hinduism." [7] To be saved from the endless succession of births and deaths is what religion means for Hindus. It seems almost hopeless, so deathlike is the grip of this theory on the mind of the people, but in one way or another they struggle on with the hope of breaking the chain at some time in the distant future.

So earnestly have the Hindus sought to find ways of being liberated from the necessity of being reborn that they have worked out three ways of salvation. Let it be carefully noted that salvation for a Hindu means liberation from samsara, the endless repetition of births to which they are bound. There is first karmamarga, or the way of works. This means that a man must keep caste regulations scrupulously, perform all the religious rites in the family and temple, and do the hundred other things which are laid down in manuals and have come down traditionally from one generation to another. But even by the most scrupulous observance of these regulations a man cannot hope to escape being born again; what he may look forward to in another life is a happier lot than that which is his in the present life.

The second way of salvation is called bhaktimarga, or the way of loving devotion to one or another of the divine beings he has chosen to worship. This second way will be discussed later.

The third and final way of deliverance is jnanamarga, or salvation by knowledge, the method of release by philosophical insight and intuition. This is the only way by which man is able to secure release from transmigration, so that he will never be born again, but enters into the bliss of Nirvana. One can see at once that this attitude toward the way of salvation by knowledge raises philosophy to the supreme place in the minds of Hindus. In India all philosophy is religious philosophy; its object ultimately is always to secure release from transmigration. It is a very practical matter, entering into the thinking of the people far more pervasively than philosophy in the Western world.

[6] *Hinduism*, p. 214.
[7] *Ibid.*, p. 217.

The earliest results of the work of the Indian philosophic mind are to be found in the Upanishads. They are very obscure, probably intentionally so. They embody esoteric teaching, secret doctrine, which is only for those who can go to a teacher for its interpretation. Nor do they present a definite system. They are "anticipations rather than completions of doctrine; they are inspirational rather than dogmatic." [8] Life has become more difficult and complex since the joyous free days of the Rig-Veda. The zest of life is gone; there is a sadder, more wistful mood. It is expressed in a refrain found in one of the Upanishads, "Lead me from darkness into light, from the unreal to the Real."

In these writings the gods are not eternal but only the temporary manifestations of one absolute being back of and responsible for all that exists. The souls of men are "sparks from the central fire, drops from the ocean of divinity," to be incarnated times without number, according to the law of karma, but in the end to find release and drop back into the boundless ocean from which they came. The only eternal, unquestionable fact in the universe is Brahman, the world-soul, and the conclusion was reached that the atman, or individual human soul, was identical with it. "Myself is the infinite self," and "The soul of the universe, whole and undivided, dwells in me," are two of the many ways in which this identity was expressed. Probably the most used phrase is "Thou art That." The object of life for these thinkers is to realize the truth of this startling affirmation. Salvation is attained by jnanamarga, knowledge, intuition, a sudden flash of insight, which will drive away the darkness and leave the man possessed of this liberating thought. Should he achieve this insight by the power of his intellect after profound meditation, concentrating his whole mind on this one thought, he was free; he would not be born again; the release was complete and final.

Look a little more closely at this absolute being, Brahman. Farquhar says that Brahman is "a neuter noun which expresses the common thought of the time, that the world-soul is an impersonal essence present in all things." [9] So enthusiastic were the forest thinkers over their "find" that they could not restrain themselves in their rapture. Brahman was to them everything good and desirable, the aim of all their longing. But when an attempt is made to describe Brahman and to state the qualities and attributes involved in the conception, the result is most disappointing. Nothing positive can be affirmed; it must all be in negatives. In fact

[8] W. S. Urquhart, *The Vedanta and Modern Thought*, p. 21.
[9] *Op. cit.*, p. 48.

he is attributeless. Of each positive characteristic one might mention the only word is neti, neti, "not that, not that." It is only by accommodation that Brahman is called "he" at all. He is impersonal, so the more appropriate term must be "it." But even more serious is the impossibility of thinking of Brahman as holy or righteous. He is presented as a being beyond the distinction between right and wrong. That would lower him, so it is claimed, and bring him down to the level of human frailty and finiteness. But the sad fact is that any attempt to posit a being for whom ethical distinctions do not exist is to bring him down to a level lower than the one we human beings occupy. This philosophical theory has crippled Hinduism through all the years and holds out little promise for the future when India needs all the moral and spiritual strength she can obtain for the task of national reconstruction which is before her—and yet this is the most deeply embedded conviction in the Indian mind.

The philosophic development which we have been considering was not completed for centuries after the writing of the Upanishads, which were finished by 500 B.C. We know little of what took place during a long period after that. What we find in the end is that six systems of philosophy arose, three scarcely deserving the name of philosophy, and yet all aiming to deliver mankind from the chain of rebirth. Only two are of sufficient importance to be described here.

The oldest is that of the Sankhya, which is fundamentally a dualism, far different from what has just been mentioned. There is a primary active substance called prakriti, which pervades the universe and is accountable for all there is in it. There are also separate individual souls, called purusha, which are eternal and distinct entities. The release from rebirth is secured by knowledge, the flash of insight in which a man realizes that his soul is essentially and eternally distinct from the active substance of the universe about him. Sankhya is atheistic and contains less hope and help than the Brahman system which has outrivaled it in securing the allegiance of Indian thinkers. It is, in fact, hard to think of two systems more antagonistic, except in the significant fact that both secure deliverance in the same way, by knowledge.

The more important system is that of the Vedanta. The word "Vedanta" means the "end" or "aim" of the Veda, that to which the ancient Vedas point and in which they have their consummation. Three great exponents of the Vedanta have arisen, differing widely from one another, yet each claiming to be the correct interpreter of the inner meaning of the ancient writings. They all teach that salvation is to be se-

100

6924

cured by knowledge though two of them make a most significant addition in declaring that devotion to a personal god is also necessary.

The first and greatest of the acharyas, or men worthy to be followed, was Shankara, whose dates are A.D. 788 to 828. He called his system nondualism. Building on the teaching of the Upanishads that there is but one reality in the universe, Shankara was forced to acknowledge the existence of the external world, the people and things which we see around us on every side. He could not deny that they had some kind of existence, but what kind of existence was it? He came to the conclusion that it was only a seeming existence, that in reality they did not exist at all. But how was even the seeming existence to be accounted for? Here he made use of an idea which came out of the Upanishads, but which he raised to a most important position. It was the conception of maya, a subtle but powerful force at work in the universe creating the mistaken notion that there was something in existence besides Brahman the absolute. This cosmic force was the power of ignorance which created the erroneous idea that people and external nature had real existence. But if maya created the illusion that things exist, what was the origin of maya? There is no way of avoiding the conclusion that it came from the only real being that exists, that is, from Brahman. And when seen in this light it certainly looks as if the Absolute was responsible for the delusion which was the cause of the entire misconception that anythng really existed besides the All itself.

Shankara made full use of the old conception that each one of us is really Brahman, if we only knew it. Hence to be saved meant getting rid of the illusion caused by maya and realizing that we are Brahman. This is to be accomplished by a flash of insight after long discipline of both the mind and the body. When this occurs and the insight has become ours, we are free; we shall never be born again; we may live a few years, but when our bodies die we have entered the nirvana of bliss. Such in essence is the contribution of Shankara, the most penetrating thinker India has ever produced.

But this teaching was not and is not convincing to many men of insight, learning, and deep earnestness. The greatest of them was Ramanuja, who lived from 1050 to 1137. His philosophy has been called qualified nondualism. He was in the tradition of the Vedanta because he believed that there was oneness in the universe. Reality did not consist of a plurality of separate and independent factors but of a united whole. "God together with the souls and matter is an organic whole," [10] but Ramanuja made a most important qualification. For him the ultimate was not the impersonal All but a personal God, and the souls of men and the nature around them are real and not destined to be absorbed by and in God. No, they are permanent, and human beings may look forward to continued conscious life in communion with God—that is, if they attain the knowledge that liberates, and if they give themselves in loving devotion to God, who comes to them with his grace to give them freedom from the fetters of transmigration.

Finally there arose Madhva, the last of the three classical philosophers. His dates are a little uncertain—as frequently given they are 1199 to 1278. His system is called dualism. He did not hold, as did Ramanuja, that the universe formed one organic unity or whole, in which God was in a way embodied in individual souls and matter—God was too transcendent for that. God was essentially different from all else in the universe, from individual souls and nature. But he is the only independent being, existing in his own right. On the other hand God is the creator of souls and things, who are thus dependent on him. Like Ramanuja, Madhva called himself a Vedantist and believed in the necessity of traveling the way of knowledge, but he believed in a God who could be counted on to save men through his grace, and this grace was the crowning cause of salvation. But India has gone with Shankara and looks upon him as the paramount figure of the entire galaxy of Indian thinkers. His influence has been tremendous, never more so than at the present time, when the Indian people are seeking a firm foundation in thought for the upbuilding of the structure of their entire life.

THE CASTE SYSTEM

Hinduism is the most amorphous of all religions. Almost anything can be said of it with the assurance that it is true, and at the same time almost anything which is said may be denied, and that with good reason. What is it, then, which makes a man a Hindu? What is the standard of orthodoxy which may be applied to determine a man's standing in the Hindu community? One of their own students, Professor Govinda Das, declares that it cannot be defined, for the reason that "Hinduism is absolutely indefinite." He speaks of it as an "anthropological process to which, by a strange irony of fate, the name of 'religion' has been given. . . . It is all-comprehensive, all-absorbing, all-tolerant, all-complacent, all-

[10] M. Hiriyana, *The Essentials of Indian Philosophy*, p. 182.

102

compliant." [11] He sets up as many as fifteen tests or standards, and finds them all deficient. A man may believe what he likes, do as he pleases, and follow any ritual or custom he chooses, and still be a Hindu. It comes down to this—that a Hindu is one "who does not repudiate that designation," or one "who says he is a Hindu, and accepts any of the many beliefs, and follows any of the many practices that are anywhere regarded as Hindu." [12] But among all these clues or standards there is one which is so important and so inclusive that there are those who feel that it is a valid criterion. It is the caste system, the form of organization obtaining wherever Hinduism exists. To be a Hindu means to belong to one of the castes and to obey caste regulations. Orthodoxy in Hinduism is then conformity to custom, petrified in social organization.

A caste is a group of people kept apart from other caste groups by regulations touching marriage, food, in some cases occupation, and also residence. Taking them in reverse order, conformity with reference to residence, which is the least important, means that a Hindu shall not travel or reside outside India. The fact that the university centers in Europe and America attract so many Hindus clearly indicates that this rule rests lightly on those who feel impelled to seek their education abroad. Yet among the stricter families a ceremony of purification with features that are offensive and even disgusting is necessary on the return from a foreign country to wash away the taint which has been incurred by travel and by association with foreigners, the men and women they have met in our colleges and universities! But so far as travel itself is concerned, most enlightened Hindus wink calmly at it and pay little attention to the prohibition.

Occupation helps to determine caste in many cases. For illustration the following may be cited: the Ahirs are by tradition herdsmen; the Chamars, workers in leather; the Chuhras and one or two others, scavengers; the Goalas, milkmen; the Kayasths, writers or penmen; the Kumhars, potters; and so on. But even in these cases not all the members of the caste follow the traditional occupation. [13] Likewise the Brahmins constitute the priestly caste but are found widely scattered among the professions and occupations, and so of many others.

In respect of food conformity is more significant. One must not eat with a man of another caste, and frequently among the higher castes

[11] Op. cit., p. 45.
[12] Op. cit., p. 57.
[13] See The Imperial Gazetteer of India (new ed.), I, 314.

THE RELIGIONS OF MANKIND

the food he eats must be prepared by a servant who belongs to the same caste. But even with respect to this regulation many a Hindu today pays scant attention to it at times. He will eat with others on a dining car and at a banquet, even though he may be scrupulously careful when he is at home. The women are more conservative and prevent the growth of more liberal ideas which the men, particularly those of intelligence, might not be adverse to introducing. At the present time, when India begins to feel the need of unity in order to build up a worthy national life, the bondage of caste become oppressive, and leading men feel the necessity of breaking away from the old customs and demonstrating the possibility of all Indians, Mohammedans as well as Hindus, sharing a common political and social life. It must be noted that especially in villages and small towns the old regulations seem to hold about as strongly as ever.

It is at the point of marriage that caste retains its most tenacious grip upon the social life of India. Hindu parents are between two fires. It is a disgrace to have daughters who remain unmarried after their early teens, and yet husbands must be found within their own caste or sub caste. This rule is absolute and unbending. A Hindu may be lax in respect of food and eating with men of other castes, but at this point he is still strictly bound. He must not marry his children to outsiders and thus "break caste." The problem which issues from this dilemma has led to customs which have been of untold injury to Indian life. Child marriage is an almost inevitable outcome of the necessity of finding desirable husbands and wives for all the boys and girls in the community. Thousands of marriages are consummated before children reach their teens, with physical and moral results which are deplorable. This custom, in a land of high mortality, has produced thousands of little widows and widowers. The boy may marry again, and usually does so, but the poor girl—her story is the saddest of all the suffering little women in the world. According to tradition she is held responsible for the death of her husband, and as she is a criminal her hair is shaved off, her dearly loved ornaments are taken away, and she is dressed in a coarse garment and becomes the drudge of the family. She may not remarry but remains until the end of her life a poor, miserable soul—unless, of course, she is the mother of sons. This lifts her to a position of honor from which she cannot be displaced.

The most commendable thing for the widow to do until comparatively recent times was to mount the funeral pyre and be burned to death with the body of her husband; and, willingly or unwillingly, this horrible custom, called sati or suttee, was carried out many thousands of times before the British government put a stop to it in 1829. In rare cases even today widows immolate themselves, unfortunately with the approval of many in the Hindu community.

Measures of reform are being enacted by the Central and Provincial governments, having as their object the raising of the age of marriage and the relief of widows by allowing their remarriage. But with all that wise reformers may say and do the mass of the people still cling to the old customs, and women still suffer from the disability of inferiority. The day of woman's emancipation has begun, but the road to the goal is a long and difficult one. A new day is dawning, but at times it seems slow, very slow, in coming.

No theory of the origin of caste is completely satisfactory. We do not know the exact number of castes and sub castes, of which there are well over two thousand. The word for caste in Sanskrit is varna, which means "color." This would indicate that the Aryan as he came into India from the north was originally fair-skinned in contrast to the dark Dravidian. In their endeavor to preserve the purity of their blood and the fairness of their skin the Aryans hedged themselves around with restrictions touching their relations with the aborigines. The earliest division we have on record separates into distinct groups the priests (Brahmins), the warriors (Kshattriyas), the agriculturalists (Vaisyas), and the menial laborers (Sudras). The three mentioned first constitute the twice-born people, those who had the right to be initiated or be born again into the religious community. The Sudras, who are supposed to have been largely of Dravidian blood, at least in the beginning, were outsiders so far as the ceremonial and worship of the twice-born were concerned. According to the theory found in the Institutes of Manu, one of the ancient books of laws and customs, the Brahmins, Kshattriyas, and Vaisyas were born from the mouth, the arms, and the thighs, respectively, of the supreme soul of the universe, while the poor Sudras proceeded from the feet and were looked upon as the menial, doing their work at the bidding of the three other orders.

The tendency at the present time is to lay less emphasis on the differences of race and color as the explanation of the origin of caste and more on occupation and division of functions. But even so the complexity of the caste system and its multiple divisions and subdivisions is so baffling that even at best most competent authorities give up the attempt to furnish anything like a full or even an adequate account of its origin and development.[14]

But while no one has been able to give an explanation of caste which is fully convincing, the most evident fact in the whole system is the pre-eminence of the Brahmin priest. He is the vitalizing force in the system and dominates it completely. All take their cue from him. He looks upon himself as inherently superior to all the others. Was he not created different, and has he not demonstrated that he is not to be classified with the common run of men? The caste system is his way of preserving his position inviolate, and he clings to it with the most serious concern. At many points he has deserved well of the people. He is rightfully recognized as the gifted leader in the higher life of the community. But, on the other hand, having little or no sympathy with those who occupy a subordinate position, and filled with unfathomable pride, the Brahmin lords it over the consciences and wills of men and exercises a tyranny unsurpassed anywhere in the world.

Some good things may be said of caste. It engenders a certain solidarity which is of great value in the precarious conditions in which most of the people of India live. In times of distress caste acts as a kind of labor union, or a trade guild, or as a relief association in giving assistance to those who otherwise would have no sense of security. There is a mutual helpfulness exercised which is good and beneficial. But the count against the system as a whole far outweighs any good which may be claimed for it. It is fundamentally divisive and stands as a strong bar against the unity which the forward-looking Hindu knows must be achieved before India can become a strong nation ready and worthy to take its place among the nations of the world. Even deeper than this, however, caste kills all sense of brotherhood. To a Hindu his "brother" is a member of his caste and no one else. He is taught to despise and look down upon the lower castes as inferior, by contact with whom he must not soil his hands. The whole system is a matter of most serious concern to every thoughtful Indian as he faces the task of making the new independent India not only a free but a united land. Everywhere there is stirring, and remarkable results have been achieved in opening the way to a liberalizing of caste restrictions, if not to their complete abolition.

When we come to the fifty millions of outcastes, or untouchables, we reach a depth of human misery and degradation almost unbelievable.

[14] See H. Hutton, *Caste in India* (1946), for a comprehensive survey of the present situation.

106

Their touch is polluting, and their very shadow falling on the food prepared for a high-caste man renders it unfit for use. Centuries of such disdain and abuse have created a race of cringing creatures who, scorned by their own proud superiors, have lost all the self-respect they might have developed and are today among the most pitiable people in the world. They constitute one of the greatest challenges to social and religious service to be found anywhere. And yet despite their name, outcastes, they are a part of a religio-social system which is responsible for their present condition. It is among these people that Christian missions have done a notable work. They have proved that an outcaste is capable of an enlarged outlook and can develop self-respect and resourcefulness of a high order. One of the best evidences of a new spirit in India is that Indian leaders are taking untouchability seriously. In all this Gandhi played an important and noble part, with the result that every political party and every group of socially-minded Indians have made the doing away of untouchability a prominent feature in their program of reform. It is of the highest significance that Dr. B. R. Ambedkar, who came directly out of an outcaste community, became one of the most important members of the Constituent Assembly, which framed the Constitution of the Indian Republic.

HINDUISM SINCE THE RISE OF BUDDHISM

During the sixth century before our era Buddhism arose in northern India. As a result of the example and teachings of Gautama Buddha the whole complexion of things religious was greatly changed. Eventually Buddhism waned, and Hinduism asserted itself anew; it was a veritable renaissance, which in the end established the supremacy of the old faith over the land. But the Hinduism which raised its head after the centuries of strong Buddhistic influence was not the same. The caste system remained intact and even developed, though it was not encouraged, to say the least, by the Buddha and his followers. The sacrificial system of Hinduism was more seriously modified. The theory remained the same, but the form was changed. Bloody sacrifices almost ceased to be offered, and their place was taken in large part by cereals and flowers. We shall have occasion to note one of the exceptions to this rule, but the remarkable change is not to be minimized by the relatively few instances of animal sacrifice which continued to exist. And, finally, the Hinduism which emerged presents a very different organization of the pantheon; it even worships a different set of gods. The same names occur, but gods who were once prominent have given place to others who held a subordinate position or to those whose names do not even occur in the ancient records.

Back in the period of the Gupta dynasty, A.D. 320-650, a strong movement came to light to look upon Brahma,[15] Vishnu, and Siva as the threefold manifestation of the Supreme, the Absolute Brahman we have met before. This triad, or Hindu Trimurti, has never entered deeply into the thinking of the people, though it is frequently mentioned in the religious literature and is at times represented in sculpture in the form of a triple head on one pair of shoulders. Brahma, the first member of this trio, is the creator, the more or less personal source of the universe and the life which it contains. He has no popular following, only one temple in all India being devoted solely to his worship. But the fact that he is looked upon as personal calls attention to the theistic tendency which has expressed itself in various forms throughout the course of Indian religious history.

The stories of Vishnu and Siva are very different. Their worship constitutes the sectarianism of modern Hinduism, the people being roughly divided between the worshipers of Vishnu and the worshipers of Siva. Vishnu was one of the celestial gods in the Rig-Veda and was associated with Indra, with whom, however, he could not compare in importance. During the centuries Vishnu increased in dignity and greatness, and took to himself some of the qualities of the great Indra himself, until in the end he easily overtopped the national god of the Aryans of a bygone age. The most marked characteristic of the worship of Vishnu is that he is not worshiped in his own person but in that of one or another of his manifestations, or avatars, in Sanskrit. Through these manifestations the worship of Vishnu absorbed many stray beliefs, even the Buddha being acknowledged as one of the avatars. An avatar is the descent or appearance of deity among men, more or less temporary, to accomplish some special task. It is more of a disguise than a revelation of what the god is really like, so it differs from the Christian idea of incarnation, which does not change and is the "very image" of the invisible God. Vishnu himself was lifted higher and higher until he was finally declared to be

[15] For convenience, a difference in spelling has been introduced to distinguish the three meanings of the word frequently given as "Brahman." The spelling *Brahman* designates the neuter, impersonal All, the philosophical Absolute. *Brahma* stands for the personal creator, also called Prajapati, one of the emanations of the Supreme Brahman. *Brahmin*, which springs from the same idea and root, is used of the priests and the priestly caste.

one with the Universal Spirit, the great Preserver, and as such fills the place of the sole god of the universe.

The most prominent of the incarnations of this great god are Rama and Krishna, heroes of the great epic poems, the Ramayana and the Mahabharata. Krishna is an avatar with a very striking history. How much of it is lengendary and how much sober fact it is exceedingly difficult to determine. He is, like Rama, a great hero, "an exterminator of monsters, a victorious warrior," but unfortunately his record is not consistent. In the Bhagavad-Gita he is pictured as a noble counselor, but in the puranas he is far from that. Much of his time is spent in impure gambols with the gopis, shepherdesses, on the hills, and even in adulterous relations with Radha, who becomes his beloved mistress. Spiritualize the account as many high-minded Hindus do, the dangerous journey through such mire to reach the heights beyond is likely to stain the soul of the purest-minded devotee. It is a sad plight in which popular Hinduism finds itself with its most exalted avatar. If the great God above is anything like that, there is little hope of raising the people to a high level of honor and purity.

In contrast with Vishnu the Preserver, Siva is known as the Destroyer and represents the dark, cruel aspects of life. He also represents the powers of reproduction and is always symbolized in his temples by the linga, or human phallus, instead of by an image. This idea is strongly emphasized in Siva worship, Nandi the bull being represented as an attendant of the god, a striking example of powerful passion and generative power. "Yet in South India there are daily sung to Siva hymns that for warmth of feeling have not often been excelled. . . . The god seems so unlovable, yet the Saivite saints are intoxicated with love for him, and call him Grace itself." [16] With all his other attributes Siva becomes to them all that any of the other gods stand for, and even ravishes their gaze as they see in him the god of love. For both the philosopher and the peasant Siva is the paragon of all excellence, for one the basis of an all-embracing world view and for the other the friendly god who will be with him in trouble.

Unlike Vishnu, Siva has no incarnations, but he is not alone in the world of gods. He has his consorts, or wives, and is very frequently worshiped in their person rather than in his own. Among these wives are Devi, "the goddess"; Durga, "the inaccessible"; Karala, "the horrible one"; and Kali, "the black one." This terrible nest of harpies accentuates the tragic feature of Siva worship and illustrates to what lengths these

[16] Sydney Cave, *Redemption, Hindu and Christian*, pp. 124-25.

poor people, on whom the struggle of life has laid its heavy hand, are compelled to go to find solace and relief. To take but one example, Kali, the goddess after whom the city of Calcutta is named, is depicted as a cruel woman who with devilish glee dances on the body of her husband, holding aloft a human head she has just cut off. She can be satisfied only with blood, and at her temple goats are killed in order to spatter her protruding tongue with the bloody sacrifice. And yet women all over India cry out to "Mother Kali" as their only hope in distress and suffering. Closely connected with the worship of Siva is that of Ganesa, his son, the elephant-headed god of wisdom and "the embodiment of success in life," whose unique images are to be seen in all parts of the country. The Saivites are numbered by the million, and by their devotion and earnestness attest the inalienable religiousness of the Indian people, who seek God even in the grotesque and repulsive forms in which Siva and his company are so frequently represented.

Intimately connected with the growth of sectarian Hinduism, which has been briefly described, another most significant development was taking place. The worship of Vishnu and later the worship of Siva took a form which became the most characteristic feature of Hinduism and which still retains a powerful influence on the religious life of India. It is called bhakti, a word which means, as clearly as we can translate it, loving devotion. It is akin to the Christian idea of faith, though bhakti is more deeply impregnated with fervent emotion, emotion of the exuberant type of excessive physical and mental agitation. Slight traces of this attitude are to be found in the Upanishads, but it was in the Bhagavad-Gita—commonly called the Gita—that it began to exercise a powerful influence. The Gita is the most influential book in Hinduism. Coming into its present form probably A.D. 200, it has had its ups and downs in popularity, but is now at a new peak in esteem. It has been called the "New Testament of Modern Hinduism," and it is well known that Gandhi went to it for comfort and uplift more than to any other religious classic.

It is impossible here to go into a description of the Gita except to call attention to the emphasis found in it on the attitude of utter devotion to Krishna. All three of the great philosophers—Shankara, Ramanuja, and Madhwa—wrote commentaries on the Gita, but it was Ramanuja who emphasized the feature of devotion to Krishna and thought to make it the key to unlock its secret. Since his time a long succession of Bhaktas has always been at war with the monistic philosophy of Shankara and his

110

followers, who have little or no place for a personal God and for a conscious and permanent relation between him and his worshipers.

Still another movement developed. The Shaktas are worshipers of Kali, the wife of Siva. A Shakti is the wife of a god thought of as the energy, the sexual energy of her husband, so the whole movement is erotic. Yet even here there is a distinction. One group of Shaktas, those of the "right hand," are respectable, reading mystic meaning into sexuality as the symbol of creativity in the universe. Another, however, thost of the "left hand," include sexual immorality as an essential element in their worship. Very fortunately this form of worship is frowned upon by most of the Hindu community, and it is doubtful if it continues to be practiced. But the very fact that these erotic forms of worship have been practiced and that a whole literature, the Tantras, exists and is popular attests that that Hinduism always runs the danger of being contaminated by practices which are entirely unworthy of high-minded men and women.

Besides these forms of religious life India has many others. When we are told that 90 per cent of all the people of India are demon worshipers, we ask how that can be when the people have been roughly divided between the two great sects. The fact is, the lines are loosely drawn and are stepped over with ease. Millions who may at times worship at the shrines of Krishna or Siva are also devotees of lesser gods and village divinities who are little better than malignant demons. The people see no incongruity in so doing. They are in want and are fearful as they look into the future—why should they not have access to any and all gods who may possibly avert the dangers which beset them? And so the worship extends out to include the worship of heroes and saints, demons and spirits, tutelary and village deities, the family ancestors, and even animals and plants and stones and other inanimate objects. There is no end to the list of sacred objects held in reverence and worshiped by the people. The cow is holy and inviolable, and to be treated with reverence. Even monkeys are sacred, with temples erected in their honor, in whose courts troops of the chattering fortunates are fed and treated like spoiled children. India is ineradicably religious and finds divinity everywhere. All the way from the lofty conception of the Supreme Creator down to the depths India has run the gamult of religious experience and doctrine. This god-intoxicated land is not to be restrained in her long quest for a satisfying conception of God and for an experience which will bring the people into vital touch with him.

111

Modern Reform Movements and the Situation Today

On August 15, 1947, India achieved her independence. The British army sailed away, and British officials in every department of government turned over their duties to Indians. At the end the change came so quickly that Indians themselves could scarcely believe that their dream had come true. This revolution affected every phase of Indian life. We are interested here in the effect of independence on religion and the religious life of the people. Outwardly the most marked result was the partition of the land between India and Pakistan. This was a religious move from top to bottom, the Mohammedan minority being convinced that they could not expect to be treated justly and to take the part which they felt they should have in the conduct of public affairs. They felt that they could not trust their Hindu fellow countrymen who formed the vast majority in the land as a whole. So India was torn in two; a new government was set up in Pakistan; hundreds of thousands of people, both Hindus and Muslims, were killed, and great hoards of refugees, Hindus from Pakistan and Muslims from India, fled from their homes and remain for the most part today displaced people cared for from public funds. The whole series of events provides terrible evidence of what bitter religious intolerance can do when animosities of long standing are unleashed.

In this chapter interest is being concentrated on Hinduism and the effect of the coming of independence on the thinking and inner life of the Hindu community. The most marked effect is a new self-confidence which has naturally accompanied the tremendous rise of patriotic fervor which the coming of independence has engendered. On every hand are evidences of what an Indian scholar has called "the Renaissance of Hinduism." [17] A sense of self-sufficiency and even of complacent self-satisfaction is abroad in the land, and Hinduism is being proclaimed with renewed confidence as the crown of the world's religions.

Dr. J. N. Farquhar calls attention to a number of phases of the influence of the contact with the West on the religious life of India. The coming of Western education, the teaching of the Christian missionaries, and their philanthropic work through hospitals, schools, and orphanages, together with the work of Western scholars in studying and revealing to the astonishment, even of Indian religious thinkers themselves, the beauties and profound insights in the ancient religious classics of the

[17] See D. S. Sarma, *Studies in the Renaissance of Hinduism in the Nineteenth and Twentieth Century.*

Sanskrit literature—all these played their part. As a result of these and other influences a number of significant movements of social and religious reform have marked the recent history of Hinduism.

The most advanced of all the groups which are seeking to bring religion into line with the new light from the West is the Brahmo Samaj. This Samaj, or "church," has had an honorable history since the day of its founding in 1828. A very remarkable man, Ram Mohan Ray (1772-1833), highly educated and well versed in the literature of Islam, Buddhism, and Christianity as well as of Hinduism, turned against the polytheism, the idolatry, the social abuses, and the moral blemishes of the faith in which he had been brought up and founded a "Theistic Church." He had few disciples, and in all its history the society has had but few members—not over five thousand at any time. Even this small number has been seriously divided and has been unable to present a united front against the social and religious abuses which it condemns. But all hold to an unqualified monotheism and a purely spiritual worship. They are social reformers, opposing caste, child marriage, and the enforced celibacy of widows, but at this point there is a division of sentiment between the progressives and conservatives. Caste feeling is too strong to be easily overcome, and one wing—the less important, let it be said—were unwilling thus to cut themselves off from the Hindu community. The "Progressive Brahmo Samaj," led by the gifted though erratic Keshab Chunder Sen (1838-1884), threw itself into the work of reform with zeal. Keshab was a deeply spiritual man and read much in the literature of Christianity. He held Christ in the highest honor, and some were even optimistic enough to look forward to his conversion to Christianity. He not only had no intention of taking this step, but in the end lost his hold on his own followers by claiming almost divine honors as a special channel of revelation. The Samaj still lives and through its numerous publications promotes the reforms for which it has stood and witnesses to its belief in the one God, who may be approached only in spiritual worship.

Of a very different sort is the militant Arya Samaj. Founded in 1875 by Dayananda Sarasvati, whose watchword was "Back to the Vedas," and who believed India could be regenerated only by a return to the ancient faith, this society has grown in numbers and influence and is a powerful factor in Indian religious life. Opposed to idolatry and with the desire to promote the worship of one God, the Samaj has stood for certain needed reforms, but caste has not been successfully opposed, and the belief in transmigration and karma nullifies what might otherwise be a worthy advocacy of monotheism. Violently opposed to Christianity and lending itself to the nationalistic agitation, the Arya Samaj has tended to become a political as well as a religious movement. Its reforms do not go deep enough to promise anything commensurate with the need, and its failure to strike at the root of the religious needs of the country gives little hope that India's regeneration will be furthered by this agency.

Toward the end of the last century a poor Brahmin priest lived in a little temple not far from Calcutta. Through his own life and teaching and even more through the work of one of his disciples this obscure man has profoundly influenced the religious thinking of intelligent Hindus in every part of India. Ramakrishna Paramahamsa (1834-1886) was a man of the keenest intelligence and yet had almost no formal education. He had a consuming passion to experience religion in vivid intimate realization. After a period of storm and stress within, he achieved inner calm and assurance. He believed he could see God with his physical eyes and have communion just as with a human personality. Strange to say, his god was Kali—could any object of worship be more incongruous? But Kali was to him the great beneficent, kindly mother, the embodiment of everything good, the greatest of the gods.

Paramahamsa's alert mind was eager to know and understand the religious experience of others. The result of his studies was that he set up shrines to the gods of other religions and worshiped them all. He had come to the conclusion "that all religions were true, that they were simply various paths leading to the same goal." [18] It is impossible to overestimate the pervasive influence of this attitude. It is one of the basic convictions of practically all educated Hindus at the present time. One of their own scholars declares: "In a way, the true starting point of the present Hindu Renaissance may be said to be Sri Ramakrishna Paramahamsa." [19]

It is doubtful, however, if his convictions would have spread so widely and have entered so deeply into the texture of the thought of modern India had it not been for his most remarkable disciple, universally known as Swami Vivekananda. He might easily be considered the most forceful personality present at the World Parliament of Religions held in Chicago in 1893, where he electrified his audiences by his vivid personality and

[18] J. N. Farquhar, *Modern Religious Movements in India*, p. 194.
[19] D. S. Sarma, *op. cit.*, p. 228.

THE RELIGIONS OF INDIA: HINDUISM

glowing eloquence. He at once became a world figure and was wel-
comed by enthusiastic audiences in Europe and America. To him India
was the home of spirituality which would die out were it not for the
saints and ascetics of India. He founded the Ramakrishna Mission, an
order of ascetic monks, an organization with branches in various Indian
cities. These monks are great believers in education, give themselves to
the conduct of hospitals, and carry on a considerable publishing business.
But with all that we are amazed that they have given themselves heart
and soul to the monistic philosophy of Shankara, so that to them God,
the final fact in the universe, is unknowable and without attributes.
Amazement increases when we discover that the Ramakrishna Mission
is the ardent defender of everything in Hinduism, yes, everything in
every form of the religion, with the one exception of untouchability. Yet
their influence is tremendous and growing, reaching out in its influence
to thousands of the intelligentsia who have no connection with the mission as an organization.

The Theosophical Society was founded in New York in 1875 by two
very colorful personalities: Colonel H. S. Olcott, an ex-officer in the
Union Army in the American Civil War, and Madame Helena Blavatsky,
a forceful Russian woman with a very dubious past. These two came to
be known as the "Theosophical Twins." In 1879 they came to India,
where the headquarters of this world-wide movement have been located
ever since. Here they were soon joined by the famous Mrs. Annie Besant,
the widow of an Anglican clergyman, a woman who lost her Christian
faith, became enamored with Madame Blavatsky, and who by her
ability and zeal soon began to exercise an amazing influence.

The story of the Theosophical Society in India is not pleasant reading.
Their relations with the occult and their claim to the possession of
magical and even miraculous power were finally investigated by the
Society for Psychical Research of Great Britain, which discovered fraud
and exposed the deception which was practiced at the séances. But the
movement went gaily on and now numbers as many as five hundred
circles or local societies in India alone. This, of course, has little or no
connection with Hinduism and would not be noticed here were it not
for the significance of Mrs. Annie Besant. Leaving Madras with its un-
savory associations she went to Benares, the center of Hinduism, and
made that her permanent headquarters. Immediately the scene shifts
and Mrs. Besant takes on the role of a defender of Hinduism. She went
very much further in her advocacy of the religion of her adoption than

the Hindus themselves. Many of them hesitated to put the stamp of their approval on features of the popular religion. Not so with Mrs. Besant; to her Hinduism was the perfect religion; there was nothing in its beliefs and practices which was not good and beautiful. She combined with this a commendable interest in education. She founded the Benares Hindu College, out of which has grown the Benares Hindu University, a great institution of learning now situated on a magnificent campus on the edge of the city. This amazing woman, as erratic as a number of her attitudes and actions were—erratic in the estimation of many Hindus as well as outsiders—no doubt played an important part in giving an impetus to the ardor and self-confidence to be found among Hindus today.

Titantic forces are at work in Indian life. Ardent patriots are still drinking deeply of the exhilarating cup of freedom, not as yet sobered by the seriousness of the problems—social, economic, political, moral, and religious—which demand drastic action. Corruption is eating its way into even the higher brackets of political life, and other evils abound, so the question arises, Does Hinduism possess the moral power to overcome this giant who stands in the way and to build up the new India on the principles of rectitude and unselfish devotion to the interests of all the people? That insistent question is beginning to be asked and must be asked over and over again to bring about a frank facing of an alarming situation.

Jawaharlal Nehru stands bravely for a state in which no faith shall be established as the national religion but with equal rights and toleration for all. At the same time eager and influential Hindus are impatient. "Everyone knows," they say, "that India is a Hindu country. Why shouldn't we act and make Hinduism the national religion under the protection of the state?" And no one can tell what the end will be. At the same time there are many who do not share this view but who look into the future with assurance that Hinduism will more and more dominate the scene in India and be recognized by all as the natural flowering of all that India means and stands for in the world. In the words of Professor D. S. Sarma:

We have no longer any fear that [Hinduism] might be overpowered by Christianity or Western civilization. It has oulived the Christian propaganda of modern times as it outlived the Muslin oppression of the Middle Ages and the Buddhist schism of ancient days. It is now able to meet any of the world religions on equal terms as their friend and ally in a common cause.[20]

[20] *The Renaissance of Hinduism*, p. 70.

The last words in this quotation indicate still another aspect of the present situation. Unlike Islam, which with intolerant zeal has so often used coercion in its expansion and has repressed and restricted other faiths which are in a minority, Hinduism, at least in the mind of many of its leaders, would live at peace with other religions and actually look upon them as allies "in a common cause." One of the most insistent notes to be heard from educated Hindus today is "The Essential Unity of all religions," as it is put in the title of a widely read book. In its vaunted liberality and tolerance the one thing which these Hindus will not tolerate is the winning of converts from one religion to another. Why should such an attempt be made when all religions are true and lead to the same goal?

It is at just this point that Hinduism and Christianity stand in the sharpest opposition. The zeal to win men to Christ is the living breath of Christianity. But Christianity as a living, growing force in the world is being challenged more strongly in India today than in any other land. India may well be called the testing ground of the religions of the world. Here more religions are present in throbbing vitality than in any other country, and here the claims of the living religions of mankind to the allegiance of men are more likely to be validated or nullified than anywhere else among men.

SUGGESTIONS FOR FURTHER STUDY

Bouquet, A. C. *Hinduism*. London: Hutchinson and Company, 1949. A short and very suggestive recent sketch.

Farquhar, J. N. *Modern Religious Movements in India*. New York: The Macmillan Company, 1915. Needs considerable correction today, but very valuable for the earlier history of the movements.

————. *An Outline of the Religious Literature of India*. New York: Oxford University Press, 1920. Retains its place as an authoritative survey. Deals with the literature of Jainism and early Buddhism as well as that of Hinduism.

Hill, W. Douglas P. *The Bhagavadgita*. New York: Oxford University Press, 1928. No better exposition exists of the *Gita* by a recognized authority.

Hiriyana, M. *The Essentials of Indian Philosophy*. New York: The Macmillan Company, 1949. Probably the best brief manual on Indian philosophy.

Macnicol, Nicol. *Indian Scriptures.* Everyman's Library. A translation of a number of the hymns of the *Rig-Veda,* of one of the most important of the longer *Upanishads,* and of the *Gita.*

Moore, George Foot. *History of Religions.* Vol. I, chs. XI, XIII, XIV.

Pratt, James Bissett. *India and Its Faiths.* Boston: Houghton, Mifflin Company, 1915. The record of a traveler with a mind trained to interpret religious beliefs and practice.

Urquhart, W. S. *The Vedanta and Modern Thought.* New York: Oxford University Press, 1928. One of the best critiques of the *Vedanta.*

CHAPTER VI

THE RELIGIONS OF INDIA: JAINISM, SIKHISM, PARSIISM

JAINISM

MAHAVIRA, THE REPUTED FOUNDER OF JAINISM, WAS AN OLDER CONTEMporary of Gautama the Buddha. His dates, according to Jain tradition, were 599 to 527 B.C. Like the Buddha this reformer turned against the pretensions of the Brahmin priesthood and repudiated the authority of the Vedas. But also like the Buddha, Mahavira could not and did not seem to want to break the shackles of karma. Fear of future rebirths remains the key to unlock the door into the secret of Jainism. All their ascetic practices, all their rules of conduct, which reach down into every act of human life, are directed to the achieving of emancipation from the fateful wheel of transmigration. Thus this religion too shows itself to be in the Hindu tradition even though it broke away and has been living a separate life for 2,500 years.

Buddhism has disappeared from India; Jainism remains. It had its day of glory when it wielded more authority and numbered far more adherents than it has at present. But it persists and shows a tenacity which is remarkable. Not numbering more than a million and a half, groups of Jains, or "conquerors," as they call themselves, are found in every part of India, where in the business world they are known as successful merchants and wealthy bankers. Strange as it may seem this religion started as an ascetic movement, turning its back on money and possessions. To quote from one of the leading authorities, "An unworldly faith," it is now chiefly found in "a class famed throughout India for their love of gain and their reluctance to part with their money. . . . Indeed it would be impossible to imagine any creed or rule of conduct which, prima facie, would seem so little likely to appeal to a constituency of cautious, middle-class bankers and shop-keepers." [1]

[1] Margaret Stevenson, *The Heart of Jainism,* pp. 7-8.

At about the age of thirty Mahavira became an ascetic and instituted an order, a community of laymen as well as monks, of women as well as men, and was so successful that at the time of his death he had a following of fourteen thousand monks. We have taken for granted that Mahavira was the founder of Jainism—but was he? There is a tradition that an ascetic named Parsvanatha, born in Benares in 817 B.C., really started the movement which received its organized form at the hands of Mahavira. Be that as it may, there are other traditions which are clearly legendary and no more. Behind the two leaders just mentioned legends tell that there were twenty-two other saintly figures connected with their religion who reach back so far that Jains have claimed that their religion is the oldest in the world. All of these personages, including Parsvanatha and Mahavira, are known as Tirthankaras, those "who show the true way across the troubled ocean of life." [2] They play a very important part in the religion today. Images of these worthies occupy a prominent place in Jain temples, where they are reverenced and even worshiped. In fact this is about the only worship feature in the religion. This community flatly denies the existence of a creator god and of any other divine beings which might deserve to be considered divinities, and yet every Jain will stoutly deny that his religion is atheistic. The basis of his denial is that he does pray and offer sacrifices to the Tirthankaras.

The Jains, whether laymen or monks, are constantly reminded that they themselves are divine, that their task is to let the essential divinity within them come to its own and shine out in its beauty. "There is no higher god than man himself." [3] Religion for a Jain is self-development with no dependence on higher powers. Hence there is little significance in worship and prayer. In their own words, "The pure, All-Conscious, Self-absorbed Soul is god and never less or more." [4] This means that there is no saving power outside themselves, so there is no such thing as forgiveness or grace coming to them from another and higher being. Jainism is really "a system of ethics rather than a religion," [5] despite the claim vigorously maintained to the contrary.

At a somewhat uncertain date about the time of the opening of our era the Jain community was split in two, divided so seriously that they have remained apart until the present day. The schism took place over the clothes versus nudity question. One of these sects is the Digambara, or

[2] Ibid., p. 42.
[3] Nichol Macnicol, The Living Religions of the Indian People, p. 188.
[4] Stevenson, op. cit., p. 297.
[5] Ibid., p. 289.

the "atmosphere-clad," that is, the nude, and the other the Svetambara, or the "white-clothed." So far as the Jain laymen are concerned there is no practical difference, but they continue to belong to one of the other of these sects, worship in different temples, and loyally adhere to the particular claims of the sect to which they belong. In A.D. 1473 a third sect arose, coming out of the Svetambara group. They are the Sthanakavasi, who took a stand against the use of images and idols, which are found in the temples of both the older sects.

The monastic institutions, where the discipline is very strict, have set the type of Jainism. Harsh asceticism and austerities are looked upon as the chief means of salvation. Mahavira is said to have set the style by plucking his hair out by the roots as an evidence of sincerity and zeal as an ascetic, and his example has been followed by the monks through the centuries. "Among austerities fasting is the most conspicuous; the Jains have developed it to a kind of art, and reach a remarkable proficiency in it. The usual way of fasting is to eat only one meal every second, third, fourth day, and so on down to half a year. Another form of fasting is starving oneself to death." [6] Of great importance are the five vows. They are (1) not to kill, (2) not to lie, (3) not to steal, (4) to abstain from sexual intercourse, (5) to renounce all interest in worldly things, especially to keep no property.

These and other vows, kept very strictly by the monks, are relaxed to a considerable degree for the laymen, but it must be understood that in Jainism the distinction between the monk and the layman is not clear cut and radical. The layman is not regarded as an outsider or as merely a patron in friendly relations with the monks. A very effective tie unites the laymen and the monks, with no very distinct boundary between the two. It is very evident of course that some difference has to be made. A layman could, however, at times renounce his liberty and become one of the monks for a longer or shorter period by becoming stricter in keeping of the regulations. But when he was at home and pursuing his vocation, it was understood that he could not escape doing some injury to animal life, something which a monk scrupulously avoided. He must do as little injury as possible—that is the layman's rule. To quote from Dr. Hermann Jacobi,

It cannot be doubted that this close union between laymen and monks brought about by the similarity of their religious duties, differing not in kind,

[6] Hermann W. Jacobi, "Janism" in Hastings, *Encyclopaedia of Religion and Ethics.*

but in degree, has enabled Jainism to avoid fundamental changes within and to resist dangers from without for more than two thousand years, while Buddhism, being less exacting as regards the laymen, underwent the most extraordinary evolutions and finally disappeared in the country of its origin.[7]

A Jain, upon being asked what his religion stands for is likely to reply that it is nonviolence. One often reads such a statement as "Nonviolence is the Supreme Religion." These people have carried the Hindu and Buddhist doctrine of nonviolence to living things (ahimsa) to the extreme limit until it seems to outsiders to be an obsession. To keep from doing violence is the chief requirement resting on the conscience of a Jain. He faces what to him is the awful fact of transmigration. Emancipation is release from the dreadful prospect of being born times without number into this world of suffering and misery. "Jainism might be defined as a 'way of escape,' not from death, but from life."

There are nine categories or concepts on which the whole system turns. These are the doctrines which every Jain knows and which control his thinking and his practice.

1) Jiva, life, vitality, soul, or consciousness. The soul is indestructible, but if the soul possesses hatred or is attached to things of the world, that is, is "fettered to Karma," it is bound to the wheel of rebirths and cannot escape. But Jiva, or life, in Jain thought includes much more than human beings. All animal life is sacred and must not be molested. It does not stop even there—inanimate things like fire and water, and even certain vegetables are thought to have a kind of life, and great care must be taken not to injure them. We are told that monks never "snap their fingers, or swing or fan themselves, lest they injure air." [8] Of course no Jain would think of killing vermin. No matter how annoying mosquitoes, flies, and ants may be, nothing must be killed, so it goes without saying that they are strict vegetarians. It is not possible here to give even a sample of the endless classifications of living things which abound in Jain literature.

2) Ajiva, things inanimate. Here there is an elaborate classification of natural objects. One subdivision is called pudgala, or "matter which possesses colour, smell, taste and form, and is perceptible to touch. . . . Jains indulge their genius for subdivision by dividing each colour by the two smells, five flavors and eight touches, and then again they divide each

[7] *Ibid.*
[8] *Ibid.,* p. 100.

smell by the five colours, five tastes and eight touches, and so on, till they get 560 divisions out of pudgala." [9]

3) Punya, or merit, the actions which lead to good karma, out of which comes peace of mind. Among these meritorious acts are giving water to the thirsty and "thinking well of everyone and wishing them well." [10]

4) Papa, or sin. And here the characteristic feature of Jainism comes clearly to light. To take any life seems to the Jains the most heinous of all crimes . . . yet the central thought of Jainism is not so much saving life as refraining from destroying it." [11] But to the Jains' eternal credit there is a list of seventeen other sins, "the next worst of them being untruthfulness." Among them are excessive love of possessions, anger, cheating, greed, quarrelsomeness, slander, telling stories of discredit about anyone, finding fault, lack of self-control, hypocrisy, and false faith. Such a list surely indicates noble thinking and high ideals. Then again we find them analyzing and listing each with a separate name, with eighty-two results of sin in all.

5) Asrava, or the way karma is acquired by the soul. This and the next four categories deal with karma. We thus are able to realize the all-pervasive influence of karma, which is implicitly accepted and underlies all else in their thinking.

We have become acquainted with karma in Hinduism; it also exists in Buddhism. But here we find it in a form quite different from that in the other religions. Karma in Jainism is conceived not as a law according to which rebirths take place or as a force or influence, but as consisting of "extremely subtle matter which pours or infiltrates into the soul, when worldly actions make as if it were an opening for it." [12] So the Jains often speak of karma matter as a real material thing/ The thought of karma underlies all the nine categories. "It is the key that solves all the riddles of this unintelligible world."/ [13] With his propensity for analysis the Jain believes there are eight kinds of karma, each of which is harmful in its own and unique way. In order to reach deliverance from its ravages the soul must ascend a ladder of fourteen steps. They are steps in asceticism. At one of the important stages the ascetic "loses all sense of humor, all pleasure in beauty of sound or form, and all perception of pain, fear,

[9] *Ibid.,* p. 109.
[10] *Ibid.,* p. 118.
[11] Macnicol, *op. cit.,* p. 180.
[12] *Ibid.,* p. 183.
[13] Stevenson, *op. cit.,* p. 173.

grief, disgust, and smells, so Jaina asceticism amounts to self-stultifica-tion." [14]

/Moksha, or complete deliverance, is the last of the categories. When a Jain ascetic has attained deliverance, he at once becomes a Siddha. What is a Siddha like? He is a being "without caste, unaffected by smell, with-out the sense of taste, without feeling, without form, without hunger, without pain, without sorrow, without joy, without birth, without old age, without death, without body, without karma, enjoying an endless and unbroken calm." [15] And yet "the Jaina Siddha through all eternity will maintain their separate identity." [16] Nearly every item in this list of qualities is negative, "without" this and that. A more positive state-ment is found in another quotation: "Omniscience, boundless vision, illimitable righteousness, infinite strength, perfect bliss, indestructibility, existence without form, a body that is neither light nor heavy, such are the characteristics of the Siddha." [17] The Siddha is all this by the power of the soul itself, which "decides its own condition, good or evil. . . . The soul is the cow from which all desires can be milked, the soul is my heavenly garden." [18]

This religion, like other faiths in India, is putting on new life and showing remarkable vigor. Each of the sects has been holding a series of conferences for several decades. The need for unity has made itself felt and has resulted in the formation of an All-India Jain Association, which organizes open meetings in various cities. An increasing number of editions and translations of their sacred books are being published. Propaganda literature in pamphlet form can be easily secured. They are eagerly making a bid for the attention of the modern man in India and elsewhere, claiming that Jainism stands for world peace, spiritual inde-pendence, individual freedom, and the universality of the brotherhood of souls. At one of these open meetings an aged but very active ascetic wanted his hearers to know that Jainism was needed in the New India now coming into being. He also urged his hearers in typical Jain fashion never to forget that they were divine. In the words of a European con-vert to their faith this appeal is sounded forth: "O you people of all lands! Here is the Truth. Live it and find your own soul." [19]

[14] *Ibid.*, p. 189.
[15] *Ibid.*, p. 169.
[16] *Ibid.*, p. 172.
[17] *Ibid.*, p. 192.
[18] *Ibid.*
[19] Matthew McKay in *Addresses and Essays on Jainism and World Problems*, p. 24.

SIKHISM

The Sikhs are found all over Northern and Central India, but especially in the Punjab, their ancestral home. In the days of the British rule in India the Sikh was a familiar figure in the port cities along the coast of China and in many of the British colonies, where he served as policeman, ever dependable and of striking appearance. According to the census of 1941 the Sikhs numbered 5,691,447 and at the present time their number is estimated to be something over 6,000,000. The Sikhs suffered with the Hindus in the displacement of population following the partition of India and Pakistan, so they help to swell the number of refugees, particularly in the Punjab, which was split in two by the separation of the two countries. But they on their part were particularly savage in their attacks on Muslims, their traditional enemies, during the dreadful days of murder and eviction in 1947.

Whence came this most recent addition to the religions of intensely religious India? We are compelled to go back to the Bhakti movement, which, as will be remembered, owes its impulse to the theistic philosopher Ramanuja, who in the eleventh and twelfth centuries of our era declared that there was one God, a being of love who was to be approached by bhakti, or loving devotion. Nanak, the founder of Sikhism, was deeply influenced by this movement. Thus we can see how the Sikhs are an offshoot of Hinduism and of the fervent devotional bhakti wing of that many-sided religion.

Nanak's dates are A.D. 1469 to 1538. He came from the Jat racial group, which has been the backbone of the Sikh religion and has furnished almost all its leadership. They belonged to the northwest of India. "Their language and their physique proclaim them to be of Aryan descent. . . . They have preserved their Aryan social heritage relatively unmixed for thousands of years and physically are among the tallest and heaviest peoples of India. Their complexion is prevailingly light brown or dark tan. They are predominantly farmers and form, perhaps, the finest rural population in India." [20]

Nanak caught the spirit of interfaith friendship and co-operation from his spiritual mentor Kabir. "His message was summed up in the words, "There is no Hindu and there is no Mussulman." [21] With such a beginning one might have expected a very different outcome. Within a few generations the growing Sikh movement found in Islam, as it was em-

[20] C. H. Loehlin, The Sikhs and Their Book, p. 2.
[21] Macnicol, op. cit., p. 209.

bodied in the Mohgul dynasty, its chief antagonist, so that bitter hatred toward Muslims has become their settled attitude. On the other hand, while Sikhism has retained its separate identity, it is quite close to Hinduism, and friendly relations exist between the adherents of the two faiths.

Nanak was an ardent preacher and might have been known to later generations only as a reformer and a leader in the revival movement of his day. But a new and most important idea—an "innovation" it has been called—came to him which had most significant consequences. Just before he died Nanak, acting on the new idea, "formally appointed a successor, and taught his people that the same divine spirit which had been in him was thus passed on into the succeeding gurus." [22] There were ten of these gurus, or counselors. A Sikh scholar says of them: "The gurus took in hand the training of a nation, and each of them at a time gave as much instruction as was needful, passing it on to the next guru when the work of one generation was complete. In this way the whole course of training extended over ten generations." [23] For two hundred years the story of Sikhism is the story of the gurus and their contribution to the life and practices of their followers.

Nanak did not appoint either of his own sons as his successor. They had, in his estimation, unfitted themselves for the succession by becoming ascetics. Thus early in their history the Sikhs were turned against austerities and the denial of life. Angad, who received the appointment, was a man with wife and children. It should be said that after the first three gurus the succession became hereditary and remained so until the line came to an end in 1708 with the death of the famous Gobind Singh.

One after another the gurus added to the deposit of teaching and practice. The second guru, Angad, constructed a special alphabet so that the words of himself and the other gurus might be transmitted in a language all their own, a sacred language, unknown to outsiders. Unfortunately it is not known as widely as it might be by the Sikhs themselves, with the result that the average Sikh cannot read his scriptures and does not know their contents. But the possession of a different written language did act as a barrier separating the Sikhs from Hindus and all others. Quite a different picture is given of the third guru, Amar Das. He became a social reformer, being vigorously opposed to the entry of caste distinction into his community and taking further steps against ascetic practices. Amar Das was very severe in opposition to sati and female

[22] Loehlin, op. cit., p. 3.
[23] Professor Teja Singh, quoted in Loehlin, op. cit., p. 3.

infanticide. He was an organizer, establishing a central place of pilgrimage with a bathing pool, so dear to the heart of the Indian. The result of the innovations was that the Sikh sect, which had been little less than a loosely organized community before, was rapidly becoming a church.

His successor, the fourth guru, Ram Das, procured land and laid out a city, the religious capital of Sikhism. At first called Ramdaspur, the city of Ram Das has for long been known as Amritsar, one of the most remarkable religious centers in India. The fifth guru, Arjan, appointed taxgatherers to raise money for building purposes. Here before our eyes is a church being turned into a state. He also built two other sacred centers in the Punjab, but even more important than that, Arjan can never be forgotten, as the famous Golden Temple in the midst of the Pool of Immortality in the city of Amritsar is his work. But probably his crowning act was the compilation, in 1604, of the Adigranth, the Sikh bible. He collected the religious poems or hymns which he and his predecessors had composed as well as those of a dozen or more Hindu and Muslim devotees, including of course those of Kabir, and made them into a single collection. The book, just as he left it, has been increasingly the center around which the religion has turned.

A complete change came over the community. The first five gurus had been men of religion and social amelioration, but the last five were pre-eminently warriors. In its early days the Moghul dynasty had not been unfavorable to the Sikhs, but as time passed opposition took the place of tolerance, and intolerance turned into fierce active opposition. What a change! Nanak had in mind bringing Hindus and Muslims together, but in a few generations the Sikhs were compelled to organize an army to fight the Muslim rulers and also to resist orthodox Hindu local princes who were jealous of the growth of a strong virile community in their midst. Two of the gurus, Arjan and Teg Bahadur, were put to death by the Moghuls, so that when we come to Guru Gobind Singh, we find him possessed with a new and fierce sense of mission, "to oppose Muslim tyranny." [24]

Gobind Singh stands out as "the mightiest warrior and greatest organizer of all the gurus." [25] He formed the Sikhs into a "military theocracy known as the Khalsa, or purified." [26] No longer must they be known as Sikhs, or "Learners," but as Singhs, the "Lions." There was an initia-

[24] Loehlin, op. cit., p. 7.
[25] Ibid.
[26] Ibid.

tion ceremony in which the two-edged dagger played an important part. After this all Sikhs should be in possession of the five distinctive marks, the five k's, (1) kes, the uncut hair on head and face, (2) khanga, the comb to hold the hair on top of the head, (3) kirpan, the sword or dagger, (4) kara, the iron bangle to be worn on the wrist to parry a blow, (5) kachh, breeches ending above the knee. All Sikhs today adhere to the first two regulations and always wear a turban. Gobind Singh also forbade the use of tobacco and this has been obeyed. As might be expected these strict regulations and the attitude back of them divided the community into the older more moderate conservatives, who continue to this day to prefer to be known as Sikhs, and the extremists, or radicals. In fact a sect arose among them who called themselves the Akalis, or the "immortals," a fighting sect who wear a garb which distinguishes them from their fellows.

But the most startling thing which Gobind Singh did was to produce another sacred book, the Granth of the Tenth Reign. This book was entirely different from the original Granth. It was composed to arouse the military spirit in the people. He had discovered that the effect of reading the old Adigranth was to make his people "feeble-minded," meek and humble, as were Nanak and the other writers whose devotional hymns are included in the older work. He wanted something entirely different. This new Granth, however, did not supersede the Adigranth though it became a kind of supplementary bible, the special scripture of the Akalis and other extreme militarists. Gobind Singh was wise in not displacing the Adigranth and thus disrupting the community. In fact he did a very remarkable and unprecedented thing when he made the formal declaration that the line of human gurus would come to an end with his death. In place of a living leader he installed the older book itself, the revered Adigranth, as his successor, "the venerable book, the embodiment of all the Gurus." Thus came to an end the line of succession of living gurus, with a book placed in the position of final and permanent authority over the Sikh people. It is actually the chief object of worship, having the central place of honor in the Golden Temple at Amritsar and at other places of worship.

The remainder of the story can be briefly recounted. By 1767 the Sikhs had carved out a land of their own in the Punjab, and had established a kingship. Fierce wars continued with the Moghuls, but the Sikhs were able to maintain themselves as a separate nation until after two wars with the rapidly growing British power. In 1849 the Punjab

128

was annexed to the British possessions and remained under British governors until India was made free in 1947. But what of the Sikhs and their martial spirit after they lost their independence a hundred years ago? During the period of the wars the British testified that the Sikhs were the "bravest and steadiest enemy ever encountered in India." Just as the Scottish Highlanders, who had been enemies of the English from the earliest day, became an indispensable addition to the British army after the middle of the eighteenth century, so the Sikhs entered the British service in large numbers and fought bravely in both World Wars and are now very numerous and very highly thought of in the new army of free India.

The significance of the story of the Sikhs is well summarized by Dr. R. E. Hume: "Politically, Sikhism is the only religion in the history of the world which has given birth to a nation, with the exception of Judaism. . . . In its case, as also in the case of Judaism, political independence has been destroyed while religiously and every other wise the people has continued strikingly able and distinctive." [27] Unfortunately a great many Sikhs today, particularly the younger men, are more interested in their community politically than religiously and show little interest in the scriptures and their religious message.

The religion of the Sikhs centers in their sacred book, the Adigranth. It holds the central place in all places of worship and is treated as a divine object. In the Golden Temple at Amritsar two copies of the huge tome are being read aloud continuously day and night, while the most revered copy occupies the place of honor and is the object of devotion. Is it actually worshiped? This seems to be the case. It is looked upon as the "living guru," and in the temple "the sacred book is installed in the place of deity, and the ceremonial of Hindu worship is rendered to it." [28] But with all that its contents have been neglected, and few Sikhs really understand its meaning. A part of this neglect is owing to the fact that the Adigranth is not only large but is composed in six languages. In the words of the chief authority on Sikhism, "The Granth Sahib thus becomes probably the most difficult work, sacred or profane, that exists, and hence the general ignorance of its contents." [29]

There is nothing distinctive in the religion which is found in the Adigranth. It is "a syncretism and adaptation of Hindu, Mohammedan,

[27] Quoted in Loehlin, *op. cit.*, pp. 14-15.
[28] Macnicol, *op. cit.*, p. 219.
[29] Macauliffe, quoted in Loehlin, *op. cit.*, p. 30.

and perhaps Christian religious ideas." [30] Unfortunately karma and transmigration are given a place, and also maya, which is a kind of "magic power, and is represented as a woman, who is in collusion with the five evil passions." [31] But of far greater importance is the conception of God, a single Being, who is personal. Professor Teja Singh makes "the essence of Sikhism as Nam and Sewa, or adoration of God through repeating his name, and service to mankind," [32] and not the worship of the book.

In stirring times when conflict is in the air the Sikhs increase in numbers and prosper, but when peace is abroad Sikhism tends to lose its vigor. There are those who believe that eventually the Sikhs will be absorbed into Hinduism. There is much of Hinduism in their religion already, and there are calls from prominent men suggesting that they go back to their origin, the Bhakti movement in Hinduism. The Sikhs, unlike the Buddhists and Jains, have made little contribution to Indian culture. This has been explained on the ground of their having faced through most of their history a hostile environment and oppression and persecution by Muslims. But it must also be acknowledged that this opposition has made the Sikhs into a self-centered people, proud of their cohesion and of their success as a fighting force. And this very cohesion may be the sign of a vitality which will keep them a distinct independent body, continuing to exist with a sense of destiny and even of mission to the motherland of India.

PARSIISM

On December 10, 1916, the Parsis celebrated the twelve hundredth anniversary of their landing in India. They derive their name from "Persia" and are proud to think of themselves as followers of the prophet Zoroaster. The exact date and circumstances of the coming of these "Pilgrim Fathers of Zoroastrianism" may be more or less a legend, but what we do know is that when the conquering Islamic armies swept over Persia and most of the inhabitants turned Mohammedan, a group of faithful men and women made their escape from the country and settled in India. Not all, however, did so. A small number who did not deny the faith remained in Persia and have retained their identity until the present day. Known as Gabars and numbering about ten thousand,

[30] Loehlin, *op. cit.*, p. 15.
[31] Macnicol, *op. cit.*, p. 221.
[32] Loehlin, *op. cit.*, p. 48.

this small remnant eke out a rather unenviable existence in central Persia.

But even the main body of Parsis in India is only a remnant, the memory of a departed glory. The contrast is striking between a proud nation, the ancient Iranians—"Iran" being the equivalent of the Sanskrit "Aryan," meaning "noble"—whose established religion was Zoroastrianism, and the little community of exiles in India, jealous of their faith and guarding it carefully against compromise with any other religion. Their total number is only about a hundred thousand, one half of whom make their home in one city, Bombay. Others are scattered in small groups, only one of which exceeds five thousand souls, in a score of cities throughout India. But in many ways it is the most distinguished community in India. Highly educated and frequently wealthy, they not only care for their own poor, but are generous in their gifts to public enterprises. As bankers and industrialists no group surpasses them. With all this they are exceedingly clannish. Contrary to the ideal which prevailed as late as the sixteenth century, the Parsis are now opposed to any extension of their faith to other nations or among the alien peoples by whom they are surrounded. What is to become of such a small and exclusive company of people is a question they are being compelled to ask ever more seriously. The danger of inbreeding faces them, and the postponement of the age of marriage, which has come with their contact with the West and the more strenuous conditions of modern life, bodes ill for the permanence of a community which has taken so exclusive an attitude.

What holds the Parsis together is their loyalty to their great prophet and leader. Unfortunately, great uncertainty exists relative to Zoroaster.[33] When he lived and where he worked are still subjects of controversy. The traditional dates are 660 to 583 B.C. However, some competent authorities feel that the facts demand an earlier date, about 1000 B.C. But Zoroaster was a real historical character despite the uncertainty in date and the locality where he worked.

When he was thirty years old, Zoroaster experienced "a divine manifestation" or vision, which was the first of seven visions which came to him during the ten years following. He was led by an archangel before the throne of God. Here he communed with God himself. He began to preach immediately after the first vision and was never deflected from

[33] This is the Greek form of the name. The original form is Zarathustra, as it is in the old Persian language.

it. At the end of the ten years the doctrine was a completed whole, a distinct message very different from the faith which had existed for long among his people. For a time his preaching produced little effect. Finally at God's bidding he went to the court of King Vishtaspa and sought the conversion of the king himself. At last he succeeded, against the opposition of the jealous priests, who for a time were able to keep him in prison and away from the king. The story is embellished with miraculous interventions, which were incorporated into the narrative later, but the one significant fact stands out, that the king, the queen, and finally the entire court were soundly converted. This is said to have occurred in 618 B.C., when the prophet was forty-two years old. It was his triumph; from that time on his work was relatively easy.[34] After many years of teaching, while engaged in the "holy wars" in defense of the faith, he was killed at the hand of an enemy, "a Turanian whose name is preserved to ill renown." Zoroaster was one of the greatest religious characters the world has known. Had he been followed by a succession of like-minded men, as was the case in the history of the Hebrews, he might have produced effects similar to that described in the Old Testament; but he was the only religious genius this religion produced, and during the centuries after his death there was a sad decline from his lofty teaching.

Zoroaster was a practical man and preached the doctrine of work, especially the care of cattle, which were to be protected from the wild Turanians of the north. But more than this, he was deeply stirred by the recklessness of the nobles, who "killed domestic animals, unheeding the requirements of rural husbandry." [35] So Zoroaster was in a true sense a social as well as a religious reformer. As Archbishop Söderblom says, "He could not bear to see robbery go unpunished and the fruits of labor spoiled."[36]

This was one side; but there was another, almost unexplicable in one so practical. He was not concrete and simple in his teaching, as was Jesus, and thus failed to win the people to himself and his doctrine. He was abstract in his thinking and seemed never to be able to come down to the level of his hearers. Despite all this he was intent on reaching all with his new conceptions and accomplished a veritable religious revolution. He hated nature worship and any form of anthropomorphism. God to him was "high and lifted up" above any likeness of anything in heaven

[34] See A. V. W. Jackson, Zoroastrian Studies, Chap. III, for further details; also Zoroaster, the Prophet of Iran by the same author.

[35] Nathan Söderblom, The Living God, p. 180.

[36] Ibid., p. 187.

or earth. He denounced all the old "heavenly ones," calling them evil powers fit only to be destroyed and put away. He spared none, not even "Mithras and his troops"; they were all to be banished. Zoroaster's god was Mazdah, or Ahura Mazda, "the wise," the wisdom in question being the "knowledge of good and evil," or, as Professor James Hope Moulton puts it, "the unerring instinct that can distinguish between Truth and Falsehood, which for the prophet were the most vital aspects of good and evil." [37] Here, then, lie close together the two great truths which Zoroaster would introduce, that God is one, and that he is holy and irreconcilably at enmity with evil. This is not far distant, surely, from the teachings of the Hebrew prophets.

So much is fairly clear, but difficulties are immediately forthcoming. Of the various parts of the Avesta, the sacred literature of the Zoroastrians, the Gathas are undoubtedly the work of the prophet himself. They are exceedingly difficult to translate and to understand. From beginning to end they contain statements about "six highly abstract conceptions," known as Amesha Spenta, or "undying holy ones." They are Vohu Manah or Good Thought; Asha, Right or Divine Order; Khshathra or Dominion or the Excellent Kingdom; Aramaiti, Piety or Holy Character; Haurvatat or Health; and Ameretat or Immortality. (The last two are always found together in the Gathas.)

What are these Amesha Spenta? They have been called "vassals," and "archangels," who help Ahura Mazda in his work of truth and righteousness. So they were without question in after years, and so they are held to be by competent scholars even in the teaching of the prophet. But Professor Moulton argues strenuously for another explanation. To him they are not outside but "within the Deity"; they share adoration with the Deity"; they are personifications, more or less real, even when they are called by their special names or titles." [38]

We must never forget that Zoroaster was not a theologian, and must not be surprised at lack of clarity, and even at what seem to us to be contradictions, in this rugged prophet of the out-of-doors. Was the teaching of Zoroaster dualistic? Undoubtedly in Zoroaster's mind the forces of righteousness and the forces of evil are engaged in an irreconcilable conflict which can be ended only in the complete victory of what is true and noble and upright. Even more than this, he held that there was a

[37] *Early Religious Poetry of Persia*, p. 56.
[38] See Moulton, *Early Religious Poetry of Persia, The Treasure of the Magi,* and *Early Zoroastrianism.*

personal spirit of evil, Angra Mainyu (Ahriman), who in the beginning chose evil as his portion and who created evil to oppose the good which exists in the world. It is very easy to see how a thoroughgoing dualism can be attributed to Zoroaster, but the point which Professor Moulton insists on time and again is "the Uniqueness of the Creator as the central feature of the faith." [39] Others like Professor A. V. Williams Jackson emphasize the ever-present dualism as being more significant than the monotheism in the teaching of Zoroaster. But even he speaks of the "quasi-monotheism in Zoroastrian dualism," especially in the affirmation of the faith of a "single great Primal Cause." It is a difficult problem at best. Another scholar, Professor M. Haug, looks on "Zoroaster's theology as monotheism, his speculative philosophy as dualism." [40]

This religion is on a high level because it gives the rightful place to morality in religion, such as has rarely been surpassed. Unfailing emphasis on "good thoughts, good words, good deeds," raises this faith and its founder to an eminent position among the world's religions. And, as Professor Moulton has said, "It is a tribute to national character that all evil should be summed up in the she-devil 'Deceit.' " [41] But at the same time Zoroaster's limitations are very evident. He was a stern prophet, unmellowed by the thought of God's love and mercy. These titles are not found among the Amesha Spenta, the personified qualities of the God he worshiped. The final victory in the universe will without question be a victory of the good—this is an essential element in all his teachings. His paradise is ethical, and only the pure in heart may enter; there is little hope for the sinner. He must cross from this world to the next over "the Bridge of the Separator," which was "broad for the righteous, narrow as a razor for the wicked, who fall off it into hell." [42] A man determines his own destiny, and as he is wicked or good goes to hell or heaven when he dies. It is very simple, but even here there is a forward look to a kind of messianic age when Saoshyant, a savior to come, will usher in a period of "renovation" here in this world when all evil will be overcome and goodness will prevail. Doctor M. N. Dhalla, a Parsi high priest, declares: "Bowing before Ahura Mazda, Angra Mainyu will hide himself with the demons in the earth. Evil will forthwith vanish and with it will disappear all evil propensities in man." [43]

[39] *Early Religious Poetry of Persia*, p. 67.
[40] See A. V. Williams Jackson, *Zoroastrian Studies*, pp. 31-35.
[41] *Early Religious Poetry of Persia*, p. 66.
[42] *Ibid.*, p. 71.
[43] *Zoroastrian Theology*, p. 183.

And, of course, in the whole universe itself the one good God, Ahura Mazda, will be completely victorious.

We do not know what might have occurred had a succession of prophets arisen in the spirit of the great Zoroaster, but there were none. We are hampered by not knowing the condition of the religion during the reigns of the Achaemenides, who ruled Persia from 558 to 331 B.C. Tradition asserts that the kings were confirmed Zoroastrians, but of this we cannot be sure. Alexander the Great conquered Persia in 331 B.C., and for a long period there was great confusion. Not until the time of the Sassanids, who ruled from A.D. 226 to 641, did the kingdom settle down again and the land have rest. These centuries, the period of the "Great Kings," were glorious days for the religion of Zoroaster, when with the revival of the faith a missionary spirit was developed and the teachings of the prophet were carried to regions as far distant as China. Then came the final catastrophe, when the Muslims conquered the land and Iran ceased to be Zoroastrian.

Changes were introduced into the religion after the time of the prophet, which are accounted for by Professor Moulton, in large measure at least, by referring them to the Magi. He looks upon the Magi as an indigenous non-Aryan tribe who lived in western Persia, and who, when they came in contact with the Zoroastrians, succeeded in winning a place for themselves as the priests of the people. They are known by their adherence to astrology, divination, and the practice of magic—which, by the way, derives its name from them, magic for Magi. All this was alien to the spirit of Zoroaster and indicates a serious declension from the high level of his teachings. "They hardened the prophet's profound adumbrations of truth into a mechanical system of dogma, therein showing the usual skill of priests in preserving the letter and destroying the spirit." [44]

These men carried the ethical dualism of Zoroaster into their theology. Instead of continuing to place Ahura Mazda over the whole creation, the one supreme Lord above all, they made "a systematic division of the world between Ahura Mazda and Angra Mainyu." All the angels of the one had demonic counterparts of the other. Even the Amesha Spenta, who had become fully developed and distinct archangels in the meantime, had their corresponding fiends in the realm of evil. So the god of righteousness and the god of evil divided the universe between them, each equally powerful and each having had his part in the original creation of the world. It must be said, however, that even in this theory at

[44] *Early Religious Poetry of Persia*, p. 78.

the end Ahura Mazda was to be completely victorious over Angra Mainyu. The good was to conquer, and the evil would be finally overthrown. Men were to choose which side they would take in the conflict, and so the ethical note was retained intact. But the keen edge of Zoroaster's moral insistence was dulled by the precise ceremonial regulations which were embodied in the Vendidad, the priestly code of the religion. The dualism of clean and unclean was carried to an extreme, until the whole of life was dominated by ideas of ceremonial purity and cleanness. The moral factor was swamped under the ceremonial. The elements of fire, earth, and water were considered sacred, and many rules were laid down to preserve them pure and uncontaminated. The religious life was reduced in large measure to overnice refinements and scrupulous care to avoid pollution.

At two points the Magi sought to introduce practices which were utterly strange to the people. In one they succeeded, and in the other they failed. The method of disposal of the dead among the Zoroastrians is to place the bodies on a framework of iron within a low circular tower, and there allow them to be stripped of their flesh by vultures, which await with avidity the uncovering of the bodies to begin their gruesome work. The purpose of this strange custom is to avoid the pollution of earth and fire by either burial or cremation. It was adopted by the Zoroastrians and remains to this day one of the most marked peculiarities of their ceremonial. Wherever there is a Parsi community of sufficient size to justify their presence, these dokhmas, or "towers of silence," are to be found, built in beautiful groves where vultures are always near at hand, waiting for their prey. The burial of the bones after they have been picked clean is not supposed to pollute the earth in which they find their resting place.

The other practice which the Magi desired to introduce and failed in doing was marriage between the closest relatives. This was considered by the Magi as "a religious duty of the most extravagant sanctity." [45] Fortunately, it did not approve itself to the good sense of the people, and although it is frequently mentioned in the Avesta, it is utterly repudiated by the modern Parsis.

The symbol of the Supreme Deity is fire. The Zoroastrians have been called fire worshipers, but it is quite certain that this is a misconception. Fire is the visible emblem or symbol of divinity and is so highly rever-

[45] *Ibid.*, p. 77.

136

enced as such that it is not to be wondered at that they have actually been called fire worshipers. But this they have the right to disclaim.

The priesthood is highly important. The most important function they are called upon to perform is the care of the fire in the temples. This is the very center of the cult, and most elaborate are the precautions taken that the purity of the flame may not be endangered. Only Parsis are allowed entrance into the inner precincts of the temple, where the urn containing the fire stands upon a stone pedestal. "Religious Parsis visit the fire temple almost daily, and on four days of each month (3rd, 9th, 17th, and 20th), those sacred to Atar, there is a very large attendance." [46]

In addition to the handicap of small and even dwindling numbers the Parsi community is rent by serious disagreement in belief. There are the conservatives, who are vigorously opposed to any change and would have everything remain as it is now. At the other extreme are the radicals, who are anxious for the future and can see no hope unless drastic reforms are introduced. And between the two are all varieties of opinion, both liberal and conservative. There is also the tendency to rationalize the faith. When this has been done with vigor, as by H. T. Bhabha, the president of the Fourth Zoroastrian Conference, held in 1913, the result, put in his own words, is as follows: "It is singularly free from dogmas, and is so simple in its tenets that it differs but little from Unitarianism or Rationalism." [47] These more radical reformers are not adverse to the admission of converts, but even they want only a few. They are afraid of being swamped by the admission of those of another race who cannot share their hereditary pride and cannot be counted on to uphold unswervingly the ancient and distinctive traditions of the community. The reformers also have in their program the use of prayers in a living language, the abolition of meaningless ceremonials and of prayers for the dead, and the mitigation of certain ceremonial restrictions placed on women, particularly at childbirth. One other tendency is at work, and this in the direction of theosophy. Dabbling in the occult and reaching out after contacts with the spirit world have affected the Parsis as similar gropings do in the West in disintegrating interest in genuine religion and magnifying the importance of the physical in the attempt to reach the spiritual.

So, after all, we cannot wonder that there should be a sense of want

---

[46] *Ibid.*, p. 145.
[47] Quoted in *The Treasure of the Magi*, p. 174.

and need among the Parsis. Their religion at best lacks completeness; there is no adequate doctrine of salvation. A leading Parsi, Dr. Jivanji Modi, says:

> A Parsee has to believe that for the salvation of his soul he has to look to nobody else but to himself. Nobody—no priest or no prophet—will intercede for him. For his salvation he has only to look to the purity of his own thoughts, words, and actions. . . . Think of nothing but the truth, speak nothing but the truth, and do nothing but what is proper, and you are saved." [48]

A stern religion with a high moral code and the example of a most vigorous champion of righteousness in their great prophet, it has failed to provide for mercy and sacrifice, tenderness and love, and by this failure has made it impossible for it to be a religion with a wide appeal to needy men and women.

SUGGESTIONS FOR FURTHER STUDY

Archer, John Clark. *The Sikhs.* Princeton University Press, 1946. A full-length study by a competent scholar, but not easy reading.

Dhalla, M. N. *History of Zoroastrianism.* New York: Oxford University Press, 1938. A detailed study by a highly educated Parsi high priest.

Jackson, A. V. Williams. *Zoroaster, the Prophet of Ancient Iran.* New York: Columbia University Press, 1901. All that is known about the prophet is found here.

Jacobi, Hermann. "Jainism" in Hastings, James, *Encyclopaedia of Religion and Ethics.* Also printed separately in *Studies in Jainism.* Ahmedabad, 1946.

Loehlin, C. H. *The Sikhs and Their Book.* India: Lucknow Publishing House, 1946. The best handbook we have, but greatly needing fuller treatment.

Moulton, James Hope. *The Treasure of the Magi.* New York: Oxford University Press, 1917. The best handbook on the entire subject.

Stevenson, Margaret. *The Heart of Jainism.* New York: Oxford University Press, 1915. The most important work in English available.

[48] *Ibid.,* pp. 205-6.

CHAPTER VII

BUDDHISM

India's Greatest Son

Gautama the Buddha was destined to influence the thought of Asia more than any other person down to our own time. His dates, as nearly as can be ascertained, were 563 to 483 B.C. At Kapilavastu, about 130 miles north of the modern city of Benares, a stone tablet was discovered in 1896 which marks the birthplace of India's greatest son. He was given the name of Siddhartha but is generally known as Gautama, the name of the family to which he belonged. He is also widely known as Sakyamuni, the "sage of the Sakyas," the name of the clan or tribal group of which his family was a member, and in which his father was a leading chieftain. Buddha, or "the enlightened one," is a title which became the name by which he is best known.

Many are the stories told of his birth and early years which are so fabulous that it is difficult to extract the modicum of truth they contain. Little is known of the life of young Siddhartha until he was about thirty years of age. We may well believe the tradition that he excelled in manly sports. His endurance and the attainment of a hale and hearty old age attest a strong constitution and a firm foundation laid in youth for a strenuous and long life. It is quite certain that he was married and had one son, of whom he was exceedingly fond. A persistent tradition repeated many times over in Buddhist literature indicates that Gautama was of the meditative and thoughtful type and possessed a nature deeply touched by the pain and sorrow of life. In these legends we are told that he was strangely moved by the sight of a decrepit man, a man suffering from an offensive disease, a putrefying corpse, and finally a wandering monk who had realized the vanity of life and had forsaken it forever to search for the deeper satisfactions in religion and philosophy. We may think of these tales as windows into the mind of the young and serious Gautama. What we do know is that about the age of thirty he left house and home never to return to the old relationships again. It has been

139

called the "great renunciation." He turned away from wife and child, from his father, and the succession to the headship of his people, from all that the future had to offer of honor and success. All these he rejected to answer the summons of an inner craving which was not satisfied and which could not be hushed.

In thus abandoning his home and becoming a penniless wanderer Gautama took the step which many before and since his day in India have taken. We know comparatively little about the next five or six years. There is good evidence that he went to one religious teacher after another, but of what they taught and what he thought of their theories we do not know very much. It seems clear that they could not satisfy the deep craving in the heart of this earnest seeker. The opposition which he showed in later years to the current philosophies would seem to have begun at the time when these teachers failed to give an adequate answer to his questions.

During this period Gautama gave himself to a severe regimen. This was also a typical Indian thing to do. By abstinence he reduced himself to a skeleton. Disciples gathered around him in admiration of his fortitude and perseverance. They were not able to follow him in the utter abandon of his efforts to extort the peace he craved by hardships and deprivations. He carried his exertion to the breaking point, and nature rebelled. He finally fell over in a swoon. His disciples thought he had died and wondered at the unrelaxing resolution they had failed to attain. But he revived, much to their surprise. Then an astonishing thing took place. Gautama calmly declared to his followers that mortification had failed to bring the peace he craved and that he would give it up. His erstwhile disciples could not understand a statement so unorthodox and forthwith took their leave and went to Benares with contempt in their hearts for one who had turned away from so time-honored a practice as self-abnegation and asceticism. And just here the originality of Gautama begins to show itself. Up to this time he had been a typical Hindu, but now he began to branch off and follow a direction all his own. Asceticism had failed to satisfy, so he turned away from it decisively.

From this time he became an advocate of the "middle way." His experience had led him to the conclusion that neither luxury on one side nor asceticism on the other could satisfy the inner craving he felt. The only thing to do, then, so far as everyday life was concerned, was to travel the middle way, not giving way to softness and luxury on one side nor undergoing the hardships of self-inflicted asceticism on the other. He

140

set men the example of simple living with only a few regulations, which were calculated to keep men from the evils and sins which would make the development of character impossible. It was good, wholesome living he inculcated—wholesome in all respects save one. Gautama had separated himself from his home and his wife, and he could not see that traveling the middle way ought to mean the avoidance of unbridled license on one hand and celibacy on the other. To him no advance could possibly be made in character, no progress could be made toward peace and satisfaction, so long as man lived in company with a woman. To make woman a stumbling block to man in the journey toward his heart's desire is to lower her condition and at the same time to keep man down to a level at which the finest flowers of individual and social life can never grow. Gautama did not see this, and his system has suffered to our own day from this defect.

But all that he had attained was negative. He had learned that the inner rest he was craving was not to be had by living a life of ease or by asceticism. The process of elimination had been at work, but nothing positive had been gained. The temptation came to give up the pursuit, go back to his home, and take up his life where he had left it on the night when he suddenly took his flight. Would this not be the best course out of the confusion in which his failure had left him? But no, that would not have been Gautama the Buddha. He found himself in a dreadful moral and mental struggle, which is described most realistically in Buddhist literature. The forces of Mara, the enemy of all that is good, charged like legions of armed demons from the front and then from the rear, seeking to break down his determined resistance, but through it all he sat unmoved, with purpose unchanged and desire unquenched. At last, under the shade of the famous bo tree, the most sacred shrine in the Buddhist world, the enlightenment came, and he was free. Thus did Gautama become the Buddha, "the enlightened." His last battle with his lower nature had been won; his doubts were dissolved; and the peace whose elusive quest he had been following so long swept over his soul, never again to be absent from his experience. He had grasped the meaning of the world's sorrow and could cure it.

Such a memorable experience and such a stupendous claim demand explanation. What was the disease which had doomed men and women to sorrow and despair? Surely the man who could not only give the correct diagnosis but also offer the cure was a benefactor the whole world was awaiting. Without doubt the strivings through which he had been

141

passing uninterruptedly for so many years and the attempts he had made from every conceivable angle to find the way out of his mental anguish account in large measure for the final conclusion the Buddha reached, but for him the whole matter was the result of a spiritual illumination or mental intuition which burst upon him like a light flowing in from the heavens. What was the cause of this sorrow and inner pain? Nothing less than desire, the lust of gold and fame and pleasure—all that made men cling to the things of life and sense. He had laid his finger on the canker that was eating the life out of his fellow men. How much of all this he had thought out before the day of concentration under the bo tree it is impossible to say. The final conclusion was that peace and poise could come only by the suppression of desire. From that hour until the end of his long life he had perfect peace within. His life was one of unruffled calm untouched by the varied experiences through which he passed.

The temptation which came to him at once was to become a solitary recluse, spending his years in quiet enjoyment of his newly found experience and thinking through all its implications. But again this would not have been Gautama the Buddha. He deliberately made up his mind to devote his time to the carrying of his message to men as far as his journeys might lead. He acted upon this determination and proceeded, after seven weeks, we are told, to Benares, where he found and won back the disciples who had so recently deserted him. In this way until the end of his long life Buddha continued to win converts until they could be counted by the hundreds and thousands. He never wearied of telling his message and rejoiced as one after another men and women came to him, were convinced, and went away with a new life open before them. He had determined "to set rolling the royal chariot wheel of a universal empire of truth and righteousness," and he never lost an opportunity to make a convert and set another soul free from the fetters of desire.

The chronology of the life of the Buddha is uncertain. The period from the time when he abandoned his home until his emancipation was probably about five years, roughly from the age of thirty to thirty-five. He died at the age of eighty, thus spending forty-five years in declaring his doctrine up and down northern India. During the four months of the rainy season he remained in one place teaching his disciples and preaching to the people who came to him, but as soon as the dry season came he was off again on his long journeys, accompanied by a group of his disciples. The story is a somewhat disconnected narrative of what he said and did in the course of the years. He met many people, men and women of all ranks and classes, and most interesting are the accounts of his replies and admonitions. He was dignified yet sympathetic, firm yet kindly, dealing in each case with insight and sending each one away with an appropriate and convincing word. No wonder he came to be idolized by his followers. They looked on him as one who could meet every emergency, as one who was not to be baffled by any carping or even sincere questioner. In the course of his tours he came to his old home at Kapilavastu and there met his wife and son. He went back several times. They may have thought to receive him back to the old relationships, but that was not to be. They were little more to him, that is, so far as his actions showed, than fellow beings who stood in need of his message. His words fell on good ground in each case, and both wife and son became members of the two orders he instituted, one for men and the other for women.

So the Buddha lived out his days, never ceasing this round of teaching from place to place. At last the end came as a result, so it is said by Professor T. W. Rhys Davids, of an attack of dysentery caused by eating a meal of rice and mushrooms.[1] Or was it pork? We cannot be sure. He lived for a number of hours, during which the time was spent in conversation with Ananda, his most devoted follower and personal attendant, and others who desired a word with the dying leader. Shortly before becoming unconscious he summoned his strength and said, "Mendicants! I now impress it upon you. Decay is inherent in all component things; work out your salvation with diligence!"

No purer character has India given to the world, one worthy of the honor which has been bestowed by countless believers in all subsequent ages and worthy of our highest esteem and admiration.

EARLY BUDDHISM

Gautama left no written records. The early literature has come down to us in the Pali language and consists of the three Pitakas, or "baskets," which contain the rules which the Brothers and Sisters are to observe, the truths which are to be taught, and the psychological system on which it is based. How much of all the teaching came from Buddha himself it is impossible to say—probably very little. No record of his teaching seems to have been committed to writing for over two hundred years. The Pitakas as we have them today are the result of a long growth lasting

[1] *Buddhism* (Manual), 1912 ed., p. 80.

through several centuries. What we have to work on is a library of about twenty-nine titles in which "the number of Pali words in the whole is about twice the number of words in our English Bible." [2]

Of the various approaches which might be made to the study of these teachings none is more fruitful than that through the Three Signs, or Fundamental Truths. The method of approach is of real importance, for the teaching is somewhat baffling, and caution must be exercised at a number of important turning points. The first of the Fundamental Signs is the impermanence of all things. To put it in the ancient phrase, "All the constituents of life are impermanent." The statement is also made, "There is no being. There is only a becoming." This is to be accepted as literally true of all things; gods as well as the atom are equally included. The passing away may be delayed for a long period, but the principle of change is the principle of all existence. Just as soon as there is a beginning, decay begins; the beginning of the end is at hand. Here in India, five hundred years before Christ, is being preached the philosophy of change. We do not live in a static universe, but one in which everything is in a state of flux. At about the same time in Greece philosophers were conjuring with the same idea. Heraclitus, about 536-470 B.C., denied that there was any such thing as permanence. "There is no static Being, no unchanging substratum. Change, movement, is Lord of the universe." [3] And we today are still discussing the same problem. Is there anything permanent, or is everything subject to change? The modern doctrine of evolution asserts the doctrine of change and links us to the ancient Greeks and to the Buddha and his followers.

Nothing is to be excluded from the sweep of this theory. It is the explanation of the atheism with which the Buddha has been charged. But he was not an atheist; he took the gods of India for granted, but it made little difference to him whether they were real beings or not. Whatever they were and wherever they might be at any time, they were bound by the same law of impermanence and change. Why should anyone look to them? They were in the possession of no powers man did not have at his disposal. The result was that the Buddha constructed a system in which no god was needed. A god might for the time being seem strong and wise, but it was only a passing phase with no assurance of continuance. So, then, worship was useless and prayer an empty form. What we have here is a system which, strictly speaking, is no religion at all.

[2] T. W. Rhys Davids, Buddhism (American lectures), p. 52.
[3] A. K. Rogers, A Student's History of Philosophy, 1916 ed., p. 15.

Just as it stands, it might well be called a system of psychological ethics. Later we shall try to estimate the meaning of this conclusion in the light of other facts which would indicate that elements of a true religious attitude were there from the beginning, even though formally everything religious seemed to be excluded. It is just at this point that one of the greatest authorities, Mrs. C. A. Rhys Davids, puts in a word of vigorous protest. She believes that there are evidences in the Pali books that the Buddha was conscious of being related to a "higher-than-man," which would place his teaching in an entirely different light.

The second of the Fundamental Signs is that sorrow is implicit in all individuality. "All the constituents of life are full of misery." The Buddha's discovery under the bo tree was that the cause of misery, which he himself had sought to escape and which he found everywhere in the world, was desire. We cannot gain what we want, and we cannot escape what we dislike, and this involves misery and sorrow. This doctrine of suffering and its cure has received classic expression in the teaching of the Four Noble Truths and the Noble Eightfold Path, which must be clearly understood as fundamental to our study.

The Four Noble Truths are as follows:

1) Now, this, O recluses, is the noble truth concerning *suffering*.

In many forms the statement is made that all human experience involves suffering because it flows from individuality, or separate conscious existence. To live and cling to life involve desire and hence sorrow.

2) Now, this, O recluses, is the noble truth concerning the *origin* of suffering. Verily it originates in that craving thirst which causes the renewal of becomings, is accompanied by sensual delights, and seeks satisfaction now here, now there—that is to say, the craving for the gratification of the passions, or the craving for a future life, or the craving for success in this present life.

So long as the enticements of the outside world have the slightest attraction for us, we are subject to pain and sorrow. Desire is the cause of suffering.

3) Now, this, O recluses, is the noble truth concerning the *destruction* of suffering.

Verily, it is the destruction, in which no craving remains over, of this very thirst; the laying aside of, the getting rid of, the being free from, the harboring no longer of, this thirst.

4) And this, O recluses, is the noble truth concerning the way which leads to the destruction of suffering.

Verily, it is this Noble Eightfold Path; that is to say:

Right Views (free from superstition and delusion)—

Right Aspirations (high, and worthy of the intelligent, earnest man)—

Right Speech (kindly, open, truthful)—

Right Conduct (peaceful, honest, pure)—

Right Livelihood (bringing hurt or danger to no living thing)—

Right Effort (in self-training and in self-control)—

Right Mindfulness (the active, watchful mind)—

Right Rapture (in deep meditation on the realities of life).

There are those who believe that this "rapture" is really a trance, almost if not entirely a state of ecstasy.

In the monastic order which the Buddha instituted the journey along the Noble Eightfold Path is carefully regularized. Monks proceed from step to step, taking a long time to reach the final stage—if ever they reach it at all. In the Buddha's day many of his disciples reached the final stage almost at a bound.

In the course of his gradual progress in the Path the Buddhist must break the Ten Fetters: Delusion of Self, Doubt, the Efficacy of Good Works and Ceremonies, Sensuality, Ill Will, Love of Life on Earth, Desire for a Future Life in Heaven, Pride, Self-righteousness, and Ignorance, each of which is treated at length in the Pali texts.

When a man has achieved the eight positive characteristics of the Noble Path and broken the Ten Fetters, he has become an arhat (also arahat, arahant) and thus has realized the Buddhist ideal of life. It is also known as Nirvana, or "the going out," "the going out of the three fires of lust, ill-will, and dullness and ignorance." So arhatship, or Nirvana, may be attained here in this life, a state of perfect mental quiet and rest, in which no desire ruffles the poise of the peaceful devotee (save, of course, the desire for more of the present satisfaction and the desire to bestow the gift on others) and no longing breaks in on his contemplation. But is there no future life, no expectation beyond the time when his body shall come to the end of its term in death? This can be answered only by a consideration of the last of the signs.

The third Fundamental Sign is that of the absence of a "soul," the "no-soul" doctrine that "all the constituents of life are without a soul."

146

We are separate and distinct individual beings now, but we have no permanent or even temporary soul as an entity in itself. It is all a delusion to think that there is such a thing as a person or a chariot or a chair. These are only names which we give to the temporary gathering together into a seeming unity of qualities or "aggregates" which are only parts of the all-embracing universe in which we live. You may ask of a chair as you mention each part, "Is this the chair?" and of course the answer must in each case be no. So at the end of the examination the Buddhist says: "Where, then, is your chair? It has eluded you. There is no chair! What you call a chair is but the name you give to the temporary collection of parts which when brought together may perform a useful function."

So of a human being. He is composed of parts which when assembled under certain conditions we call by a name, but there is no real person there, no you or I or he. The parts which make up a human being are called skandhas, or "aggregates" and they are five in number. The first consists of the material properties, in short our physical bodies. Then follow four mental qualities, which, as nearly as we are able to designate them in the terms of modern psychology, may be given thus: sensations, or feelings; abstract ideas, or perception; potentialities, or the elements of consciousness; and thought, or consciousness taken as a unified whole. We, to speak of ourselves, are merely the name which is given to the five skandhas when they are thus unified. What holds them together is what might be called the thread of life. When at death the thread is broken, the skandhas fall apart, never to reassemble. That individual being has ceased to be and will never come into existence again. There is no essential soul, so how could he?

We are to understand that the person now living inherits from the person who preceded him the results of his moral achievement or failure. He may rise higher in the scale or sink lower than his predecessor according as he adds to or subtracts from the moral content which he inherited. What causes him to be born at all if he is not the same person who had lived before? So long as anyone dies and desire or craving is left in his heart, another set of skandhas is bound to assemble and constitute another person who must take up the task where his predecessor left it. And so it goes on from one to another until in the end the series to which they have all belonged comes to an end forever when the hoped-for result has been achieved, that is, when one arises who succeeds in crushing out desire, becomes an arhat, and enters Nirvana. His body

147

may keep on living for years, but when it dies the skandhas fall apart, and there is nothing to require another set of skandhas to gather again, for there is nothing left around which they may assemble. Karma simply ceases to function in this case.

This is the Buddhist law of karma. According to this law new individuals are born one after another until in the case of an arhat all desire is used up. So with all the changes taking place in the universe and in every particle of matter in it. There is an unchanging law according to which all this takes place. It is impersonal and works by a kind of blind necessity, inevitable and unchanging, the one great compelling power in the universe. But the Buddha gave no evidence that he ever thought of these final questions. He made the statement many times that he was concerned with one thing only, sorrow and the curing of sorrow. All else was irrelevant. Then when an arhat has in this life attained Nirvana, what becomes of him when his body dies? What becomes of a candle flame when it is blown out? The Buddhist is likely to answer at this point by saying that whatever happens nothing essential is lost. We of the West are not satisfied and insist, "Is not consciousness lost, and personality, and without these what remains?" And still the Buddhist replies, "Nothing is lost." But still, what is the final state? It is often called Pari-nirwana or final Nirvana. But what is it like? On the surface the only answer would seem to be annihilation, and some assent to this, but others protest vigorously. If not complete annihilation, what can the answer be? It is a condition of "bliss," but the word has little content. Still others would simply say they do not know, but they are sure it is not annihilation.

The question arises, What keeps the whole process of the round of rebirth going since there is no god who creates and sustains the universe? The Buddhist has recourse to what he calls the law of "dependent origination," also known as the "chain of causation," a kind of impersonal law of cause and effect which starts with ignorance and is controlled by the action of karma, which of course is impersonal too. And this theory is declared to be an adequate substitute for "childish 'creation' stories!" [4]

Surely, all this could not be expected to find lodgment in the minds of the common people, and it never did. Attainment was possible only to those who separated themselves from ordinary life and became monks, living a life apart in communities so that all their energies might be con-

[4] C. H. S. Ward, *Buddhism*, I, 88.

centrated on attaining the end desired. The order was not a priesthood standing between god and men. The gods were negligible; man must secure his attainment by his own powers, so a priesthood would have been an anomaly. The order was merely a means to spiritual attainment on the part of its members. During the whole history of Buddhism the order of monks has been the key to its expansion and its power in every land to which it has gone. The monasteries, large and small, in every Buddhist country attest the hold of the idea of salvation through self-discipline on the minds of men and women. Lifeless and even degenerate though they may have become in many cases, the monastic institutions still continue to thrive and influence the lives of the people.

The Buddha, the doctrine, and the order were the three anchors of early Buddhism. When the candidate for the order went before the abbot of a monastery, he repeated this formula:

> I go for refuge to the Buddha.
> I go for refuge to the Law (dharma).
> I go for refuge to the Order (sangha).[5]

This is about as near a prayer as early Buddhism achieved. The monasteries were not to be the permanent home of the monks in the original intention. They were supposed to be penniless wanderers (bhikshus), depending on the gifts of the laity for their daily needs. Only during the rainy season were they to be located in a definite place. But the temptation was great to possess a permanent seat, and there arose great institutions in magnificent surroundings wherever the religion was carried. A monk himself might possess nothing of this world's goods, but the monastery could. As a result they became powerful and had immense influence, like the monasteries in Europe in the Middle Ages.

The equipment of the monks was exceedingly simple. An alms bowl, in which to secure food on the daily round; the three vestments, so that the entire body might be covered; a staff, a needle, a razor, a toothpick, a water-strainer, so as not to destroy animal life while drinking—and he was fully furnished. There was little variation in the daily routine: early morning recitation of the sacred books and meditation, the round for alms in the midmorning, the simple noonday meal, rest and meditation again, closing the day with service and recitations in the hall of the monastery. There were no services for the public and no real worship. The monk was bound to obey the Eight Precepts:

One should not destroy life.
One should not take that which is not given.
One should not tell lies.
One should not become a drinker of intoxicating liquors.
One should refrain from unlawful sexual intercourse—an ignoble thing.
One should not eat unseasonable food at nights.
One should not wear garlands nor use perfumes.
One should sleep on a mat spread on the ground.[6]

The first five are manifestly on a different plane from the last three. The Buddhists recognized this and when inculcating moral principles among the common people required of them a strict observance of the first five only. So while the Buddhist did not believe in a soul, he set high store on moral discipline. It has gone with Buddhism into the Eastern world as a steadying influence and doubtless explains in part its favorable reception into many lands which might otherwise have turned away from its teaching.

HINAYANA AND MAHAYANA

The Buddha lived in the sixth and fifth centuries before Christ. The first date in Indian history of which we may be sure is when Alexander the Great invaded India in 326 B.C. We do not know much about the condition of Buddhism until the reign of Asoka, who ascended the throne in 273 B.C. and ruled as the first real emperor of India for about forty years. The significant fact is that Asoka became a Buddhist and ruled his wide dominions according to the precepts of the faith. The most notable contribution he made to the cause of Buddhism was the sending of embassies or missions to various countries to carry the teaching. In this way many countries were reached, notably Ceylon, whose history began with the coming of Buddhism. Again there is a long period about which little is known. At about the time of Christ a king arose in the far northwest of India named Kanishka, who was not an Indian at all but belonged to one of the peoples of the great central Asian plateau. He began to rule in A.D. 78, embraced Buddhism, and took much interest in the faith and its development. Again there is little information for cen-

[6] *Ibid.*, p. 139.

turies, until Chinese pilgrims, men who had become Buddhists, made journeys to India to visit the historic places where the Buddha had lived and died and to carry back relics and books to their home in China. We learn from the volumes these men wrote that Buddhism, which had been very strong, was on the decline in the land of its birth. There may have been some persecution, but the real cause of the deterioration was that Buddhism was not distinctive and rigid enough to escape being drawn back into the Hinduism from which it had emerged. By the time of the Mohammedan incursions into India, which began in the year 1000, Buddhism had about disappeared, and now in the land of its origin and early power the faith of Gautama the Buddha, her most illustrious son, is little more than a memory.

Such, in brief, is the sad story of the disappearance of a faith from the land for which it promised to do so much. These outward changes and vicissitudes, however, are of lesser interest than the inner development and transformation which befell the faith itself. The evolution cannot be traced with any accuracy; about all we know is that at a certain time the faith was one thing, and then again several centuries after it had become something very different. Councils were called to decide questions on which the monasteries differed, but much obscurity hangs over these assemblies. We can be fairly certain that a notable council was held under the patronage of Kanishka about A.D. 100, after which a deep cleavage is apparent between two schools of thought, the Hinayana and the Mahayana.

The terms need defining. Hinayana means the "little vehicle," fitted to carry only a small number on the way to salvation, and Mahayana means "large vehicle," a means of salvation sufficient to accommodate all who would come. Manifestly, the name "Hinayana" was given to that school of thought by opponents, who desired to call attention to their own superior doctrine. But long before these two schools separated the earlier teaching had changed at a number of points. Gautama had turned his back on the gods of India and constructed a system without worship, sacrifice, prayer, or any sense of dependence on a higher power. But he had essayed to do the impossible. The need of help in the struggle of life and the tendency to turn to some being who is powerful enough to render assistance is too strongly entrenched in human nature to be thus eradicated.

Even in his own lifetime the Buddha was raised to an exalted position by his disciples. They came to look upon him as almost omniscient and

151

all-wise, ready to meet any emergency. He carried himself with a dignity which forbade undue intimacy. He was a man apart from other men. Despite his democracy, which is undoubted, his elevation and disinterestedness in the ordinary things of life cast an atmosphere of aloofness about him, which was only increased by the sanctity which seemed naturally to belong to one who was so kind and pure and good. He was almost their god while he journeyed with them intent on teaching them that there was no need of gods. Little wonder is it that in the centuries after he had passed away the Buddha himself should have been raised to the position in the spiritual world where men could look for his assistance and raise hands to him in prayer. This became true in Hinayana. There was a tendency toward theism, though it never became clear and distinct. The Buddha was raised to a place of pre-eminence even above the divine beings. He was looked upon as sinless; the doctrine arose that he had been born of a virgin, that he was perfect in wisdom and power, and that he had been able to perform wonders during his earthly life. The theory arose that Gautama was the last of a long series of Buddhas who had preceded him, and that there was one yet to come, Maitreya Buddha, the gracious god who would restore all things. This is the form of Buddhism which with many local differences prevails in Ceylon, Burma, and Thailand, and is frequently spoken of as Southern Buddhism. It must be made plain, however, that the educated monks seek most strenuously to preserve the pure, and what they consider to be the uncontaminated, teaching of the founder as contained in the Pali literature.

Recent research discloses the fact that both the Hinayana and the Mahayana were developed in monasteries in North India. Indeed, there is reason to believe that in some cases both teachings were held by different monks in the same monastery. They are both Indian products, but the Mahayana seemed specially adapted to the life and thought of the people of the north. At any rate that is where the Mahayana is now found, while the Hinayana traveled south and found its permanent habitat there.

Much thought and work must have been put on the system of the Mahayana before it was complete. Its complexity and extent are amazing. The differences between the two schools are radical and profound. It might almost be said that, instead of two schools in one religion, there are two religions—except for the fact that every branch of Buddhism looks upon Gautama the Buddha as its founder and as uttering sayings which can be interpreted as the starting point of the special teaching of each school. Among the striking differences between the Hinayana and the Mahayana three may be pointed out as containing the teachings which distinguish the two and keep them apart.

The first of these is that Mahayana developed into a full-fledged religion, completely furnished with gods and other divine beings and with all the paraphernalia of an elaborate worship, in ornate temples presided over by a hierarchical priesthood. The salvation offered was all-embracive, fitted to the needs of men whether they might enter the portals of a monastery or not. Influenced no doubt by the bhakti doctrine in Hinduism, Mahayana began to teach the message of salvation by faith—faith in a gracious god who when they died would take those who put their faith in him to a paradise in the heavens. Instead of an unconscious Nirvana as the goal of endeavor the Mahayana has substituted a paradise where men and women may live in conscious blessedness and peace. The idea of the soul has come back. Mrs. Rhys Davids believes that Gautama never went to the limit of declaring there was no soul; she holds that the no-soul theory, as well as the complete denial of a higher power to whom men may go in worship, was the work of unimaginative and pedantic monks who distorted the original teaching. Be that as it may, Mahayana preached a very different doctrine. As might be expected a hell was brought in for the wicked as well as a heaven for the faithful. Actually a number of heavens and hells are provided. Are they everlasting? Hardly. The grip of karma and the influence of the conception of an impersonal Nirvana were too strong to be completely broken. And yet the ordinary man was satisfied with the prospect of a peaceful heaven and did not trouble his head with anything further.

What about the gods who were worshiped? When once the process was started, the creation of gods and other divine beings went on apace until they could be counted by hundreds of thousands! So Buddhism, which in the early centuries was a godless religion, became a polytheism with "gods many and lords many." Most of the divinities are nameless and form the retinue of the great gods and enhance their dignity and prestige. Several of the gods were especially notable and rose to the highest rank and dominated the minds of men far more than others. The most prominent of all was Amitabha, the Lord of the Western Paradise, whom we shall meet in China under the name of O-mi-to Fu, and whom we shall find under the name of Amida as the overtowering figure among the Buddhist gods of Japan. Different schools arose and constructed complicated hierarchies of divinities, beginning with an eternal being not entirely unlike the Brahman of the Vedanta systems. Several descending grades of divinities take their places, the lowest rank being that of manifestations in the world of men. One of these manifestations is Gautama the Buddha, relegated in this scheme, as almost always in Mahayana, to a subordinate position. He was a Buddha, but there were many other Buddhas far above him in majesty and power. The monks preferred to scale the ladder of speculation and make gods of their liking rather than raise the historic Gautama to the place of supreme authority.

The second point of marked difference between the Hinayana and Mahayana is the difference in the ideal set before men. In Hinayana it is the career of an arhat which lures men on to enter a monastery and undergo the discipline of the Noble Eightfold Path. In Mahayana the ideal is quite different. It is called the career of a bodhisattva, or a "future Buddha." The term is to be found in the early Pali literature, where it is applied to Gautama. Here in Mahayana, however, it is used to designate a host of beings in the heavenly world who are on their way to final Buddhahood but who resolve not to allow themselves to enter that final stage so long as there are beings, men in this world and also beings in the heavens, who need their help. Their purpose is unselfish and altruistic, and lifts Mahayana to a much higher level than Hinayana, in which the ideal is to win arhatship and Nirvana for oneself with no responsibility for others.

The bodhisattva is a being in the heavens, but the ideal for which he stands may be espoused by men here below. By resolving to become bodhisattvas in the next world they accept the ideal of service here and now, and gain an enlargement of mind and heart beyond that of the ordinary monk and layman. Thus they become "future bodhisattvas" in this world, with the hope of becoming real bodhisattvas when they pass into the heavenly world. How much this affects the lives of these Buddhists, making them more unselfish and helpful, it is hard to say. But the ideal is there and gives evidence of noble purposes in the minds of many devoted men.

The third point of difference is that Mahayana developed several systems of philosophy which were altogether foreign to the Buddhism of the Pali books. Attention has been called to the reticence of Gautama when it came to metaphysical questions. What did not make an immediate contribution to the overcoming of desire and entering on the path toward arhatship did not concern him. At the same time many of

154

Gautama's statements really had most profound metaphysical implications but they were not developed by the Buddha or his earliest disciples. Even before the separation of the religion into Hinayana and Mahayana, Gautama's followers had split up into as many as eighteen schools, but the points of difference were more or less trivial, having to do with minor matters of discipline. It remained for the Mahayana thinkers to work out systems truly philosophical which have influenced Buddhist thinking in all Eastern Asia. We hear of Nagarjuna, who in his mountain monastery in Kashmir was not only a leading figure in starting Mahayana on its way but the father of one of the leading schools of thought.

The Buddhist philosophers found themselves dealing with the age-old problem of the nature of reality. The eternal Buddha, the source of all that exists, was thought of as existing in three forms or bodies, the highest of which was called dharmakaya, or "body of the law," and dharmakaya was reality. But what is reality in its essence? What does it consist of? Two schools had answers which differed widely. One school, that of the Madhyamikas, which owned its origin and a part of its prestige to its founder Nagarjuna, held that dharmakaya or reality was sheer void of vacancy. They are the philosophical nihilists of Buddhism. "Everything is void," was their watchword. The other school, that of the Vijnanavadins, were idealists, claiming that the only real existences are thoughts, ideas which do not stand for any objective reality. Thoughts can think themselves without a thinker and have no reference to anything outside themselves. It is an eternal illusion that object and subject exist; only thoughts have any existence whatever. Of course the Buddhist laymen knew little about all this high-flown thinking. It was confined to the monasteries and even there to that smaller group of thinkers who had the ability to give themselves to this kind of difficult intellectual labor.

BUDDHISM TRAVELS ABROAD

The Buddhism of Ceylon, Burma, and Thailand is Hinayana. The religion was carried in this form to Annam, Cochin China, and Cambodia, in the far southeastern corner of Asia. It also made its way to the island world of the East Indies and took root in Java, Bali, Sumatra, and other islands. This was long ago, for when Islam penetrated the eastern archipelago in the sixteenth century the religion of the Buddha disappeared. Driven out of Java, those who remained true to their faith fled to the little island of Bali, but even there most have become Hindus, and little Buddhism is to be found. Strange to say, it is a question whether the Mahayana or the Hinayana was the more prominent in the islands, for both give evidence of having been preached successfully. It is exceedingly interesting to find the ruins of magnificent Mahayana buildings so many hundreds of miles away from the lands in the north where this form of the faith had its characteristic growth and development. Differing from the experience in India proper, Buddhism, after a desperate conflict with Hinduism in Burma, Thailand, and the other lands of Farther India, came out victorious and remains in possession of the field to this day.

But is it really the religion of the people? Outwardly it would seem so. All these lands are filled with the paraphernalia of the Buddhist religion; temples and monasteries, pagodas and images, are to be found everywhere. Each country has its own characteristic forms, but each gives ample evidence on every hand of its Buddhist allegiance. The monks are there, and services and festivals are held, to which the people come in gala dress, enjoying the occasions to the full. With all this, however, the hold of Buddhism on the inner lives of the people is precarious. A man's inner convictions are revealed in the time of crisis, when sorrow and suffering and loss stare him in the face. Which way does he turn for help and comfort then? The testimony from these southern lands is that it is not to the monks and the Buddha, but to the old spirits and sprites of the animism which belonged to the people before the coming of Buddhism. A recent writer has said, "But even in these lands where, to the visitor, there appears to be so true a devotion to the Buddha, all the Buddhists have other religions to which they turn in time of trouble." [7]

In Burma the religion has penetrated more deeply than in any other of the Hinayana countries. This is doubtless due to the fact that education has been in the hands of monks, who thus are able to instill Buddhist ideas into the minds of the people while they are young and impressionable. It is also customary in Burma for a young man to give a certain time to monastic life. These features of the religious life of Burma have succeeded in keeping the people in close touch with their religious teachers. In Thailand or Siam, the king is the chief patron of Buddhism. The heads of the order must be nominated by the king, who honors the monks and supports them lavishly. In Ceylon and Burma there is a reform movement, made up of cultured people who desire to go back to

[7] C. H. S. Ward, *Outline of Buddhism*, I, 129.

BUDDHISM

the simplicity of the practice and teaching of the Buddha and also to interpret the faith more in accord with Western culture and the teachings of the schools. They have preaching halls with sermons and the recitation of a creed.

In the north Buddhism has penetrated China, Korea, and Japan. The faith here is of the Mahayana type and is frequently called Northern Buddhism. But besides these countries, the religion has taken deep root in the great elevated plateau, the hinterland of Asia. Beginning its career in Tibet, it has pushed farther and farther to the north and northeast until one arm has swung around and comes into contact with Chinese Buddhism in the capital city of Peking. This form of Buddhism has been given the name of Lamaism, from the monks, who are called "lamas." The peculiarity which at once attracts attention is the doctrine of incarnation, known nowhere else in Buddhism. It did not become a fully accepted doctrine until the seventeenth century. Since then it has been held that the Bodhisattva Avalokitesvara was incarnate in the Dalai Lama, chief ruler of the country. Other Grand Lamas have their seats in different sections, all claiming to be incarnations of Bodhisattvas, but none can approach the Dalai Lama in influence and power. When the Dalai, or "Great," Lama dies, the rule is placed in the hand of some young boy who gives evidence (by strange and varied signs) that Avalokita has taken up his abode in him. He is then acclaimed as the new incarnation, and he holds sway, religiously and politically until his death.

The gods and spiritual beings of Lamaism form a populous and strange pantheon. All the Buddhas and Bodhisattvas of the Mahayana are there. The center of the religion is, of course, the monastic life. There are said to be over three thousand monasteries, or lamaseries, in Tibet, the largest in the capital, Lhasa, containing as many as ten thousand monks. Waddell emphasizes the terrible effect of Buddhist monasticism on Tibet. The country has steadily declined in power and numbers, the population now being less than a tenth of its former size. He declares there is "one monk for every three of the entire lay community, including the women and children. . . . The population is, presumably as a consequence of overmonasticism, steadily drifting toward extinction." [8]

Buddhism has raised the people out of certain depths of savagery, but the notorious impurity of the monks and the hardness and cruelty of nature and man in this forbidding land have done little to inculcate high ideals of life. The idea of recompense in heavens and hells and the

[8] "Lamaism" in Hastings' *Encyclopaedia of Religion and Ethics.*

fear of evil spirits have taken strong hold, until the religion is one of fear and terror. All the poor layman wants of religion is to secure charms against these spirits. It has become almost pure magic. He repeats sacred formulas; he writes them on paper and swallows them; he inscribes them on cloth and allows them to flutter in the wind; he devises so-called "prayer cylinders" and mechanically grinds out the charmed petitions as he walks or works; he even harnesses them to water wheels, and thus nature assists him in his "devotions." Influenced by the Shakti form of Hinduism as found in the Indian tantras, Lamaism has a corrupting erotic taint, the only form of Buddhism against which this charge can be made.

The story of Buddhism in China and Japan is very different from that just recounted and must be told in the chapters dealing with those countries. It is a far call from Ceylon to Japan; it is even farther from Gautama to present-day Buddhism. The remarkable part of it all is that we should still continue to call by the name of the Buddha a religion which is so varied and contains such contradictory elements. What the Buddha taught is denied, and what he repudiated is practiced by those who would never admit the charge of unorthodoxy. They speak of these changes as developments which lay in germ in the mind of the great master! All recognize that Gautama was the founder of the faith of which historically they are a part. All believe that his ideas were living and germinal, and that it is possible to live in general agreement with the inner meaning of his purpose even though the actual doctrines may seem to contradict much that he taught. They find sorrow in the world as he did and are seeking to cure it; they are quite willing to follow his ethical demands as far better than anything they have known; they look to him as the pure example of loving service and find it difficult to measure up to his unselfish life. In all these regards they are true followers of Gautama and consider it an honor to be known by his name.

SUGGESTIONS FOR FURTHER STUDY

Hackmann, H. *Buddhism as a Religion*. London: 1910. A good volume on the developments in the faith in the various lands of its adoption.

Poussin, Louis de La Vallée. *The Way to Nirvana*. New York: The Macmillan Company, 1916.

Pratt, James Bissett. *The Pilgrimage of Buddhism and a Buddhist Pilgrimage*. New York: The Macmillan Company, 1928. A complete discussion of the religion in all the countries in which it is found except Tibet.

Rhys Davids, Caroline. *A Manual of Buddhism*. London: 1935.

Saunders, Kenneth J. *Epochs in Buddhist History*. Chicago: University of Chicago Press, 1924.

————. *Gotama Buddha*. New York: Association Press, 1920.

Thomas, Edward J. *Early Buddhist Scriptures*. London: Kegan Paul, Trench, Trubner and Company, Ltd., 1935. Selections of translations with brief introductions.

————. *The Life of Buddha as Legend and History*. New York: Alfred A. Knopf, 1927. An extensive discussion of the problem of the life of the Buddha and his teaching.

Ward, C. H. S. *Buddhism; Vol. I, Hinayana*. London: The Epworth Press, 1948.

CHAPTER VIII

THE RELIGION OF CHINA

The Early Religion

We are on safe ground when we speak of the religion of China. It is commonly stated that there are three religions in the country, not to mention Mohammedanism and Christianity, which have always been looked upon as strange and exotic. The three religions are Confucianism, Taoism, and Buddhism. A Chinese sees no incongruity in feeling that he is closely related to all three. He always wants to be thought of first of all as a Confucianist. He is more proud of that than of his relation to the other faiths, but when he is in trouble he does not hesitate to have recourse to Taoism, and when death visits his family he is almost sure to call in Buddhist priests as having especially close relations with the spirit world of the hereafter.[1] But underneath them all and expressing itself through them all is an animistic attitude which had existed for centuries before the formal religions arose and which has not been changed essentially by them. This introduces us to a feature of the Chinese character which must ever be held in mind, the thoroughgoing conservatism which has been a marked trait of the people throughout their history. We live in the period when for the first time in their recorded history these lovers of antiquity have come to realize that their

only hope lies in a change of front. What the ultimate effect will be no one can even guess. The incoming of Communism makes the question even more problematic than it was before.

The most characteristic form of early religion in China was crudely animistic. All nature and all its parts are possessed of spirits, good and bad, strong and weak. They are to be found everywhere—on the mountains, among the trees, in the ground, and under the water. Everything that happens is accounted for by the action of spirits. Sickness is caused by demons within the body which must be exorcised. A child drowns,

[1] See Francis C. M. Wei, *The Spirit of Chinese Culture*, pp. 135 ff.

160

not by any natural cause, but because a fiendish spirit seizes the child and draws him under. These spirits flit about through the air, invisible but exceedingly real. Streets must be made crooked because these imps move in straight lines and can be stopped in their wild career by a wall. Houses must be so constructed that a solid wall will be opposite every gate and door and window. The whole life of the people is governed by their fear of these dangerous beings, and much of their religion consists in attempts to drive them away. Exorcism, then, plays a large part in this low and yet all-prevalent superstition, and many are its forms.

The spirits are divided between those that are good and benevolent (shen) and the evil-minded (kwei). To secure the assistance of a powerful shen is the best means of chasing off the harmful kwei. The sun is a shen of the highest order, and to secure his co-operation is to have the benefit of a most powerful influence. Everything connected with the sun is efficacious. By a subtle magic the peach blossom, because it appears as the harbinger of the spring, when the sun again assumes control of nature, is an omen of good. The actual blossoms are often replaced by red paper, which has the same value. So, again, the blood of the cock may ward off danger, and cocks are used as charms and in the making of medicines, all because the cock crows as the herald of the rising of the sun! Bonfires, firecrackers, torches, lanterns, candles, all kinds of noises, scorching and cauterizing the skin—whatever suggests or is derived from fire may be used to bring good luck or prevent misfortune. Whatever else he may be, religiously the Chinese is a believer in spirits and in the necessity of exorcism. He may be ashamed of his belief, but he has recourse nevertheless to the exorcists when he gets into a tight place. He wants at least to be on the safe side in a world so strange and fearsome.

Another side of this animistic attitude which is even more important is ancestor worship. Men participate with nature in being possessed of spirits which make them what they are. Even a living man, like the governor of a province who has done well by his people, may be deified and accorded religious rites with no sense of incongruity. But especially men are worshiped after their death. It takes the form of the worship of ancestors and is so universally practiced and so implicitly believed in that it has been looked upon as the very center and nerve of Chinese religion. Death in no sense breaks the bond between the members of a family. The family consists of its dead as well as its living members, and, strange enough to us, the dead members are more important than the

161

living. All the arrangements of the household must be made with the well-being and the comfort of the dead primarily in mind. It is carried to the extent that it becomes an intolerable burden. The funeral must be as elaborate and expensive as the family can afford; frequently they go beyond the bounds of reason and plunge into debt. The sacrifices are carefully prescribed, and the utmost care is taken to see that all the rites are carried out to the letter. The choice of a site and the time of the burial are of tragic importance, and frequently large sums are squandered on Fung-Shui, or "wind-and-water," doctors to determine the lucky spot for the grave and the propitious time for the interment.

The ideas that lie back of these practices are the important thing. Filial piety is the first of the Chinese virtues. It is extended beyond the grave because the dead parent continues to be as much a part of the family as before. To all the inducements which existed while the parent was living to show him reverence and honor is added the inducement of the uncanny and mysterious fact that the soul has passed out into the unknown land of the shades and may possess powers and influence even more potent and surely more incalcuable than he possessed in life. To the motive of respect must be added that of fear. Above all the other duties that of being married and having sons in order to continue the sacrifices through the generations is the most urgent. Mencius, the great follower and interpreter of Confucius, declared, "Three things are unfilial, and having no sons is the worst." This deeply ingrained conviction has driven the Chinese to two practices, polygamy and adoption. The effect has been that woman has been looked upon as of little value in herself; only as she fulfills her function and becomes the mother of sons is she considered worthy of honor. In a real sense a man's possessions belongs to his ancestors, so no living man has the right to dispose of what in the final analysis is not his. Shall we call this whole attitude toward ancestors one of worship or something of lesser significance? The large majority of firsthand investigators have no hesitation in calling it worship in the most real sense. As Professor J. J. M. DeGroot puts it, a Chinese "may renounce all other gods, but his ancestors he will renounce last and least of all." [2]

The all-prevailing animism and ancestor worship which have been described do not complete the round of early Chinese religion. There is a state religion, based on the same principles but with a very different development. It shows the mind of the Chinese in a far better light.

[2] *Religion of the Chinese*, p. 86.

If we go back to the days before records were kept, the animistic attitude of mind laid hold on the greater objects of nature, personified them more or less, and raised them to a dignity not possessed by the other objects of worship. The heavenly bodies, the earth and its subdivisions and, above all, the incomparable heavenly sphere became the great gods of China. These objects were not supposed to be worshiped by the people themselves, who were restricted to their own ancestors. The august worship of the great gods became the official duty of government officials, of governors and the emperor. To the last alone was reserved the worship of high heaven, the supreme religious act of the old Chinese religion. It must be remembered, however, that in each case the emperor performed the rites, not for his own sake, but on behalf of all the people. He was looked upon as the father of those over whom he was set to rule, and as a father he worshiped for them.

The climax of the whole system was the worship of heaven, performed by the emperor at the capital city on the occasion of the winter solstice. With beautiful suggestiveness it was performed at that time because it was when the forces of cold and darkness in the world had done their worst, the time when again the shortening days ceased to become shorter and the kindly influences of the sun began again to regain power and give the first promise of the coming glory of spring and summer. Here under the open sky upon a circular terraced marble platform was performed one of the most remarkable religious sacrifices known in the whole range of religious history. There was a sublimity about the ritual which betook a high conception of its significance. The worship was offered to heaven, or Shang-ti. The term Tien is also used. So lofty is the conception that "Shang-ti" has been agreed upon by Protestants as the word by which the Christian conception of "God" should be translated into Chinese. There is nothing unworthy in the conception in any way, although it will take time for the term "Shang-ti" to carry the full meaning of the biblical conception of "God." Now that China is no longer an empire, the old worship has of course ceased to be performed. But the grand altar of heaven in the old capital of Peking remains as a memento of a glory that is no more.

CONFUCIUS AND HIS CONTRIBUTION

Confucius lived from 551 to 478 B.C. These dates can be accepted with considerable assurance. But great uncertainty shrouds the so-called facts of Confucius' life. During the past half century scholars, both Chinese and Western, have been led to believe that many things which had been asserted about the life and teaching of Confucius cannot be depended upon. They were written many years, even centuries, after his time and are colored by the changes which developed in the teaching of men who were proud to call themselves Confucianists but had departed, at places, very far from the actual teaching of the great sage himself.[3]

It is only when we come to the period of the Chou dynasty, 1122-256 B.C., that definite dates can be assigned with any confidence. Confucius lived in this period, when China was divided into many small states, frequently at war with each other and owing not much more than nominal allegiance to the weak authority of the central government. In the midst of these unsettled days—when there was almost perpetual warfare, when education was not known, and when plague, pestilence, and famine stalked through the land—Confucius was born. His birthplace was in the state of Lu, in the western part of the modern province of Shantung. He came of a highly respectable family but at this time far from being prosperous. His father was an old man of seventy when he married a young woman who soon became the mother of the sage. His lot as a young boy was not easy, his father dying when his little son was only three. Confucius was married at nineteen and had one son, who appears at intervals in the story and seems to have become one of his disciples.

One of the strands in the old tradition about Confucius is that he held a number of public offices in his native state, the last being one of large responsibility. As a result of his wise guidance the state of Lu became the envy of surrounding states because of its prosperity and humane government. He is said to have lost his position because of a serious disagreement with his prince and never held office again. All of this is controverted by the verdict of the best scholars today. Confucius may have held several minor offices but none which gave him a directing voice in public affairs. When finally he found it was hopeless for him to expect an adequate opportunity in his native state, he spent ten years wandering from one feudal state to another trying to induce the princes to let him try his schemes and bring peace and order out of the chronic confusion. He never succeeded, but with all his discouragements he never lost heart and became pessimistic. He was convinced until the

[3] See H. G. Creel, *Confucius: The Man and the Myth,* especially Chap. I, "Tradition and Truth."

end that he possessed the secret of statecraft and could make any kingdom prosperous by the sincere co-operation of the ruler in the application of his principles. But he failed to convince a single prince and was compelled to abandon his purpose and return to his native state and his early home. There he lived the few remaining years of his life surrounded by an enlarging circle of admiring disciples, students who sat at his feet and so profited by his instruction that through them his teaching was transmitted to future generations. There in the year 478 B.C. at the ripe old age of seventy-two Confucius died and was buried. His tomb is well marked at the present time, is visited by thousands of pilgrims each year, and is destined, one may surely say, to increase in interest, not only among the Chinese but among men of every nation as they come to recognize the noble example and the high ideals represented by the sage.

We do not know very much about the compilation of the classical literature already in existence nor of his own contribution. What we really know about Confucius is to be found in the famous Analects or Dialogues between the master and his students and others. The authentic part of this work was put together by scholars of the men who were in direct contact with Confucius and knew him intimately, so they come from the second generation following the sage himself.

What was his contribution? Very little religiously. All that has been described as the early religion of the people was in full force in his day as it is in our own time. He did not condemn it; he did not criticize it; he did not add to it. He simply took it for granted. His temper of mind was essentially practical; he seemed always to be averse to any discussion of spiritual or purely philosophical matters. He claimed to be agnostic concerning the next life and the world of the gods. His mind was immersed in the affairs of this life—with conduct, the development of character, the relations of man with man, with the state and all the complicated affairs of government. On these he considered he had an opinion worth while, of which it would be well for men, from the ruler to the humblest peasant, to take earnest heed. Confucius was a political reformer, and his ideas were based on an original and revolutionary theory of government. Instead of arbitrary authority exercised by a dictator prince or ruler, Confucius would have a state ruled by those who had proved their right to exercise authority by showing the qualities of intelligence and industry, by those who believed that "men of all classes possessed worth in themselves." [4] He held that "the most virtuous and

[4] *Ibid.*, p. 128.

capable should rule in the interests of the whole people." [5] This did not mean that the people as a whole should control the government, but that they should be ruled by an aristocracy not of birth or wealth but of virtues and ability.[6]

Along with this conviction about the ordering of the state Confucius had the deepest convictions about the cultivation of personal character, the development of the ideal or "superior man," the "gentleman." While he was very modest and did not claim to have attained his own ideal, Confucius, in the estimation of the Chinese, was himself its best exemplification. He was well balanced and withal self-confident, courteous, and not without a sly sense of humor despite his dignity and sobriety. Above all the master was most insistent on deep sincerity. He believed in "allegiance to principle rather than to persons" [7] and would under no provocation compromise his honor and integrity. No wonder he did not secure public office in a time when intrigue and dissoluteness were rampant in the courts of the Chinese feudal princes, with no consideration for the common people, their rights and their happiness! Altogether it is a pleasing picture we get of the strict old moralist who at the same time took delight in music and could unbend sufficiently to win not only the admiration but the personal devotion of his followers. Great injury has been done the sage by writers of later generations who have made him out to be a traditionalist standing for the old regime and defending the feudal institutions of his day as the ideal form of government.

In the estimation of Confucius human nature is naturally good. The function of rules and regulations is to guide the development of the individual in the right channels and thus prevent the deterioration which might ensue if the wrong course should be followed. A man must depend on his own unaided powers to achieve maturity of character, but this is not so hard, because of his innate goodness. He must seek to develop by the unfolding of his own inner nature and thus be true to himself. Confucius was compelled to recognize that the task was easier for some than for others. Some seem to possess the necessary knowledge and ability almost intuitively; others learn easily but must nevertheless apply themselves to learn; still others are able to acquire knowledge with difficulty; while there are those who will not learn, through either indifference or willful ignorance. But whatever condition may confront

[5] *Ibid.*, p. 157.
[6] *Ibid.*, p. 166.
[7] *Ibid.*, p. 129.

a man, the admonition of the sage is to make the very most of himself. Religion, it is quite evident, did not enter into his scheme of human life. Very little prayer would suffice, and sacrifice had only a subjective influence. He confessed that he could not enter into the meaning of the yearly sacrifice to Shang-ti. He did not object to ancestor worship, because it encouraged and enforced the obligation of filial piety, and such conduct was the cornerstone of his system of relationships.

But with all his interest in the development of individual character Confucius was primarily interested in society and the state. He believed that man could not live alone, but that he had relationships which were necessary and inevitable. All his theories were to be measured by their value in relation to the state and the condition of the people in it. He felt that if the sage and the sovereign could be combined in one person, all would be well. One of his greatest doctrines in statecraft was the power of personal example. The welfare of the state depended more upon the rectitude of the ruler than on any other factor. Evil in the ruler means eventually a ruined country, and integrity and sincerity on his part are the sure cure for a country's ills. It is almost pathetic the lengths to which this principle was believed to be applicable. With a great truth at its center it laid too heavy a responsibility on a single pair of shoulders and failed to take into account the perversity of human nature no matter how good an example might be set. Confucius believed in reciprocity as the basis of all relationships. He would have men take care not to do to others what they would not want done to themselves. He desired peace of mind and happiness for all men. This must come through education—which was always for Confucius education in character, in self-control, and above all the cultivation of sincerity. His benevolence extended to all men. "Within the seven seas all men are brothers" expresses the width of his sympathies.

Much that has come down to us under the name of Confucianism was the work of later teachers who both understood and misunderstood the mind of the great sage. Confucius was most careful, even punctilious, about the dignity and the courtesies of social life. He had been interested as a boy, so we are told, in playing etiquette, and as a man he insisted on correct procedure in the contact of man with man. Everything tended to be regularized. Later his teachings on the essential relations of human life were systematized in what are known as the Five Relations, those of Father and Son, Ruler and Subject, Husband and Wife, Elder Brother and Younger Brother, and Friend and Friend, or better, Patron and Client or Beneficiary. In each case the first named is the superior. By inherent right the father, ruler, husband, elder brother, and patron possess an authority which is not to be questioned. It undoubtedly made society static and immovable, but it has also been responsible for gross injustice and abuse.

About a hundred years after the time of Confucius, China's second greatest scholar-teacher arose. In Mencius we come down to a lower level than that occupied by Confucius, but he was so filled with admiration for his predecessor and master that he became his great advocate and lifted Confucius out of the neglect into which he had fallen. He was an even greater believer in the doctrine of the innate goodness of human nature than Confucius, but in practice could not measure up to him in character and originality. He was conceited and lived so far as he was able in style and even in luxury, but on the other hand stood for the principle that a ruler should be upright and should govern with the good of the people as his chief concern.

With each successive ruler the old Chou dynasty was steadily disintegrating. It finally went to the wall in 249 B.C., to be followed by the short-lived but memorable Ch'in dynasty, which lasted for only fifty years. The one great ruler during these years was Shih Huang Ti, who has been called the Napoleon of China. He abolished the feudal form of government and effectively established a centralized empire in the form which lasted down to the destruction of the Manchu power and the setting up of the republic in 1911-12. He is also to be remembered as the builder of the Great Wall, which was intended to be a barrier to protect the empire from the encroachments of the wild nomadic tribesmen always watching for the opportunity to sweep down on the rich country to the south. He is also remembered by the Chinese with execration because in vain conceit he attempted to destroy the classical literature and by so doing inaugurate a new era which would begin with himself and his period. It may be remarked in passing that the name China is said to be derived from the name of this dynasty, the Chin.

The short period of the Ch'ins was followed by that of the Han dynasty (206 B.C. to A.D. 220). Especially memorable is the reign of Emperor Wu Ti (140-86 B.C.). Cruel and superstitious as he was, Wu gave state recognition to Confucianism, was concerned for the common people, and is "celebrated for the rediscovery of the ancient literature, especially the Confucian classics." [8] Since that time, with all the ups and

[8] *Ibid.*, p. 234.

downs in the story and the disasters which overtook one dynasty after another, there has been a succession of scholars and teachers who have been proud to call themselves Confucianists, even though their teaching has been very different from that which Confucius himself expounded. In the words of a great Chinese scholar of our time, Hu Shih, "This Confucianism was not at all what Confucius taught or Mencius philosophized about." [9] Only one of these later teachers can be mentioned. Chu Hsi, who wrote during the Sung dynasty (A.D. 960-1280), rationalized Confucianism. To him "the mind is the perfect guide." [10] Chu Hsi and his followers have set the type of Confucian thinking since their day. Reason is the final arbiter, and in consequence a "naturalistic explanation of good and evil" [11] and all else has been the general attitude of Chinese thinking since their day.

We are to think of Confucianism not only as an ethical system, calculated to regulate the life of the individual, society, and the state, but as a part of China's religious life. Temples dedicated to Confucius are found all over China, particularly in provincial centers where under official auspices honor and worship are offered to the greatest of all Chinese. The temples are simple and beautiful. There is no image but only the table carrying the name of the sage. An attempt was made after the unseating of the emperor in 1911-12 to recognize this worship as the state religion, but it came to nothing. No, Confucius will continue to be reverenced but not in this way. He will live in the thought of the Chinese as a true patriot and as a worthy example of uprightness and unselfish devotion to the welfare of the people of his beloved land.

LAOCIUS AND TAOISM

"Laocius" is the Latinized form of Lao-tzu, just as "Confucius" is of K'ung Fu-tzu, the philosopher K'ung. Very little is known about the life of Laocius. In fact a strong tendency in our day is to cast doubt on his very existence. The few "facts" which follow about his life may be legend and nothing more. He was born in 604 B.C., about a half century before Confucius. Once the two met while the younger man was on his wanderings from state to state, but they could not understand each other; they were so utterly different in their whole outlook on life. Laocius is said to have been the keeper of the archives at the imperial court of

---

[9] *Ibid.*, p. 243.
[10] E. R. and K. Hughes, *Religion in China*, p. 88.
[11] *Ibid.*

the Chou dynasty. He became more and more discouraged as he saw everything going to decay, and finally resigned and retired. But still he was in the midst of the dismay caused by the warring of the feudal states and the supineness of the central power, so he determined upon an even more drastic step. He started off into exile and reached a noted ford in the mountains where the boatkeeper induced him to put down in writing the philosophy which he had worked out and which would otherwise be lost. As a result he remained long enough to put into written form the Tao Te Ching, a writing containing about five thousand Chinese characters, which he entrusted to the keeper of the ford, and then he passed on and disappeared. Thus runs the tale for what it is worth.

The Tao Te Ching has been translated into English a number of times, but so difficult is it to understand and render into coherent language that the various translations differ almost hopelessly. The difficulty starts in the name itself. Beginning with the last word, "Ching" means "writing" or "classic," "Te" means "duty," "virtue," or "human responsibility," but what does "Tao" mean? Many definitions have been given, very divergent and in some cases most confusing. The shortest equivalent has been given as the "Way." Another is "Nature," and still another "Providence." It has also been conceived of as the "Order of the Universe," the "Rotation of the Seasons," and even "Time," and more recently as "Reality." It may be that Dr. Soothill's statement is about as helpful as any that can be found: "Tao, then, may be considered as the eternal and ubiquitous impersonal principle by which the universe has been produced and is supported and governed." [12]

The aim of this original and very remarkable work is to indicate that human duty consists in imitating Tao or "way" of the universe. Now, what Laocius saw as he looked out on nature was quiet, humility, self-effacement, placidity, emptiness, and freedom from effort. It was the passivity of the processes of nature which impressed him, and man was to follow nature as closely as he could. He must live a life of "inward spontaneity"; he must not be headstrong or self-willed; he must be possessed by a "spirit of inanition." He must not even teach his doctrines; they must shine for themselves. Is there any wonder that Confucius, the apostle of strenuous endeavor, and Laocius, the preacher of the gospel of inactivity, should have been incomprehensible to each other? Confucius has won the day, and China has gone with him and not with

[12] The Three Religions of China, 2nd ed., p. 16.

Laocius. But the quietist has had his followers too, men who retired into the mountains alone and gave themselves to the discipline of nature. They thought they might by so doing become etherealized and even enter the company of the gods. They fasted, believing that a saint needed no food, and became sadly emaciated; and when this did not have the desired effect, they sought drugs and elixirs to induce the spiritualized condition they were in search of. They thought that by absorbing the good in nature they might live long and even achieve immortality. They practiced breathing exercises to drink in the good influences of the atmosphere. These strange ascetics did not grow in number nor thrive greatly. Buddhism was abroad in the land and had a more positive aim and a better organized monastic discipline. But these seekers after Tao, the true Taoists, had some influence in China and helped to bring in the belief in immortality, which had been sadly lacking despite the ancestor worship which was constantly in touch with another world.

But this is not what we know as Taoism today. The modern variety, which still goes under the old name, is a mass of puerile superstitions. It is the worst side of Chinese religion. Taoist temples exist everywhere. Theoretically, the business of the ignorant priests is to help the people live in accord with Tao, but practically it is magic run mad. Soothsaying in every imaginable form—by the almanac and combinations of lines, by magical religious ceremonies, incantations, and what not—is carried on by a priesthood which has become skillful in working on the superstitious fears of the people and by so doing keeping them in subjection and terror.

The beginnings of Taoism as a formal religion go back to one named Chang Taoling, who was born in A.D. 34. He discovered, so it is said, the elixir of immortality, founded a priesthood and hierarchy, and set up a state in the far western province of Szechwan, which was put down with much bloodshed. Descended from this ambitious priest a line of so-called Taoist "popes" has come down through the centuries to our own time. They have for many years been situated far away in an inaccessible mountain retreat in the province of Si-kiang. The "pope" does not exercise the kind of authority his title would indicate, but he is looked upon as the spiritual center of a system which in its sublime beginnings gave promise of a better sequel than the poor excuse of a religion it is now. "Taoism has had a demoralizing influence. . . . There is little doubt that Taoism is dying out in China, especially with the

171

spread of modern education, but it may be a long time before it becomes entirely extinct." [13]

CHINESE BUDDHISM

The Chinese are practical, and Confucius ministered to that bent with such insight and wisdom that the whole life of the people has been built up around his ideals. He did not feel the need of more than the meagerest amount of spiritual influence and believed that could be supplied out of the religious life which already existed. But he was mistaken. The Chinese have deep spiritual longings and capacity for mystical religion which many are not likely to appreciate. Taoism so soon descended to the level of quackery that all it could do was to trade on the superstitious fears of the people. But still there was an unreached depth to the Chinese heart which nothing in China had been able to touch. This was the opportunity of Buddhism. Coming for the most part in its Mahayana form with the assurance of being able to bring men into vital contact with the spiritual world, Buddhism touched the hearts of many Chinese. There is no other explanation of the career of Buddhism in China, where it has persisted despite the bitterest kind of persecution. The presence of a million Buddhist monks and nuns today speaks eloquently of the hold of the religion on the Chinese mind and heart.

These monks and nuns are scattered widely over the country. They are to be found in little temples in the cities and villages, but here the conditions are not ideal. The usual contempt in which the Buddhist monk is held in China is to be accounted for largely by the conduct of these men, who are in the world and also unfortunately of the world. We are assured that there are monks who deplore the condition. They would not for a moment risk their reputation in such a company amid such surroundings. To them Buddhism is a gospel to be sincerely followed. They betake themselves to the monasteries where ideals are higher and where laxity is less frequently tolerated. They are not all ideal by any means, but the contrast between them and the Buddhist centers in most of the cities is very striking. In such retreats they find others like-minded and are able to give themselves uninterruptedly to meditation and worship. Here are pure souls seeking emancipation, who resist wrongdoing and lewdness, and who are reaching out in every way they know how to find the light.

[13] Wei, *op. cit.*, p. 142.

The monks are divided into various groups or sects. To secure correct information on these different groups is difficult. Many of the monks themselves are not intelligent and add to the confusion. There are today six schools of thought which fall into two essentially different groups, and between the two the difference is "profound and radical." The members of the first group are the adherents of Ch'an-tsung, "Ch'an" meaning "meditation," and "tsung" "school" or "sect." They make inwardness the one method of attainment. This school in its denial of soul and of any higher power is not unlike early Buddhism and can scarcely be called Mahayana. It was founded by the patriarch Bodhidharma, who came to China from India in A.D. 528. He opposed the use of any sacred scriptures and all outward ritual—the "inward look" was sufficient. The attempt was made to empty the consciousness of every idea. It was to be a subjective experience with no objective content; it was pure abstraction. Bodhidharma was called the "Wall Gazer," because of his habit of looking intently at a blank wall as he sought to divest his mind of thought and make it as blank as the wall itself. Everything outward was considered superfluous; even the distinction between right and wrong was held to be the imperfection of a lower standpoint above which meditation would lift the seeker. A monk thus becomes indifferent to everything. This school was split up into five subdivisions, each of which became a school or sect. They do not vary greatly, though one, the Lin Chi, took the lead and spread all over China and even into Japan, where we shall meet it under a different name.

The second group, Ching T'su-tsung or Pure Land sect, opposes the absolute subjectivism of the Ch'an school and teaches that salvation is attained by faith in O-mi-to Fo, the Chinese equivalent of the Indian Amitabha. This teaching was also carried to Japan, where, as we shall see, it had a remarkable development.

Buddhism has a real hold on the life of the people who come to the temples and have recourse to the monks. They know nothing of the distinction between the schools. They are taught that there are gods, loving O-mi-to Fo and the merciful Kwan-Yin, who will hear their prayers and receive their sacrifices. They are also told that there is a heaven of bliss which they may attain and dreadful hells which they may escape by throwing themselves on the mercy of these benevolent beings. There is no message like that in the other Chinese religions, so it answers the craving and the fear in their hearts. They do not throw over their other religious practices in thus coming to a Buddhist temple. It has been said that the several religions of China answer to moods in the Chinese soul.[14] Confucianism makes plain their duty; Taoism ministers to their superstitious fears; and Buddhism opens up the spiritual world and gives them the promise of future blessedness. Buddhism has also accommodated itself to ancestor worship and has incorporated various features from Taoist teaching. It offers prayers for the dead and adds its comfort to the friends and relatives who are concerned about the welfare of their departed in the next world. Buddhism exists in China also in many lay communities or secret societies, about which not much is known. The members try to assist each other on the road to salvation. The monastic idea is not insisted on, but the five moral commandments of the Buddha must be kept. In spite of persecution these societies are very numerous, showing the hunger which exists for the message of a spiritual religion.

Like everything in China, the outward aspect of Buddhism is dingy and run-down. Here and there repairs have been made and at places extensive alterations undertaken, but in general it is the need of renovation which strikes the eye of the visitor. But when this has been said, one must hasten to express unbounded admiration for the artistic sense and the eye for the appropriate which have been displayed in choice of temple and monastery rites. Whether on the rock-bound island of Puto, where the waves are never still, or the Little Orphan Island, which raises its sharp crest far above the waters of the mighty Yangtze which surround it, or the lovely stillness of the shaded crest of Kushan Mountain near Foochow, it is always the same. By an unerring instinct the pioneers of Buddhism in China found the places of beauty and claimed them for the practice of religion. The Chinese may be practical and materialistic, but this is only half the tale. There is a depth to their nature which Buddhism has touched, a love of beauty and a craving after the things of the spirit.

What of religion in China today? The revolution of 1911-12 under Sun Yat-sen swept the Manchu dynasty from the throne and substituted what was intended to be a republican form of government. This is not the place to trace its history. The significant fact is that the Chinese have not been permitted to work out their problems unmolested. Japan stepped in and threw the entire land into confusion. This lasted until the end of World War II in 1945. During this period of political upheaval all kinds of intellectual, moral, and religious movements were launched in various parts of the country. There was for a time a vigorous

[14] W. J. Clennell, *The Historical Development of Religion in China*, p. 13.

anti-Christian campaign which was paralleled and frequently joined with an antireligious movement. Nationalism has had many of the same results found in Western lands. It almost became a religion, with Sun Yat-sen as its chief divinity. There were also all kinds of liberalizing tendencies which would reinterpret Confucianism and Buddhism and bring them into line with modern scientific thought. The last act of the drama, the coming of Communism, is still being enacted. To the surprise of all, those self-styled "liberators" have overrun and conquered the entire country, all but the island of Formosa, where in 1950 the discredited Kuomintang party had a precarious hold. What the end will be no one can say, and what will become of the religions of China is completely hidden. A comment by an old resident of China may be as pertinent as any other word that has come out of the chaos: "The Chinese have a remarkable way of not doing what they do not want to do."

SUGGESTIONS FOR FURTHER STUDY

Creel, H. G. Confucius, the Man and the Myth. New York: John Day Company, Inc., 1949. A pioneer in the new interpretation of Confucius.

de Groot, J. J. M. The Religion of the Chinese. New York: The Macmillan Company, 1910. A very valuable short manual.

Goodrich, L. Carrington. A Short History of the Chinese People. New York: Harper & Brothers, 1943.

Hodous, Lewis. Folkways in China. London: Arthur Probsthain, 1929. Valuable for the animistic background of the religions of China.

Hughes, E. R. and K. Religion in China. New York: Longmans, Green and Company, 1950.

Reichelt, Karl L. Religion in Chinese Garment. London: Lutterworth Press, 1950.

————. Truth and Tradition in Chinese Buddhism. Rev. and enlarged ed. New York: G. E. Stecher and Company, 1927.

Soothill, W. E. The Three Religions of China. 2nd ed. New York: Oxford University Press, 1923. Valuable in itself and needed to correct certain statements made by de Groot.

Waley, Arthur. The Analects of Confucius. London: 1945.

Wei, Francis C. M. The Spirit of Chinese Culture. New York: Charles Scribner's Sons, 1947.

Yang, Y. C. China's Religious Heritage. New York and Nashville: Abingdon-Cokesbury Press, 1943. By a Chinese scholar who is a Christian.

CHAPTER IX

THE RELIGIONS OF JAPAN

SHINTO

JAPAN RECEIVED HER CIVILIZATION FROM CHINA. IT IS NOT KNOWN when the influence began, but the process was complete by the end of the seventh century of our era. About everything cultural came to Japan from across the sea, from China, the mother country of all Far Eastern culture. By way of the peninsula of Korea these influences came flowing in until in the end Japan had entered the stream of history, and her course can be followed step by step from that time on. The cultivation of the silkworm, the written language and literature of China, the ethical system of Confucius, and the religion of the Buddha—all these and much else came in and transformed the country and the people. Not, then, for the first time in her history did Japan in the nineteenth century show eagerness to receive from other peoples what was necessary to take her place by the side of the progressive nations of the world. She was doing only what she had done before, thus proving her willingness to learn from others whenever it is to her advantage to do so. But by the side of this characteristic must be placed another which is just as important if we are to understand the meaning of Japanese religion and civilization. On everything which Japan has ever received from the outside she has not failed to put her own stamp. The sign manual of Japan is indelibly attached to all she produces, making it her own unique output. There must be, then, a very distinctive and tenacious Japanese racial fiber, which, while assimilating with avidity all that may be offered, succeeds in giving it a character which no one can mistake. At no point is this to be seen to better advantage than in Japanese religious development. This makes it essential to study with care the religious life of the people before the coming of religion from China.

The early religion is known as Shinto. This is a Chinese word, or two words, both of which we have met before. "Shin" is the same as the

176

Chinese "shen," which means "good spirits," while "to" is the same as "tao," the "way," as it may be translated. The religion, then, is the "Way of the Good Spirits," or the "Way of the Gods." The equivalent name in pure Japanese is Kami no Michi, "Michi" meaning "way" or "road," "no" being the possessive, and "Kami" meaning the "deities" or "gods." The word "Kami" is the clue to the whole system. It denotes that which is above, any power or influence which can accomplish what man cannot prevent and is stronger and wiser than he. It is something he must look up to as possessing strength. All the evidences of power he saw and felt around him in wind and storm were proof of the existence of what was higher than he could attain. There are many Kami, presiding over all the phases of life. Thus it is seen that as in all other countries the earliest form of religion in Japan was nature worship. The cult was exceedingly simple. Unpainted, unadorned wooden shrines were the centers of worship. No images were present in the early day, though the presence of the spirits was indicated by fluttering pieces of notched paper. A gong above the entrance could be sounded to call the attention of the spirits to the coming of worshipers. Lustrations preceded the clapping of hands and offering of brief prayers. There was no sacred book, no doctrine to be believed, and no code of laws to be followed. Of all the religions of primitive peoples none has ever been found more simple and unencumbered than the early religion of Japan.

Yet the people were intensely religious. Wayside shrines were numerous, and various lesser divinities like the Kitchen God presided over their home life and the daily task. The God of Plenty and the God of Health had their place, as did a hundred others, each with its designated function. Ancestor worship was everywhere prevalent. To this day no Japanese household is complete without its god shelf with the tablets of the deceased before which prayers and sacrifices are offered. Another aspect of Shinto which grew up in the early period was reverence for the ruling house. It was fully developed by the time the continental influences had done their work and remained as the most characteristic feature of Shinto until January 1, 1946, when the emperor disavowed his divinity. As Dr. G. W. Knox phrased it, everything in the ancient religion might be summed up in the injunction, "Fear the gods and obey the emperor." It was "essentially nature worship married to the worship of the imperial house." [1]

[1] *Development of Religion in Japan*, p. 66.

A closer glance is necessary at this point. In A.D. 712 a book was written called the Kojiki, the "Record of Ancient Matters," which has been called the bible of the Japanese. This was followed in 720 by another work, the Nihongi, or "Chronicles of Japan," which covered much the same ground but showed more of the Chinese influence than the earlier volume. The object of the writers was to trace the history of Japan and the imperial line back to the beginnings. We read there of the divine beings Izanagi and his wife Izanani, who produced many of the Japanese islands as well as the Japanese race; also various tales of gods and goddesses, among whom was the great sun goddess, Amaterasu-o-mi-Kami. She ruled in the heavens in brilliant light, the highest divinity of the Shinto pantheon. Not only so, it was her "grandson" Jimmu Tenno, who assumed the rule in Japan, so it is said, in 660 B.C. and inaugurated the line of emperors. Remarkable to say, the present sovereign, Hirohito (1926-   ) is the one hundred and twenty-fourth in direct descent from Jimmu Tenno, the grandson of the sun goddess! We may be sure the line has not been broken since records began to be kept in the fifth century, and how long before that we cannot know. Suffice it to say that the Japanese were taught as the first fact of history that their reigning emperor was directly descended from Amaterasu, the sun goddess. Little wonder that patriotism was for them a part of their religion and allegiance to the imperial house the highest obligation they knew.

Then came Buddhism, and it all but swallowed Shinto. It would probably have done so had it not been for the reverential attachment to the ruling dynasty. This was their most tangible connection with the gods and the world of divine power, and held them fast during all the centuries. Even though through most of their history the emperor has been little more than a figurehead so far as actual rule is concerned, the Japanese have always looked on him as the representative of the gods, as the final source of all authority. In the year 1868 a revolution occurred, and the emperor was restored, for the first time in many centuries, to his rightful place as actual ruler as well as theoretical sovereign of his people. The Japanese have rallied around him with passionate devotion. No theory of "the divine right of kings" was ever more far-reaching and complete than with the Japanese. But it went a step further and asserted the actual divinity of the very person of the emperor. He was their divine ruler and commanded their loyalty and obedience by a right seldom claimed in all history and never elsewhere in modern times. The

178

patriotism of the Japanese may readily be interpreted as religion, and in fact was about all the religion many Japanese had.

Shinto, then, was saved from almost complete extinction by its connection with the ruling house. What became of all the gods and goddesses of the early religion? In a comparatively short time after its arrival Buddhism became the dominant religion and overtopped the simple faith of the early days. Pure Shinto remained little more than the ritual and ceremonial of the court, in which the people were only slightly interested. But we must always remember that even a simple faith like Shinto has its roots deep down in the life of the people and cannot be torn up and thrown away at will. So it was in Japan. The people mixed their Shinto and their Buddhism together, and the result was not altogether incongruous. It was known as Ryobu, or "Dual," Shinto. The mixture almost became a compound when, by a happy thought or a stroke of genius, a celebrated Buddhist priest named Kobo Daishi (A.D. 774) began to teach that the old Shinto deities were in reality Buddhist bodhisattvas! What they had been worshiping in ignorance of their true greatness he now made known to them, and from that day the two religions have lived side by side in peace, though it must be said that Buddhism got the lion's share and received all the glory.

Because of its connection with the imperial cult Shinto was given a place of honor at the restoration in 1868 but declined rapidly, until in 1899 the priests of the sacred shrine at Ise, the shrine dedicated to Amaterasu, the divine "god-mother" of the emperors, took steps to make Shinto a purely secular organization. But Shinto continued to be the embodiment of the spirit of patriotism. It expressed their confidence "that there is a something more than their present strength and wisdom which directs and aids and on which they may rely." [2] Besides this aspect of Shinto, however, the old religion has had an independent existence. Buddhism had not entirely obliterated the ancient priesthoods and the purely Shinto shrines and forms of worship. Thirteen sects, not greatly different and yet separate and distinct, make their appeal for the allegiance of the people. And besides, in recent years all sorts of movements, often with the claim to heal the sick and frequently led by women, have vied for support. They come and go, at times having as many as a million adherents and then again dwindling to small size and lessened influence.

[2] Knox, op. cit., p. 79.

The Coming of Buddhism

The conquest of Japan by Buddhism was not without opposition. After its introduction from Korea in A.D. 538 the new faith had its ups and downs before it was able to prove that it possessed larger power and could give greater material assistance to the Japanese than their indigenous Shinto. When the cause of the new teaching had been embraced by the Prince-Regent Shotoku Taishi (572-621), the opposition ceased, and Buddhism was accepted as belonging to the country. From those early days to the present Buddhism has remained the great religion of the masses of the people. For the last three hundred years other influences have taken possession of the minds of the cultured, and Buddhism has been more or less neglected in these circles. Still it has been the great religious power in the land, thoroughly acclimated and with a development which is peculiarly Japanese.

The contrast between Shinto and Buddhism is sharp and complete. Shinto is simplicity itself, in the lack of all outward adornment as well as of inner content. There was almost nothing to believe and very little to do in the old faith. Buddhism is the exact opposite of all this. It is elaborate and complex in every feature. It has temples ornate and profusely decorated without and full of images and the paraphernalia of worship within. It has its books and its ceremonial, its priests with their vestments; everything we associate with color and form in religion came into Japan with Buddhism and made the country over again. Art was stimulated, and the beauties we associate with Japan began to appear. But more than these outward manifestations, it was rich in inner content. It opened up a spiritual world to the wondering gaze of the simple Japanese. They had never dreamed such a world existed, peopled with beings so magnificent and resplendent that they could not help winning the awesome reverence of a backward people. Here for the first time was the hope of immortality and contact with merciful gods who were all-powerful yet interested in the salvation of men. The imagination was stimulated, and the glories of a paradise presided over by the gracious Amida became real. In short, the hitherto undeveloped capacity of the Japanese for all that a spiritual religion could supply found its satisfaction in Buddhism. It could not be otherwise when the Japanese mind was beginning to expand under the influence of culture from the continent.

As in China but more so in Japan, the rise and growth of schools or sects became a marked characteristic of the development. Some of the sects were introduced directly from China, but those which have put a

180

distinctive mark on Japanese Buddhism were born and grew up in Japan itself. This does not mean that they are not related to the Buddhism across the sea. Japanese Buddhism has preserved the historical continuity of the faith, and even in the sects most distinctive of the country the connection with older teachings is close and vital. In a number of cases Japanese monks went to China and brought back the nucleus of what they embodied in their own systems. But it may truly be said that in the Japanese sects Buddhism has reached its farthest bound in doctrine and practice. Here Mahayana has developed to the point of greatest divergence from the teaching of Gautama Buddha. The sects number about a dozen, but, if all the subsects are counted, the list comes to about thirty. The most important—to bring out characteristic features—are six in number: Tendai, Shingon, Zen, Jodo, Shin, and Nichiren.

Tendai arose early in the ninth century. It sought to be comprehensive in its attempt to gather in teachings of all sorts, but later in its career it changed and chose to be eclectic. Its chief claim to distinction is that of being parent of several other important sects. Out of its great establishment on Hieizan, a mountain near Kyoto, overlooking the beautiful expanse of Lake Biwa, have come a number of the great historic leaders of Japanese Buddhism. Not satisfied with the doctrinal stand taken by its leaders, they withdrew and founded schools of their own, which have become more famous than the mother of them all. It had a stormy history. In the days when feudalism was in power and monks could be soldiers, Hieizan became a veritable fortress, sending out its armed men to help this side and then that in the interminable strife of the feudal lords. Finally in the sixteenth century Nobunaga, the national dictator, suspecting that the monks of Hieizan were against him, made an attack and after bloody fighting cleared the mountain and burned every building on it. The sect never recovered from this blow, and now peaceful Hieizan is the summer home of beauty-loving Japanese who are glad to escape from the heat of the city.

Shingon arose in the same period, being founded in 806 by Kobo Daishi, whom we have already met. The core of his teaching is "that man can even in this present life attain Buddhahood since he is essentially one with the eternal Buddha." [3] This Buddha is Dai Nichi (in India, Vairochana), early developed in Mahayana. He is the all, inclusive of everything. The system, then, is pantheistic. Man came out of this all, is essentially one with it now, and will be reabsorbed; this is what it

---

[3] A. K. Reishaver, *Studies in Japanese Buddhism*, p. 94.

means to attain Buddhahood. There are two methods of attainment, one by meditation and knowledge and the other by a righteous life. So there are two worlds, one of ideas, "unchangeable and everlasting, having existence only in universal thought" and the other a world of phenomena, the world we see and touch. Vairochana is the center of both, but, of course, the latter is only a seeming world, destined to pass away. The real world, everlasting and eternal, is the ideal world to which all will attain in final salvation. Unfortunately, belief in the efficacy of the magic word, the spell, the posture, has worked evil in the sect, only partially saved by the idealistic philosophy on which it is based.

The Zen, founded in 1191, is by no means the most numerous of the sects, though it has the largest number of temples. It lays great stress on contemplation, thus being somewhat in harmony with the Buddha's way of virtue. It harks back to the patriarch Bodhidharma in China, who would have nothing to do with any scripture or form of worship but gave himself to meditation. Thus he would arrive at the state of emancipation, a state which when reached baffles description. Great emphasis is laid on discipline of the body in order to attain the control which makes mental concentration possible. But it is not by reasoning processes that the desired end is achieved. The purpose of the intense concentration is to discover the futility of reaching the goal through the intellect. By intuition, by the flash of intuitive insight alone, is one emancipated. And when this aim is reached, it cannot be described. How could it be when description is an intellectual process? As Sir Charles Eliot remarks, "when a sect boldly states that its doctrine must be felt and not read and that every attempt to state it in speech or writing must be *ipso facto* a failure, the expositor need say no more." [4] D. T. Suzuki, one of the highest authorities in Zen, declares: "There are in Zen no sacred books or dogmatic tenets. . . . If I am asked, then, what Zen teaches, I would answer, Zen teaches nothing. . . . Anything that has a semblance of an external authority is rejected by Zen. Absolute faith is placed in a man's own inner being." [5] So, of course, there is no higher power, no sacred book, no prayer, no worship. Yet with all this, Zen has in recent centuries exercised a remarkable influence on thoughtful men in Japan—and also, more than any other form of Buddhism, on scholarly writers in Western lands. The discipline which it considered so important made Zen attractive to the Samurai, the scholar-soldiers of

[4] *Japanese Buddhism*, p. 399.
[5] *An Introduction to Zen Buddhism*, pp. 14, 21.

the regime before the revolution of 1868, who learned its lessons of physical control and of disdain of hardship and suffering. The widely known Japanese system of self-defense called jujitsu had its origin in Zen. The key to the system is balance, through which one's opponent is made to defeat himself by a quick turn or twist. And finally, Zen made a great contribution to Japan's cultural refinement, the use of tea and the ceremony of serving it with an exact and beautiful ritual being a part of the gift of Zen to these decorous people.

With the advent of the Jodo we find ourselves in another atmosphere. Founded by Honen-Shonin in 1174, it promulgated the doctrine of the western paradise, or Pure Land, which is presided over by the great Amida. The way of salvation is by faith. Amida promises to deliver all those who trust in him. But paradise cannot be assured without the repetition times without number of the Nembutsu, or prayer formula, which runs thus, "Namu-Amida-Butsu." The rosary thus becomes an important article, as the prayers are told off one by one. Of course it becomes a meaningless and lifeless form, even though merit and a nearer approach to the heaven of Amida are the reward of faithfulness in its performance.

Another step must be taken for the "faith doctrine" to come to its own, and that was taken by Shinran Shonin, the founder of the Shin sect. This remarkable man had his introduction to Buddhist doctrine in the Tendai monastery on Hieizan. Dissatisfied with the teaching, he left, determined to seek a more satisfying way of salvation. He went to China and traveled from center to center, and doubtless while there made his discovery and formulated his distinctive doctrine. Coming back to Japan, he founded a new sect in 1224. He gave it the name of Shin or Shinshu. It is also known as Jodo-Shin, or True Pure Land, also the Hongwanji Sect. He built directly on the teaching of the Jodo, with its emphasis on the western paradise of Amida. He made much of Amida's vow. It is said that this spiritual being, going on to the perfection of Buddhahood, solemnly vowed that he would never allow himself that last and crowning experience so long as there were people in this world of suffering whom he might help. He would give them an immediate salvation, the earnest of what was in store for them in the great beyond. Shinran was very emphatic that there was no other salvation, and that it could be attained by faith, and faith alone. Here is where he parted company with the Jodo. There was no possibility of accumulating merit by anything a man might do, not even by repetition

183

of the Nembutsu. Only by putting faith in Amida and believing that he would receive any who came might a man hope for salvation. Even the faith which we exercise is not in our own power but is graciously bestowed by Amida. Not even prayer avails; there is no merit in any form or "works"; it is solely by the mercy of Amida, who looks with compassion on the heart of anyone who is willing to trust him. There is no difference between the priesthood and the laity. To enter a monastery or to practice meditation is as useless to secure salvation as it would be to storm the battlements of heaven. The theory which is now being increasingly accepted is that this doctrine arose in North India, where the bhakti doctrine was being preached, and that Shinran found it already an accepted teaching in certain monasteries in China which he visited. He took it, however, and filled it with a new vitality when he came back to Japan.

But who is this wonderful being Amida in whom men are asked so implicitly to place their confidence? Trace him back through China to India, and there as Amitabha he appears as one of the Buddhas of Contemplation. In the triple scheme worked out in the early Mahayana days there was Amitabha, and under him Avalokita, the Bodhisattva of Contemplation, and lastly Gautama, the earthly manifestation. It is all an imaginary scheme whose only sure historic foothold is Gautama, here a very inferior being. So men are asked to pin their faith on Amida, a figment of the imagination, placed in the heavens as a savior because man felt the need for what such a being could offer, but with no assured existence in the world of spiritual beings. Speaking of the difference between Amida and Jesus Christ, Professor Arthur Lloyd says, "But the one is an idea, the other a Person—the one a creature of theological fancy, the other a Being whose history is well defined." [6] There is no place in the history of religion where the difference between a genuine historical revelation, which Christianity proclaims in the fact of Jesus Christ, and a conception with no basis in history can be seen more clearly than just here.

The Shin sect is by far the largest and most popular in Japan. Shinran was an innovator. Monasticism meant nothing to him, so, like Luther, he broke the bonds and married. Celibacy could bring a man no nearer the goal, so he would have none of it, and to this day the priests of the Shin sect marry like their parishioners and live among men like their fellows. They dress like the laity except when attending to their priestly

[6] *Praises of Amida*, p. 150.

duties. They are in close touch with the people and are seeking to accommodate their practice to the demands of modern life. They are opposed to Christianity but pay it the high compliment of copying its methods. Preaching halls have been provided, and sermons are delivered. Sunday schools are conducted, provided with the helps and apparatus of similar Christian schools, sometimes with a pathetic inability to put in the original touch which would make them soundly Buddhistic. Young Men's Buddhist Associations have been organized in various cities, and a periodical literature attempts to meet the intellectual needs of alert young students and the cultured men and women. They are careful students of all that is being developed in Christian countries in religious education. They are a force to be reckoned with, with an enormous following and a readiness to make almost any move to meet new situations as they arise.

There is one more sect, the Nichiren. It was founded by a remarkable man of that name in 1253. He was scandalized by the neglect which was being shown the person of the historical Gautama, and wished to reinstate him in his rightful position. The Jodo and the Shin, recently formed, had almost entirely neglected the great founder and had placed other deities in his place. But with all his enthusiasm for the person of Gautama the historical Buddha was to be conceived of mystically and not as a living, concrete personality. "The true Buddha is a greatness permeating all being, the great illumination we must find in ourselves." [7] What is to be gained by a return to the historical Buddha when he is not to be taken historically is a question. The sect has been noted in Japan for its vigorous opposition to all rival sects and other religions. It condemns Buddhist sects which preach a different doctrine almost as violently as it does Christianity. It will not appear on the same platform with any other sect but prefers to go its own noisy way, fighting here and resisting there wherever an enemy appears. But with all its misdirected zeal the movement seeks to follow the example of Nichiren, who was one of the most picturesque personages and noblest patriots Japan has ever known. Living in a time when the country was in danger of an invasion by the hordes of Kublai Khan, the Mongol emperor of China, this Buddhist monk was the prophet of preparedness and had much to do with the vigorous and successful defense which kept the invader from landing on the sacred shores. Several times he was exiled for patriotically resisting the evil counsels of men in power. His life was

[7] H. Hackmann, *Buddhism as a Religion*, p. 292.

in danger, but with singleness of purpose he went his way, seeking to lead men aright both politically and spiritually. Latterly he lived in the mountains of central Japan, in a little shelter he built for himself away from the confusion of a troubled time. The inspiration of his name is still powerful as the story of his unselfish devotion to native land is recounted in story and song.

So much for the sects, to one or another of which the people belong. They are not concerned about the philosophy of the sects; they call the priests in to officiate in times of need, and give themselves to such performances as are prescribed. When it is remembered that Buddhism is the religion of the village people, who comprise 80 per cent of the entire population, it is easy to see that it is the religion par excellence of the Japanese.

Buddhism has continued to pay a price for its militant interference in affairs of state during the Middle Ages. The Tokugawa rulers, who assumed control late in the sixteenth century and retained it until the restoration in 1868, curtailed the aggressiveness of the sects and reduced them to comparative impotence. The religion lost the hold it had on the gentry and became more exclusively what it had always been and is today, the religion of the common people of the country. In recent decades various sects followed their adherents to Korea, Manchuria, China, Canada, the United States, and even to South America, and built temples and ministered to the needs of their people. Since the end of the war in 1945, they are completely out of other Asiatic countries but retain their hold in the Western continent.

THE ADOPTION OF CONFUCIANISM

Buddhism provided a moral code with rules and regulations for the monks, and also to a certain extent for the masses of the people. But at the same time Buddhism came into Japan the teachings of Confucius also made their way from the mainland. When the Japanese mind had finished its work on the Confucianism which came from China, it was considerably altered. It was compelled to fit into the Japanese mold, and in doing so received an impress which would have caused Confucius himself to recoil strongly against it. The conditions in Japan were entirely different from those in China. Confucius based all his practical injunctions on the family. The first relation was that of father and son. But in Japan it was somewhat different. The first relation was, rather, that of ruler and subject. The state is first; loyalty, and not filial piety, is the first virtue, though filial piety is of high importance.

In China, again, peace is held in the highest esteem, and the scholar is considered the first man in the social scale. The men who produce are put first, and the scholar is a producer of the highest and finest sort. The soldier, on the other hand, is looked on as a destroyer and as such is put down to the lowest plane, beneath the farmer, the artisan, and the merchant. But in Japan the soldier always comes first. In China the emperor ruled as the Son of Heaven so long as he ruled in accordance with the principles of virtue and benevolence. He might forfeit his right to the throne and cease to be considered the Son of Heaven by unseemly conduct, provided, of course, the aggrieved people could find a leader to organize them for victory, sweep the old tyrant from the throne, and take the place himself as the accredited ruler of the people. The voice of the people was in a real sense the voice of God. Dynasty after dynasty in China was hurled from the throne by just this process. But the Japanese looked at the matter quite differently. The emperor was the Son of Heaven by right of descent from Amaterasu—such was the theory. But, more practically, he ruled by right of conquest and the power of the sword. His ancestors had won the first place in the land, and he intended to maintain the position against all comers. The imperial family must be secured on the throne at any price; peace, then, was of secondary importance and has never been looked upon as a particularly desirable thing in Japanese history. As a consequence the soldier became the first man in Japan, and underneath were ranged the farmer, the artisan, and the merchant in that order. By an interesting turn the soldier was also the scholar. The uniting of these two characters, which are separated by the whole width of the social scale in China, in one individual was one of the unique features in Japanese life in the old regime.

When the Confucian ideal was brought into contact with a condition so strange to its essential genius, the resulting "Confucianism" had a changed face. There gradually developed out of the transformation a new code which was admirably fitted to the feudalism which prevailed in Japan until 1871. In China, on the other hand, feudalism had been abolished in 221 B.C. by Shih Huang Ti. The code in Japan was called Bushido, "Bushi" meaning "warrior" and "do" being another form of the "to" or "tao," with which we have become familiar. Here it might again be translated the "way," making the whole word mean "The way of the warrior." Much has been written about this old code—"Code of

Honor," we might call it—in praise and admiration. It deserves about as much praise—and condemnation—as the old code of the gentleman of the South, with its dueling and its oversensitiveness on questions of personal honor. Its great virtue was loyalty. A man must sacrifice everything to loyalty, usually to his feudal lord. Life itself was of little value compared with firmness and steadfastness in this allegiance. It applied equally to the gentlewomen in Japan, who were taught to sacrifice everything, even their honor, if by so doing they might exhibit necessary loyalty in a time of danger or crisis. Japanese literature is full of examples of men and women who forfeited their all for the cause of their liege lord. Loyalty to parents was also included—in fact, loyalty in every relationship where it might be called into play. There was little chance for the development of individuality and a well-rounded personality; the individual counted for almost nothing.

Other sides of Bushido will throw it into bolder relief. Coupled with loyalty were hardness and stoic indifference to suffering and loss and death. Simplicity was admired in adornment and taste. Frugality in food and clothing became a rule; the Samurai came to loathe money; to him it was literally "filthy lucre." Laconic in speech, courtly in manner, reserved among friends, and dignified at all times, he led a life which had been forced into a rigid mold with little opportunity to relax and be his natural self. Never appearing in public without two swords, he was inured to the thought that at any time he might be called on to use either or both, the keen long blade on an enemy and the short dirk on himself. For in Japan suicide was raised to a virtue, if performed to escaped an ignominious death at the hands of an enemy or if no other way remained to vindicate one's honor. Is there any wonder the sword was called "The Soul of the Samurai"? Is there any wonder that Japanese are fierce fighters and that martial virtues have been held in such high esteem among them?

Such was one side of Confucianism when it had become domesticated in Japan, but there was another. The Chinese classics and the ethical system based in them were being studied with deep insight. Confucian ethics is not utilitarian. It is built on the profound conception that behind our workaday world there is another in which what we strive to attain in moral conduct is based on an immanent principle. The ethical system we seek to follow is an essential part of the eternal nature of things, and as such there is a binding quality to its obligations which no merely utilitarian system could command. This thought stirred the soul of men here and there, and a literature grew up which rooted ethics in

188

the very heart of a universe whose inner essence is righteousness. To be righteous ourselves is to express in time and under mundane conditions what the universe is expressing in the solemn majesty of its mighty processes. This sobered many a man and led him to reverence the universe of which he was a part. It became a religion for many who were not to be satisfied with the philosophy and practice of Buddhism. As might be expected, there could be no propaganda, no enthusiasm to establish a kingdom, but the calm dignity of quietism. Men lived carefully, but, more than that, they felt hushed in the presence of a world order which was the embodiment of all they admired and could respect. This high type of Confucianist theory could be the cherished possession of only a few. Yet it was and still is the inner groundwork of belief of conservative men who have not been able to ally themselves with any of the aggressive religious organizations which are seeking to win the allegiance of Japan.

Between the restoration in 1868 and the opening of World War I in 1914 Japan reached out her arms to take all she could assimilate of a civilization and culture to which she had been a complete stranger. We have no way of determining what course the old religions would have taken had Japan been left to herself any more than a would-be prophet could have predicted what would have become of Shinto just before the influences from the Continent began to flow in during the fourth or fifth century. Japan became a new nation, the first people of the East to take her place at the councils of the nations on an equal basis. So rapid was the speed of the transformation in the eighties of the last century, and so completely was she assimilating Western culture, that there were deluded optimists who predicted that Japan would soon become a Christian nation. They did not realize that with all the changes which could be seen on every side there was another movement, one of radical reaction, which was at work and would ultimately be the undoing of Japan herself.

Rabid militarists were most displeased at the growth of democratic feeling and of other liberalizing movements among the people and firmly set themselves against them. They forged the mighty power of patriotism as a foil against the Westernizing tendencies, basing this new nationalism on an old conviction which they refashioned into a powerful instrument to fit their purposes. They had ready at hand the ancient reverence for the imperial house, and this was made the touchstone of loyalty to Japan and everything Japanese. This reverence and loyalty were so built up that they became a religion, with all the deep fervor which religious devotion elicits. Dr. Basil Hall Chamberlain, who knew the Japanese as well as any man living, spoke of this movement as "the making of a new religion." It became the most living thing in the land, about all the religion many Japanese had. And it may rightly be called a religion, for was not the emperor a divine being, and was he not in direct unbroken descent from the great sun-goddess herself? Everything was made to bend to this supreme loyalty. Every student and school child in the empire was required several times each year to repair to a designated Shinto shrine and there at a given signal make a profound bow—to whom? To the emperor and his ancestors, to the spirit of Old Japan, to the loyal dead who had gone before. All of these were mingled together, as the object of their patriotic obeisance.

Was this act worship or the reverence of patriotism? The Japanese government declared that it was an act of patriotism and was not religious. But it caused serious misgiving in the minds of Christians who took the government at its word, yet knew that the exercise was performed at a Shinto shrine where immediately after the act of mass reverence was over the old worship would go on in the old way. So it went on for decades, the military party constantly strengthening its grip and leading the country into one act of aggression after another, until finally by 1942 Japan was ruling an expanse of territory from Northern Manchuria, through China, all the way to the lands of southeast Asia and far out into the island world of Indonesia and the western Pacific. Their ambition knew no bounds, and with sublime self-confidence they banked their faith on the undoubted fact that Japan had never been defeated in a war and the assumption that they could never be defeated.

Then came the disastrous end when in abject humiliation Japan surrendered unconditionally on August 14, 1945. Her defeat was complete, and without exception everyone in Japan as well as elsewhere knew that she had been crushed. The great significant event which marked a total round-about-face took place on January 1, 1946. In an official edict the Emperor Hirohito disavowed his divinity and also the claim "that the Japanese people are a race superior to other races and therefore destined to rule the world." [8] "Throughout their long history no greater change than this has ever come to the Japanese people. The Japanese state had been not merely a secular entity. It has been a sacred church as well." [9]

[8] Quoted from the edict by D. C. Holtom, *Modern Japan and Shinto Nationalism,* rev. ed., p. 220.
   [9] *Ibid.,* p. 174.

And now Japan still lies dazed and crushed, with only the beginnings of life along new lines showing themselves, and it is too soon to be able correctly to interpret their significance and to gauge their power and be sure which direction they will take.

SUGGESTIONS FOR FURTHER STUDY

Anesaki, Masaharu. *History of Japanese Religion.* London: George Routledge and Sons, Ltd., 1930. The best survey we now have.

———. *Nichiren, the Buddhist Prophet.* Cambridge, Mass.: Harvard University Press, 1916.

Braden, Charles S. *Modern Tendencies in World Religions.* New York: The Macmillan Company, 1933. Ch. 4, "Modern Tendencies in Japanese Religions."

Eliot, Charles N. E. *Japanese Buddhism.* New York: Longmans, Green and Company, 1935. The most complete discussion in English; to be sought in libraries.

Holtom, D. C. *Modern Japan and Shinto Nationalism.* Rev. ed. Chicago: University of Chicago Press, 1947.

———. *The National Faith of Japan.* New York: E. P. Dutton and Company, Inc., 1938. An authoritative study of Shinto.

Reischauer, Edwin O. *Japan, Past and Present.* New York: 1946.

Suzuki, D. T. *Essays in Zen Buddhism.* New ed. of first series. 1949.

———. *An Introduction to Zen Buddhism.* Boston: Marshall Jones Company, 1934.

Watt, Alan. *The Spirit of Zen.* Wisdom of the East Series. London: 1938.

CHAPTER X

JUDAISM

The Heritage of the Old Testament

THE PEOPLE WHOM WE KNOW AS THE HEBREWS, OR ISRAELITES, BECAME a separate people during the period following the exodus from Egypt, which probably occurred during the thirteenth century B.C. On this "birthday of the nation" a number of Semitic tribes who had been in Egypt for many years and had there suffered severe hardships escaped and began to make their way toward their future home in Palestine. They were under the guidance of a leader named Moses, who proved to be one of the world's greatest heroes and nation builders. He led them to a mountain in the wilderness in or near the peninsula of Sinai, where, not many months before, he had come to know the name of a wonderful God, who appeared to him "in a flame of fire out of the midst of a bush" (Exod. 3:2), and who called him to go back and lead out his people from Egypt. This God had undoubtedly been known before, else the people would not have received him, but the account in Exodus would indicate that he appeared as a new revelation to Moses and to the Israelites when they sojourned in the region of Sinai. This God Yahweh, or Jehovah, as we have incorrectly transliterated it, seems to have been a God closely connected with the mountain near which Moses kept the sheep of his father-in-law Jethro. He manifested himself in thunder and lightning and storm, a "God of battles," who fought for his people and led them on to victory. True, this is not the conception we get of Yahweh in the prophets and the psalmists of a later age, but it is necessary to remember that it was by gradual stages and only after a long development that the idea of God became what we see it in Jeremiah and Isaiah. Yahweh was to these early tribesmen the divine Being who had his residence in the sacred mountain and who was to become their special protector as opposed to the divinities of other peoples.

The relation between this God and his people was based on a covenant, or agreement. This covenant was not founded on blood relationship, as though Yahweh was bound to them by the indissoluble bonds of kinship. The covenant was a mutual agreement or contract in which each side assumed certain obligations which it was bound to carry out so long as the other party to the contract remained true and loyal. And when it is remembered that this agreement was morally conditioned, its uniqueness and greatness become evident. The conditions laid down, which the people of Israel were bound to recognize and obey, demanded of them rigid adherence to moral principle. Here lay the possibility of the moral and spiritual advance which marks Judaism as the religion of which more could be expected than of all the other religions of the ancient world. This covenant was interpreted in ethical terms more and more as the centuries passed, until Jeremiah could affirm that the covenant was no longer to be considered as an outer law written on "tables of stone," but as an inner law, a spiritual principle, written in the hearts of men. But in the early day everything was crude and materialistic. The presence of Yahweh was assured by the outward symbol of the Ark of the Covenant, which was taken from place to place, which went before them into battle, and which must be protected on pain of losing the divine help and presence.

When after many years these people with their desert training came into the land of promise, they ran the danger of fusion with the peoples already in the country and losing the distinctiveness of their covenant relation with Yahweh. The book of Judges shows how great this peril was. They had been nomads living a wandering life in the open and free desert; now they began to accustom themselves to the more settled life of agriculture, and this meant a change in all their habits and ways of looking at things. And since they were learning so much from the Canaanites among whom they settled, was it not to be expected that they might also absorb much of their religion? It was a real danger, seen in its true light when we know the kind of religion it was, with licentious-ness and cruelty practiced in the very places of worship. This danger remained a menace through hundreds of years, as is clearly seen in the writings of the prophets, who were called upon time and again to resist the encroachments of these morally enervating practices. During this long period Yahweh was looked upon as the "Lord" of their land, but the gods of other peoples and lands were recognized as having their territory and people too. An incident is recorded of David, when he reasons with Saul, urging him not to drive him out of the land of Yahweh, on the ground that such an act on Saul's part would virtually mean that David must go out of the territory of Yahweh and "serve other gods" (I Samuel 26:17-19).

The religion of Moses was saved from the threatened absorption by the judges and the guilds or "schools" of prophets, bands of patriotic men who kept alive in the people their loyalty to the God who had been with them and delivered them in times past. Wandering bands of men, working themselves on occasion into an ecstatic state, as the narrative in Samuel indicates, they accomplished their purpose and must be judged by this achievement rather than by our judgment as to what a prophet or spiritual leader ought to be. The founding of the monarchy under Saul and its extension under David and Solomon gave material assistance in the same direction. But even then the worship was crude and not without contaminating features, being conducted in many shrines at the old centers of Canaanitish worship and containing elements which were only gradually set aside as the spiritual perceptions of the people became sharpened. This took place under the inspiration of prophetic leaders who began to appear even before the division of the kingdoms and who in the end ushered in a new era of religious history.

Elijah stands out as one of the great commanding figures in the history of religion. In his time in a marked degree the danger of serious contamination by contact with the Baal worship of the Phoenicians menaced the people and their religion, and Elijah suddenly appeared as the heroic patriot who was not afraid to use the most drastic measures to prevent the threatened corruption. He was fearless in the presence of both Ahab and his Sidonian queen Jezebel. He was a man of action, adding little or nothing to the religious conceptions of his people, but there is no more stirring recital in the history of religion than when this dauntless champion of Yahweh won a complete victory over the howling, desperate priests of Baal. He performed a most necessary task, but there was much left to be done by other and very different men. The prophets who appeared first in the eighth century took the ideas of religion already in the possession of the Hebrew people and refashioned them into the sublime faith which was worthy to be the foundation of the teaching of our Lord and the writers of the New Testament. When Amos came into the city of Bethel and proclaimed the judgment of the God of Israel on all the nations round about, and on Israel and Judah as well, a new day had dawned. True monotheism, founded on God's right to judge all peoples on the basis of a single moral standard, began to come to its own and, in

194

the hands of Jeremiah and Isaiah and the gifted though unknown "Evangelist of the Exile," received a statement so complete and so sublime that ever after and to this day men have been compelled to go back to these inspired utterances to drink in the full meaning of the unity of God and his ethical character. This is the great gift of the Jewish people to the religious life of the world, a permanent possession which can never be superseded. This is the priceless heritage of the Old Testament which has influenced the whole subsequent religious development of the human race, wherever it has been made known.

The messianic hope, the universalism of the prophets, the development of the Law, the spiritual experience of the psalmists, the wisdom of the wise men, the apocalyptic vision—these and other features of the Old Testament revelation have not been and cannot be treated here. All that has been attempted is to trace, and with extreme brevity, the development of the central message, the supreme gift of the Old Testament to the progress of religion in the world. The belief in one God who hates sin and loves righteousness, a belief which the Jew has never been tempted to forget since the days of the Babylonian exile, is the indispensable foundation on which any faith which claims to be universal must be built.

JUDAISM SINCE THE TIME OF CHRIST

Since the days of the Babylonian Captivity the Jews have been a scattered people. During the period of the Maccabees (beginning 175 B.C.) they formed a short-lived independent state with Jerusalem as their capital, a state which was soon incorporated in the Roman empire. Subsequent revolts in A.D. 70 and 132 not only failed but resulted in the destruction of Jerusalem and the driving of the Jews out of their homeland to the ends of the then known world, and now in our day the Jewish people have again established themselves in Palestine and are laying claim to Jerusalem as their city by right of long possession in ancient days and their presence in the city now. It would seem that the state of Israel has real prospects of permanence. It has attracted devoted Jews from all over the world, though it has offered little inducement to prosperous Jewish people in America and England.

Their history has been a sad one. Success has attended their commercial ventures, but unfortunately they have been the prey all too often of avaricious princes and kings. Disliked by almost all the peoples among whom they have settled, they were driven off by themselves into ghettos, where for hundreds of years they lived a life apart. Not satisfied by such treatment, the populace and their leaders have frequently vented their rage in bloody persecution, and frequently this has been done by those who profess the Christian name. The enmity between Jew and Christian dates back to the first century and has continued unabated through the Middle Ages and into modern times. In the days of their weakness the Christians were the ones to suffer at the hands of the Jews or at their instigation, but the tables were soon turned, and the growth of Christianity and its assumption of power boded ill for the Jew. This enmity has continued to our own time. Until a few years ago it was thought that the persecution of the Jew had come to an end, except in Eastern Europe and particularly in Russia, where the hatred seemed not to be relaxed and where at any time bloody pogroms might be expected.

But alas, even in Central Europe the old antipathy broke out afresh. Under the lead of Adolf Hitler the pent-up hatred toward the Jewish race vented itself in the most horrible and abominable persecution known in human history. A few fortunate Jews escaped and became refugees in other parts of the world. The greater number, however, were put to death in the most terrible manner in both Germany and Poland. As a result of these mass murders the Jewish people, who at the beginning of World War II numbered about sixteen million, were reduced to an estimated ten million, five million of whom are in the United States, with more than two million in New York City alone, thus making it the largest Jewish community in the world.

It was exceedingly unfortunate that for so many centuries the Jew should have been compelled to live with little intercourse with the Gentile world. Not only was the European intolerant; the Jew was clannish and narrow; he preferred to live his life alone. But since the liberating days of the French Revolution, Jews have broken through their isolation and begun to share the life of the people around them. Thanks to one of their greatest leaders, Moses Mendelssohn (1729-86), the Jewish people were led to see that their future must lie in sharing the common life of the people in the midst of whom they live. During all the years of their isolation they had preserved a vigorous intellectual life, but it was closely concerned with their own circle of interests, their history, their Law, and their religion, but now a change took place. Entering the universities and feeling the force of the intellectual currents of the time, the Jew became a citizen of the world. His brilliant gifts, which had been but slightly known and appreciated, began to be manifest, and after no long period he appeared in positions of leadership in varied forms of activity.

He took his place by the side of his fellow citizens in every walk of life. He is distinct from but one with his neighbors in nationality. With unparalleled tenacity he has clung to his distinctiveness, and has done so because it it bound up so closely with his religion, which to him would be lost if he did not preserve his uniqueness as a people.

The loss of nationality and the destruction of the Temple and the sacrificial system by the Romans caused a profound change in the Jewish religion. Other means had to be found to maintain the unity of the people and preserve their religious life. Deep in their breasts was the belief in the one God of Israel; they could no longer be alienated from him. In their hands was the Old Testament, the Torah, or Law, which became the more precious as they were scattered far and wide and needed the support of a divine revelation. Common worship on the holy Sabbath day was possible through the recurring feasts which bound them together and the institution of the synagogue, which had become a part of their life during the exile in Babylon, where they were deprived of the ministries of the Temple. Not only so, but the people of Israel, wherever they found themselves, felt certain that their old covenant with Jehovah held good and would last forever.

Judaism has always been a religion of law and remains such today. It is easy to misinterpret the term and accuse the Jew of being a narrow legalist. That this danger has not been averted is freely acknowledged by leading Jewish scholars, but to use it as a term of reproach and as the chief characteristic of the religion would be unjust. As in the Old Testament period and at the time of Christ Jewish men and women had penetrated behind the form to its inner spiritual principle, so down through the ages the spiritually-minded have found God and have been nourished, not on the dry husks of legal formalism, but on the living manna which has come down from heaven. But when we have said this, the fact remains that to be a Jew has always meant and means today the keeping of the Law. Obedience to a written code has been the mark of the religion. Everything in conduct, even down to seemingly insignificant details, was determined exactly, and to fail in the observance of the written word was unthinkable in a well-regulated Jewish household.

The most prized possession of Judaism is the Old Testament Scriptures. These are divided into three parts: (a) the Law or Torah, the first five books of the Bible; (b) the Prophets, which include the historical books as well as those we commonly think of as prophetic; (c) the Writings, comprizing the remaining books of the Old Testament and including Daniel, Ezra, Nehemiah, and the Chronicles. Of these three parts the most important is the first, the Law, which becomes "the real foundation of the Jewish religion." Here was God's voice speaking his message in a form never to be superseded.

But the sacred Scriptures needed interpretation for practical and homiletic purposes, and this was done in a long series of expositions accumulating through many centuries. It finally assumed a written form in the Talmud, which is the great codification of Jewish law, civil and religious. The Talmud exists in two recensions, the Palestinian and the Babylonian, the latter being later in time and by far the longer of the two. It was completed about A.D. 500. This great body of law is the mine from which Jewish scholars in all subsequent ages have found the precious truths and traditions on which the people have been nourished. Based on the accumulated stores to be found in the Talmud, collections of laws have been formulated.[1] Among them is that of the great Spanish rabbi, Maimonides (1135-1204), who in 1180 produced a code of law and custom called the "Strong Hand," which has been very influential among the Jews to the present time. Most Jews today, however, live under the "Table Prepared," which was compiled by Joseph Caro in the sixteenth century and is a résumé of the whole traditional Law. But with all that has been done to revivify the Law and make it appear as a living expression of the will of God, the great problem is to make it an abiding force in the advancing Jewish community today. There is revolt, especially in Western lands, against the binding character of the multitudinous rules and regulations, which not only touch on the fundamental moral obligations, but cover an immense range of ceremonial observances and customs. These have become exceedingly irksome to the more or less emancipated Jew in the Western world, who does not want to be marked off from his fellow citizens by obsolete and meaningless practices.

Judaism may be said to have no definite articles of belief. A man's actions and conduct are most carefully regulated, but his beliefs are without any authoritative ecclesiastical sanction. This has led to laxity in belief along with great strictness in conduct. Dogmatic tests could not be applied, and few have been excommunicated for heresy. Notwithstanding this, attempts frequently have been made to formulate the beliefs of Judaism, but never have they been successful. Mendelssohn

---

[1] For a discussion of this literature see Oesterley and Box, *The Religion and Worship of the Synagogue*, 2nd. ed., Chaps. III-V.

used his influence to discourage anyone from any further ventures in this direction. To him religion was life and not creed, and could not be compressed within the bounds of a formula.

But Judaism has believed and believed with great earnestness in a few great doctrines. First and transcending all others is the unalterable belief in one God, high and lifted up, the Creator and Sustainer of the universe, who at the same time is a Father brooding over his children with tender love. He is the God of justice and truth who will brook no lowering of the moral standard, and who will one day judge the world in righteousness. A list of thirteen articles of faith was constructed by Maimonides, "the one and only set of principles which have ever enjoyed wide authority in Judaism." [2]

These are: (i) belief in the existence of God, the Creator; (ii) belief in the unity of God; (iii) belief in the incorporeality of God; (iv) belief in the priority and eternity of God; (v) belief that to God, and God alone, worship must be offered; (vi) belief in prophecy; (vii) belief that Moses was the greatest of all prophets; (viii) belief that the Law was revealed from heaven; (ix) belief that the Law will never be abrogated, and that no other Law will ever come from God; (x) belief that God knows the works of men; (xi) belief in reward and punishment; (xii) belief in the coming of the Messiah; (xiii) belief in the resurrection of the dead.

Maimonides was deeply influenced, as were many thinkers in the Middle Ages, by Aristotle. He believed in the revelation to be found in the Old Testament, but sought to show that the truths of revelation were in harmony with reason and could be thoroughly rationalized.

Down through Jewish history have come these two streams of law and creed, one stringent and the other lax, but there have been other tendencies. The Cabala was a revolt against the intellectualism of the schools. It was a system of occult knowledge and mysticism which exercised a strange fascination over many minds in both Judaism and Christianity. By uniting man and the divine Spirit through the practice of virtue and the overcoming of evil, preparation would be made for the coming of the Messiah, who will restore all things. But here too there was excess in emotion and in mystical vagaries, and the inevitable reaction came. It was not really Judaism at all, despite its influence on many Jews. A new intellectualism arose with vigorous advocates. The

[2] Israel Abrahams, *Judaism*, pp. 31-32.

limit was reached by the famous philosopher Baruch Spinoza (born 1632), who, depending on pure thought, reduced the whole system of the universe to a thoroughgoing pantheism. He was excommunicated from the synagogue in Amsterdam for his heresy.

With all these currents streaming through its life Judaism emerged into the activities of the modern world. A new era opened out before the Jew which has profoundly affected the religious life and thought of the people.

ORTHODOXY AND REFORM

When Judaism came into intimate contact with modern thought, a crisis was inevitable. There were those who sought to keep their religion true to the traditions of the past and were scandalized by the thought of change. They have continued down to our own time and form a very considerable part of the people. But even among these conservatives the modern world has had its effect, and all degrees of modification of the old standards can be discovered. On the other hand there is the Reform school composed of liberals who believe that the only hope of the race and the religion is to admit frankly that changes more or less drastic must be introduced and that Judaism must accept the obligation to reinterpret itself in the light of modern knowledge. It is admitted on both sides that the differences do not constitute a schism but may best be denominated as "schools." In the words of the late Dr. Solomon Schechter, a leader of the conservative wing, each party might look upon the other as "His Majesty's Opposition" [3] in one great parliament of Judaism.

There is complete agreement in both parties on certain fundamental points. The primary and inalienable doctrine of the faith is the unity of God, and, of course, there is not the slightest hesitation here. Judaism stands or falls on the platform of monotheism. So sure is she of her ground that leaders make bold to claim that her two "daughter" religions, Christianity and Islam, have each done despite to this central doctrine. Christianity, they declare, has ceased to believe in the essential unity of God by its doctrine of the Trinity, and Islam has played fast and loose with the moral ideals of both Judaism and Christianity, even though it has been an unswerving witness to the one God as an indivisible unity. Another point of agreement is the unshakable conviction that the Jewish

[3] *Seminary Addresses and Other Papers*, p. 239.

people are the Chosen Race. The ancient call of God to Abraham and his descendants in biblical times holds good and is a cardinal point of emphasis today. The race must be preserved intact and all intermarriage with Gentiles severely condemned. And when it comes to the acceptance by any member of the race of the claims of Christianity, the anathemas which are heaped upon the heads of these "perverts" are the bitterest of all the invectives of which the Jew is capable. But with all this agreement the conservative is not quite convinced that the liberal has not let down the bars to such an extent that fusion with the surrounding community may ultimately result and the Jews as a distinct people may cease to exist.

Since the days of the Babylonian exile, when the unknown prophet gave expression to the splendid universalism of the latter part of the book of Isaiah, that note has not been lacking in Judaism. True, a narrow particularism has more often been victorious than the more liberal, wider view, but it has been there nevertheless. At the time of Christ the schools of Hillel and of Shammai were in conflict, the former standing for the broad and generous policy which furthered the winning of proselytes, the latter being narrow and exclusive, and opposing all efforts to reach out after others. The school of Shammai was finally victorious, and with the loss of nationality the Jew has not sought to win converts to his religion.

This condition has obtained down through the centuries, and even today, when a different outlook has become the ideal of the more liberal Jews, no missionary propaganda is contemplated. Still the universal note is being sounded, and the mission of Israel to the nations is earnestly acclaimed. The form taken by this ideal differs among the Orthodox and the Reform Jews. Holding fast the prophetic vision of a coming Messiah who shall be born of their race and be established in power and righteousness in Jerusalem, the men of orthodox faith see all nations coming to do him honor and acknowledging his rightful sway over the world. They shall all worship the one God and spread his name far and wide until his knowledge shall cover the earth as the waters cover the sea. But in it all the Jew remains distinct and stands first, the chosen of God, his messenger peculiarly fitted to do his bidding and accomplish his desires. Such is the hope and expectation of the more conservative wing of Judaism.

The Reform Jews, on the other hand, have a different ideal. Universalism is far more prominent as an immediate possibility than among

201

the orthodox. According to several declarations of conferences of American liberal rabbis, "The Messianic aim of Israel is not the restoration of the old Jewish state under a descendant of David, involving a second separation from the nations of the earth, but the union of all children of God in the confession of the unity of God, so as to realize the unity of all rational creatures and their call to moral sanctification." [4] And again, "The Messianic idea now means to many Jews a belief in human development and progress, with the Jews filling the role of the Messianic people, but only as *primus inter pares*." [5]

Fear is expressed on the part of the conservatives that their liberal brethren are breaking down the wall of partition between Jew and Gentile. It is possible now for one who belongs to another race to ask for admission to a Reform synagogue and be received. This to a conservative is rank heresy. Their fundamental beliefs may be the same, but these strange notions are sure to wreck the hopes of the children of Israel. But even the most liberal are strongly of the opinion that since monotheism has not yet prevailed and Christianity has not succeeded in keeping the doctrine unsullied, their witness is essential to the religious development of the world, and that this can best be accomplished by the preservation of a separate and distinct people living among others but not of them through marriage and group amalgamation.

In the matter of the ceremonial law and the historic festivals there is also a deep cleavage. In different degrees the orthodox hold fast the ancient traditions and with reluctance allow modifications to be introduced. The Reform Jew, on the other hand, takes the position that ceremonies must prove their value under the conditions which now prevail; that they must not be retained merely because they have come down out of the past and have historical sanction. In fact, he takes everything in Judaism—law, creed, ceremony, and custom—and subjects it to a searching criticism. He desires his religion to be relevant to the present day, and is willing to lay aside any item which may seem to him an encumbrance. The pragmatic test is applied with vigor; that which cannot be shown to be of practical service in the modern situation must be discarded. What is happening before our eyes is inevitable, but we may be sure that with all its transmutations Judaism will long remain a religion among the religions of the world. With their belief in one God, a God of moral concern, whose influence has pervaded every relationship,

[4] Abrahams, *op. cit.*, pp. 93-94.
[5] *Ibid.*

given sanctity to the home and dignity to the individual life, a belief which has made prayer and praise a constant practice of the people and has held them together through appalling experiences which might have shattered a spirit less tenacious, the Jews are with us today believing in themselves and in their destiny. Not accepting the idea of a mediator between God and men, and rejecting the claims of that Man of Jewish race who might have led his people into a fulfillment of their highest ideals, they have been kept apart from a fellowship which might have brought in the era of peace among the nations generations or even centuries ago. What the future has in store we cannot say, but trusting in the same God and reading the same Scriptures of the Old Testament, the Christian cannot help believing that the revelation of that God which is contained in those writings may yet assume to the Jew a new glory when seen in the face of Jesus Christ His Son.

Suggestions for Further Study

Abrahams, Israel. *Judaism.* Chicago: Open Court Publishing House, 1907. A splendid little summary of the entire development.

Cohen, A. *Everyman's Talmud.* New American ed. New York: E. P. Dutton and Company, 1950.

Joseph, Morris. *Judaism as Creed and Life.* 5th ed. London: 1925. A statement of the faith by one who would be a mediator between extreme schools.

Moore, George Foot. *Judaism in the First Centuries of the Christian Era.* 2 vols. Cambridge, Mass.: Harvard University Press, 1927. An authoritative work by a master.

Oesterley, W. O. E., and Box, G. H. *The Religion and Worship of the Synagogue.* 2nd and rev. ed. London: 1911. A very important work, almost encyclopedic in scope.

Oesterley, W. O. E., and Robinson, T. H. *Hebrew Religion, Its Origin and Development,* 2nd, rev., and enlarged ed. New York: The Macmillan Company, 1937. Most valuable for the period of the Old Testament.

CHAPTER XI

MOHAMMEDANISM

The Prophet

Islam,[1] the religion of Mohammed, arose in Arabia, the followers of the prophet fondly believe that their religion is a new creation, handed down bodily and in finished form from heaven. But even a rapid survey of the origins of the faith is sufficient to show that, with all Mohammed added, the religion was firmly rooted in the past and received a number of its characteristic features from the pre-existing heathenism of Arabia. The isolation and inaccessibility of the peninsula provided the conditions in which a development could take place hidden from the rest of the world until it was ready to start on its victorious march almost to the ends of the earth.

Wellhausen speaks of the old gods of Arabia as a "rubbish heap of the divine names"; that is, paganism was in a state of decrepitude. There were many of these deities, the most prominent of which was Allah. He was regarded as "the God," the supreme being, having three daughters, the significance of which will appear later. Mohammed did not invent his Supreme Being; he clarified the conception and rid God of "partners," but the monotheistic idea was not new to Arabia when the prophet arose. Mecca was already a sacred city, the most sacred in the land, with the cubical building, the Kaaba, the center of worship. Near by was the holy well Zemzem, from which all pilgrims still drink. The whole ritual of worship which is now followed was already in existence and was taken over complete into his religion by Mohammed. Islam was not a bolt out of the blue but an adaptation of much that was old, thinly disguised, and still persisting.

Mohammed, "the Praised," was born in Mecca, the posthumous son

---

[1] "Islam" means "to submit," and is the religion of submission to the will of Allah. "Muslim," "one who has submitted," is the name frequently used of the followers of Mohammed. Differing spellings of the name of the prophet, his religion, sacred book, and other names need not concern us in this volume.

of Abdallah, of the tribe of the Koraish. When was he born? The traditional date is A.D. 570, and in the absence of agreement on the part of scholars, some of whom give an earlier and some a later date, we may accept it, of course, tentatively. His mother died when he was a little lad, and he was given a home first by his grandfather and then by his uncle Abu Talib. As a young child he was sent by his mother to be nursed and cared for by a Bedouin woman in the desert. Mecca was not a place where children could be expected to thrive physically, so she was following a well-known custom. His mother's death, which probably occurred shortly after his return, made a deep impression on the boy. He never forgot that his mother had been left a widow and he an orphan. Throughout his life Mohammed was always solicitous that widows and orphans should be cared for, and it has left an abiding mark on the religion which he founded. As a boy he doubtless tended his uncle's sheep. As he grew older, he must have joined the caravans, which, with the entertainment of the pilgrims at the time of the feasts, were the source of Mecca's wealth. It is quite certain that he made at least one trip to the borders of southern Palestine. This period of his life is so obscure that few statements can be made with confidence. He seems to have been well thought of, earning the name of Al Amin, the "Trusty," by some service faithfully rendered or by his habitual trustworthiness.

At about the age of twenty-five a most important event took place. A distant relative of his, the wealthy widow Khadijah, was looking for some person to take charge of her business affairs on one of the great caravan journeys on which she as a woman could not go. Her attention was directed to her kinsman Mohammed, and the arrangement was made. He not only performed the service to her great satisfaction but was so pleasing to her in person and manner that she offered him her hand. He accepted and they were married, Mohammed a young man of twenty-five and she his senior by fifteen years. Yet with all the difference in age these two lived happily together until her death twenty-five years after. He never forgot her and always mentioned her with gratitude and respect to the end of his life. She must have been a remarkable woman. During the long period of their married life Mohammed did not take another wife. Several daughters were born of the union, only one of whom outlived him, the celebrated Fatima, who became the wife of Ali, one of the earliest of Mohammed's followers and famous in the early history of Islam.

Mohammed's marriage to Khadijah changed the whole course of his life. He had been a poor young man, but now, married to a wealthy woman, he had leisure. Naturally of a pensive disposition, he could give full rein to his inclination with no anxiety concerning his daily bread. What took place during the next fifteen years we have little means of knowing. He must have brooded long and earnestly over the moral tragedy of the universe and the issues of human life. Other men in Arabia at this time had become dissatisfied with the old paganism. We have some hazy knowledge of these seekers after truth, Hanifs, as they were called. They were seeking to find a pure religion and had a strong drawing toward monotheism. Eventually these men became either Christian or Muslim. But what influence they exercised on Mohammed must have been slight. The Christianity with which he might have come into contact was unfortunately so covered over with formalism and so lacking in vitality that there was little chance of his being drawn in that direction.

In A.D. 610, so it is said, while Mohammed with his family was sojourning on Mount Hira, near Mecca, during the most trying season of the year, he had an experience which made him into a different man. He thought he heard a heavenly voice commanding him to convey a message. We may have a reminiscence of this experience in the ninety-sixth sura or chapter of the Koran:

> Recite thou, in the name of thy Lord who created;—
> Created man from Clots of Blood:—
> Recite thou! For thy Lord is the most Beneficent,
> Who hath taught the use of the pen;—
> Hath taught man that which he knoweth not.[2]

Doubtless the Meccans had recently learned how to read and write, and it was considered an evidence of divine favor. God was almighty; he had created man from "clots of blood," which was their way of saying that God had created man out of some very insignificant thing. The climax of the revelation was that Mohammed was to proclaim a message—"Recite thou." The participle of this verb is "Koran," "that which is recited," and appropriately becomes the name of the sacred book of the religion. It is literally the collection of inspired utterances of the prophet which he was to recite to the people.

Mohammed was deeply agitated by his experience. He could not be sure of himself and was in doubt about the reality of the call. He waited

[2] Rodwell translation.

206

for another revelation to confirm the trustworthiness of the first, but it did not come. Khadijah comforted him with the assurance that God had really spoken to him and would do so again if only he would have patience. But still there was no voice, and he was driven almost to desperation. He is said to have attempted to make away with his life by throwing himself to sure death over one of the precipices which abound on Mount Hira, but his good angel Khadijah interposed and kept him from carrying out his purpose. At last another revelation came. Again it is thought that we have a clear echo of what came to him at that time in the seventy-fourth sura of the Koran:

> O thou, enwrapped in thy mantle!
> Arise and warn!
> Thy Lord—magnify Him!
> Thy Raiment—purify it!
> The abomination—flee it!
> And bestow not favors that thou mayest receive again with increase;
> And for thy Lord wait thou patiently.
> For when there shall be a trump on the trumpet,
> That shall be a distressful day.
> A day, to the Infidels, devoid of ease.[3]

What we may be sure of is that gradually, through a period, long or short we do not know, Mohammed arrived at the conviction that he was the mouthpiece of Allah. Once having reached that conclusion, the prophet never doubted that he was in immediate contact with God. Revelations were forthcoming whenever circumstances called for an authoritative word. He now had a divine commission to "arise and warn," to preach the message of God whether men were pleased with it or not, to herald the coming of the Day of Judgment, when unbelievers would find themselves in dire distress.

But why that strange phrase, "O thou, enwrapped in thy mantle"? There is much obscurity relative to the physical accompaniments of the revelations. They came to him in various forms and under different conditions. Here it seems to have been while he was closely blanketed. Was it during a seizure, say of epilepsy or a kindred malady? There are many who find evidence that Mohammed was subject to such attacks, and they say that this accounts for many things which otherwise would have no

---

[3] *Ibid.*

explanation. They think of Mohammed as a "pathological case";[4] they think that he was not quite normal physically and mentally, and that the enigma of his character and personality is to be solved partly on that supposition. On the other hand it is just as confidently asserted that the prophet was a perfectly normal human being, deeply sensitive to suggestions which came to him from what he felt assured was the spiritual world, but none the less normal for that.[5]

If the so-called second revelation came in the year 612, the remainder of his life falls into two periods of ten years each, the first of which was spent in Mecca, the latter in Medina. Mohammed immediately began to preach to his friends in Mecca. The burden of his message was that there was but one God, Allah, that he would not tolerate the worship of any other gods ("adding partners to God" was the phrase used), that idolatry was an abomination, and that a Day of Judgment was coming when all those who refused to hearken would be hurled into the raging fire of Hell. Not many listened to him. Khadijah became his first convert. She was followed by a few others of the best people in Mecca. There were Abu Bakr, Ali, and finally Omar, all of whom became Caliphs or "successors" of the prophet. But aside from these and a few others the Meccans turned a deaf ear to his warnings. A small group of slaves and lowly people accepted his leadership, and these, because they had no standing in the community, were made the butt of ridicule and abuse. It was carried to such an extent that with Mohammed's consent they left the country and found a refuge in the Christian kingdom of Abyssinia across the Red Sea. Once they came back on hearing that a better feeling existed between the prophet and the citizens of Mecca, but it was so short-lived that they hastened back to their exile.

This better feeling was occasioned by a temporary willingness on the part of Mohammed to recognize that the "daughters" of Allah, believed in from of old by the Meccans, might be considered as "intercessors" between men and Allah. The Meccans thought they had gained a point and were willing now to listen to the preaching of their fellow townsman. He repented, however, of his weakness almost at once and withdrew the concession entirely. This made the Meccans all the more bitter, and the breach between Mohammed and them widened. It came to such a pass that a ban was proclaimed against Mohammed and his people. They were ostracized and lived precariously and more or less alone. This period

[4] D. B. Macdonald, *Aspects of Islam*, p. 60.
[5] Tor Andrae, *Mohammed, the Man and His Faith*, pp. 67-68.

lasted, it may be, for two years. The climax was reached for Mohammed in the year 620 with the death of his faithful companion Khadijah and of his protector Abu Talib. His uncle had never embraced Islam, but stood by his protégé until the end. No one could lay hands on Mohammed while Abu Talib lived. So it was a serious matter when Mohammed lost the protection of his powerful uncle. But even more serious was the loss of his wife. She had been his balance wheel for many years. Her wisdom and judgment, coupled with her devotion, undoubtedly had saved many a difficult situation. Now she was gone, and Mohammed was never quite the same again.

The question of the sincerity of the Prophet of Islam has been a difficult problem—for others than Muslims. The evidence up to this point does not justify an adverse judgment. It would be impossible to explain the calm assurance of Mohammed on any other basis than that of complete sincerity. The early utterances in the Koran have the ring of genuineness. To call him the "False Prophet," as has so often been done, cannot be justified, especially in the early period in Mecca. He preached his doctrine unhesitatingly despite the opposition of the Meccans. Political expediency would have dictated a different course. The compromise with the Meccans was a momentary weakness. His deliberate judgment is to be seen in his return to his former position, from which he never deviated afterward. He chose the unpopular way whether it brought him success or not. The problem becomes more complicated, however, as we follow him from Mecca to Medina. Professor Tor Andrae finds it "difficult to think of the lengthy and often quite sober and prosaic decrees of the last years at Medina as the product of genuine and immediate inspiration." [6] and yet the same claim is made for these utterances as for those which came earlier.

The prophet had come to realize that Mecca offered him no field; he must go elsewhere if he was to secure the favorable hearing he desired. He began to look around. He went to Taif, not many miles away, to try out his message, but was stoned out of the city. But about this time he discovered that two Arab tribes in Medina which had for many years been in a jealous contest for supremacy were now anxious to compose their differences under a common leader. This was a splendid opportunity, and Mohammed seized it. Medina was the city from which his mother had come, and he was not unfamiliar with its problems. It took some time to make such arrangements as would be acceptable to all

[6] *Ibid.*, p. 69.

parties, so it was not until the year 622 that the transfer was made. In the middle of that year, after his followers had slipped away in little groups, the prophet and Abu Bakr left Mecca secretly and made their way by a roundabout route to Medina, two hundred or more miles to the north. This "Flight," or Hegira, marks the year 1 A.H. (Anno Hegirae) in Mohammedan chronology, or A.D. 622. It is a date of which we can be certain. Mohammed settled down and made Medina his home until his death in 632.

While in Mecca, Mohammed had been a preacher of righteousness, a "warner" of the wrath to come. He stood as a prophet of God much as the Old Testament prophets, whose successor he felt himself to be. Now in Medina it was different. He was a civil ruler, a potentate, with administrative problems on his hands and with a position to maintain against his enemies. He became perforce a soldier, making war and resisting attack—a very different role all around from that in Mecca. And the difference within would seem to have been as great as that of the outward circumstances.

For these ten years Mohammed led a strenuous life, which it is impossible here to follow in detail. He began as the ruler of Medina with the very doubtful allegiance of a few surrounding tribesmen; he ended his career as the recognized ruler of all Arabia. Mecca had been captured with no bloodshed, the people opening the gates of the city and receiving their old townsman with open arms. The sweep was complete. But it had not been accomplished without opposition and bloody contests. Mohammed gave himself to practices—breaking the sacred months of truce, assassination of personal enemies, raiding the caravans of the Meccans— which may have been necessary in order to secure the mastery of Arabia, but which are hard to defend when they are the deeds of one who is a preacher of righteousness and who claims to be voicing the inner counsels of God. The battle was not always in favor of Mohammed, but steadily and persistently he followed his course, whether circumstances were for him or against him and by fair means or foul, until he had attained his ambition. It is claimed by some that with Arabia at his feet he looked out on new worlds to conquer, and the great campaigns which were carried on after his death are said to have been born in the mind of Mohammed himself.

When the prophet went to Medina, three tribes of Jews occupied a special section of the area which made up the larger community or settlement. They thought Mohammed might accept their faith because he claimed that he was restoring the true religion of Abraham. Mohammed on his side thought the Jews would accept him as one of their prophets and receive his message as a divine revelation. Both were soon to be disappointed. For one cause or another Mohammed took aggressive action against the Jews. Their tragic fate is one of the darkest blots on the reputation of the prophet. Two of the tribes were sent into exile, and the third suffered a more terrible fate. Under circumstances which do little to mitigate the horror the women and children were sold into slavery, and the men—six or eight hundred of them, according to early accounts—were butchered in cold blood. The prophet of God gave his sanction to this unbelievable cruelty with no compunctions and with no diminution of his claim to be the obedient servant of the God of justice and mercy!

Whatever may have been in his mind before the death of Khadijah, Mohammed took no second wife while she lived. But when she died, he soon married again and continued to increase his family until he had twelve or thirteen wives, not counting slave girls, in his harem. Whatever we may think of polygamy, such conduct on the part of the prophet did not affect his followers. They simply took it for granted as an accepted institution. But the conditions under which he took several of his wives were such as to make it impossible for us to doubt that Mohammed was displaying sure signs of being a sensualist. In one case, when he married the wife of his adopted son Zeid, who divorced her that she might become the wife of the prophet, even his followers were scandalized, and only the prompt arrival of a revelation from Allah saved his face and made it right for him to do as he had done. Only by such a terrible expedient did he cover the all-to-controlling passion which lay so near the surface of his life. The prophet was very jealous; he feared that others might be enamored of his wives, and this has been said to be the real motive which led to the seclusion of women. Again we are on dangerous and uncertain ground. We know that wherever Islam has gone women have suffered by being secluded from social relations with men other than closest relatives. How much Mohammed himself was responsible for this is uncertain. He was, it is true, a man of his time, but woman's emancipation has been made more difficult because of his attitude. There is a saying credited to the prophet which shows the strange contradictions in his character: "Three things have been especially dear to me in this world. I have loved women and pleasant odors, but the solace of my heart has been prayer."

211

We must go a little further. Here is a seemingly sincere preacher of righteousness, and now in the last ten years of his life there is a period which Professor D. B. Macdonald speaks of as "the last terrible ten years." [7] What is the explanation? Are we not justified in saying that the loss of his wife Khadijah and the accession of power as a ruler in Medina reveal another side of his nature, and that that which had been held in control before now gained the ascendancy and made him into a different man? It is evident that the loss of a moral stay in his wife and the rapid increase in power touched the two weak spots in Mohammed's character, lust for power and love of women. Yet with all that may be said on this side, the prophet appeared to his followers and must, as we see him through their eyes, likewise appear to us as a reformer. He found the Arabs practicing female infanticide, and he put an end to this effectively and for all time; he found the Arabs torn and weakened by the blood feud, and he welded them into a single brotherhood; he found them worshiping many gods, and when he died they were acclaiming Allah as the one God Almighty. He even curbed the sexual proclivity of his Arab followers and did away with the promiscuity which had been so common. He was a reformer, but he failed at the crucial point of personal character. The pathos is that his greatness should have blinded the eyes of his followers so that this very human man is held by them to be a model, the very paragon of excellence. It has been a weight on the religion which has kept it down on a low level of moral attainment and aspiration.

FAITH AND PRACTICE

When Mohammed died in 632, the Koran had not been compiled. It could be recited by those who had been his close companions, but very little had been reduced to writing. When quite a number of the prophet's "companions" were killed in a desperate battle about a year after his death, it became evident that something must be done, or the inspired words would soon be lost. One compilation was made by Zeid, Mohammed's former amanuensis; and, when disputes arose over various readings, a recension was made by Zeid and several members of Mohammed's own tribe, and this has been the standard version down to the present day. The finished work, written in Arabic, the "languge of the angels," is about as long as the New Testament. It consists of 114 chapters, or suras, of very unequal length. They are arranged in general with

[7] *Aspects of Islam*, p. 74.

212

the long suras first and the short suras last, but this order is almost the exact reverse of the chronological order. The lack of a sufficient number of names and dates by which the various sections can be identified and correctly placed in the life story of the prophet renders the Koran a most difficult book to use historically. Yet it is our chief source on Mohammed. It is his book; it undoubtedly came from him and is a correct transcript of his mind and the development of his thought. The frequent repetition of the word "say" indicates that in Mohammed's mind God is the speaker and dictates to the prophet what he is to "say" to the people. The Muslim theory of the origin of the Koran is the most extreme illustration in any literature of plenary verbal inspiration. The accepted doctrine in the Muslim world is that the Koran is the uncreated word of God, which has always existed at the right hand of Allah and was delivered to Gabriel, who in turn was to convey it piecemeal to the prophet as need should arise. Professor Henri Lammens says that the Koran is uncreated "in the sense not only that it reproduces a copy conforming to the prototype of the divine revelation, but that in its actual form, in its phonetic and graphic reproduction, in the linguistic garb of the Arab tongue, it is identical and coeternal with its celestial original." [8] There are many lofty passages filled with poetic fire and the burning passion of righteousness; but when the "awful machinery of divine inspiration" is used to cover his own sensuality and to compose petty difficulties in his harem, the sincerity of Mohammed is severely strained, and the Koran becomes a very human document, of great interest withal because it opens the way into the mind and heart of one of the most compelling of men.

The Koran is the chief foundation of Islam, the authority par excellence on doctrine, ethics, and customs. But much that Mohammedans believe and practice is taken from the Traditions, the Sunna, as they are called. The term signifies "the custom, habit, usage of the prophet." [9] They cover all phases of life and are believed in by all the faithful. They are literally "traditions," handed down by word of mouth in the early day until they were put down in writing. They differ in authority, depending on the trustworthiness of the persons from whom they have been derived. Collections of the Traditions have been made, which are received as standard by the people. In recent years the tendency among European scholars has been to discredit a large number of the received

[8] *Islam Beliefs and Institutions*, p. 37.
[9] F. A. Klein, *The Religion of Islam*, p. 24.

traditions, some going to such extremes that little confidence should be placed in any fact concerning Mohammed and his life unless it can be verified from other sources. These two sources, the Koran and the Traditions, are called the roots of Islam; there are also two Branches.

Should the followers of Mohammed agree on any point which is not specifically covered in either the Koran or the Traditions, then "Agreement," or Ijma, is accepted as authoritative. Now, of course, practically, it is the agreement of the doctors of the law, the recognized leaders of Mohammedan opinion, but with Islam divided as it is today even this is not easy to achieve so there shall be any real consensus on any subject. Space is taken to mention it here because any advance or change in thought and practice the religion may make in the future depends upon this possibility. The statement is frequently made that a changed Islam is no longer Islam, but Islam has changed in the past and, with the pressure of a new world situation, is changing rapidly before our eyes. The fourth and least significant of the sources of Islam, one of the Branches, is Qias, or reasoning by analogy. The learned doctors may deal with new problems which arise by comparing them with similar cases already settled. The decision must be based on the Koran, the Sunna, and the Ijma to be valid, but it does keep open the way to change and advance. In these ways do the Mohammedans seek to meet new situations as they rise and still be true to the original faith of Mohammed.

Islam's religion is separated into two main divisions, practical duties and doctrines to be believed. The duties are five in number, called the Five Pillars of the Faith. There are other lesser duties, but these stand out as the cardinal points of practice, necessary for one who claims to be a follower of the prophet. The first is the repetition of the creed, "There is no God but Allah, and Mohammed is the Prophet of Allah." The simplest of all creeds, to be learned quickly and never to be forgotten, its hold on the Muslim world has been tremendous. It is repeated at sundry and all times until it eats its way into the inner core of a man's being, never to be eradicated. The historian Edward Gibbon speaks of it as "an eternal truth and a necessary fiction." The idea of one God is the eternal truth, but Islam needs more; the apostleship of Mohammed is essential if Islam is to be Islam at all.

The second duty is the observance of the five stated daily prayers. These prayers must be preceded by ceremonial lustrations, with water if it is to be had, otherwise with clean desert sand. The prayers are to be said in either public or private and always in the direction of the sacred

Kaaba in Mecca. The times for these devotional periods are highly important—just before sunrise, at high noon, in the later afternoon (at the "yellowing" of the sun, as it is known in the desert), just after sunset, and lastly when night shuts in. At these times the Muezzin, or crier, ascends the minaret and summons the faithful to prayer. The human voice is the church bell in Moslem lands. There are other prayers, but these are the regularly designated times when without fail all must turn toward Mecca and go through carefully regulated acts which accompany the repetition of the well-known formulas. The hushed stillness of reverence is upon a Mohammedan as he bows before Allah and makes his requests known to him.

The third Pillar is the thirty days' Fast of Ramadan. During this sacred month the faithful are to abstain from food, drink, and bodily pleasure from sunrise to sunset. It is carried so far that one is supposed not to swallow his own saliva. The fast is not a severe hardship when the month comes in the cool season, but when it falls in the torrid season it becomes a real burden. Mohammed, probably out of sheer ignorance, would have nothing of intercalated months, with the result that the months move slowly through the seasons and do not remain fixed. The Ramadan fast is strictly observed, but, like so much in Islam, the observance is purely formal. Those who fast all day are likely to feast all night. It makes no difference so long as the letter of the law is kept.

The fourth duty is that of almsgiving, which is expected of every Muslim. In an Islamic country under Muslim officials the alms are collected like a tax, but there are few countries under Muslim rule today, so it becomes a matter on each one's conscience. Let us give the Muslims credit for taking care of their poor. This practice harks back to the prophet himself, who set the example of charity and kindness to those in need, particularly widows and orphans.

The last of the five duties or Pillars is pilgrimage to Mecca. It is the duty of every Muslim once in his life to undertake the journey. If a man cannot go himself, it is meritorious to send someone and thus go by proxy. The pilgrimage must be made at the appointed season. The details of the ceremonies connected with it are quite elaborate. They include the wearing of the Ihram, or two seamless wrappers, which must be put on as the pilgrim comes to the borders of the sacred region; standing on Mount Arafat, near Mecca; going around the Kaaba seven times, during which each must kiss or touch the holy stone, which is fixed in one corner of the building; tasting the waters of the well Zemzen; and doing other strange and unique things, all of which have a well-known significance.

Another recognized duty, not included in the Pillars, is that of Jihad, or the Holy War, which Muslim powers wage against unbelievers. The last attempt to declare Jihad was in the fall of 1914, when the sheikh ul Islam, the spiritual head of Islam in Turkey, obeying the orders of the Sultan, called upon all Muslims everywhere to turn against the enemies of Turkey and fight the battles of the faith. It was a Holy War so evidently "Made in Germany," as Professor Snouck Hurgronje put it, that its call was heeded only as far as Germany's influence extended and fell on deaf ears in most of the Muslim world which remained true to the Allies.

The essential doctrines of Mohammedanism are as definitely stated as the duties. They are again five in number, the first being that of God, which we shall discuss last. The second of the doctrines is that of angels, the servants of God, whose one desire is to love and know God. They are free from all sin and act as intercessors for men before God. Besides the angels are the jinn, who also must be believed in. They are the genii of the *Arabian Nights*, some of whom are believers and some infidels. They were inherited, like so many other things in this religion, from the superstitions of pre-Islamic paganism. The third doctrine is that of the books. The chief sacred books are the Koran; the Pentateuch; the Zabur, or Psalms of David; and the Injil or Gospel of Jesus. The orthodox believe that all previous books are abrogated by the Koran, thus practically rejecting the Old and New Testaments, although every reference to the Bible in the Koran is favorable to a belief in its inspiration and authority.

The fourth doctrine is that of the prophets. Many are mentioned, but the leading names are Adam, Noah, Abraham, Moses, Jesus, and Mohammed. It is held that all the others were sent to their own people while Mohammed was sent to all peoples. Jesus is recognized as a prophet, the only sinless one among them according to the Koran and the traditions. His death on the cross is denied as beneath the dignity of one of God's chosen ones. But the one overwhelming fact enunciated by this doctrine is that Mohammed is the prophet superseding all others. They led up to and pointed toward him, and only by accepting his claims can one be true to the essential messages of them all. Then follows the fifth doctrine, that of the resurrection and the last day. There will be the sounding of the trumpets, the descending of the books, the weighing in the balances, and the crossing of the narrow bridge, from which the wicked fall off into the fiery pit below. All mankind, good and bad, will

216

be raised and will answer for their deeds. All Muslims will in the end be saved no matter what their record may have been. The last state is in heaven or hell, both of which are pictured with vivid imagery, calculated to appeal to the imagination of the dweller in the desert.

The first great doctrine, that of God, is so important that it occupies nine tenths of the space in Mohammedan works on theology. There is but one God, Allah, and he is the omnipotent Creator and Ruler of the universe. He has many qualities, which the Muslim expresses by repeating "the ninety-nine most beautiful names of God." Of these attributes, or qualities, what are called the essential attributes are life, knowledge (absolute omniscience), power, and will. The doctrine of the foreordination of good and evil follows logically from the emphasis which is put on the almightiness of Allah. It has had an interesting history. The prophet was no theologian and gave expression to contradictory views in the Koran, but as the suras are studied in chronological order predestination becomes more marked. There the beginnings are found of the fatalistic pall which has always hung over Islam, which has tended to smother moral enthusiasm and to render difficult any movement toward social reform. Was it not all predetermined by the almighty Allah? So what can we do about it?

Only once was the doctrine seriously challenged. For thirty-four years at the beginning of the third Islamic century, that is, about A.D. 825, a party flourished in Bagdad which denied divine predestination and asserted free will in man. These Freethinkers in Islam, Mutazilites, or "Seceders," as they were called, held other unorthodox doctrines, such as the creation of the Koran. They possessed great influence until they were overcome and in turn suffered the persecution they had inflicted on the more orthodox. They were discomfited in debate and were unable again to lift up their heads, through the victory of al-Ashari, the orthodox champion who had once been a Mutazilite himself. He was a master of dialectic and brought over into Islamic theology the methods of the scholastic philosophy. He gave great impetus to orthodoxy, which retains its almost undisputed hold today. No feature is emphasized with more insistence than the doctrine of God's unchangeable decrees, predetermining all that happens in the world of nature and of men.

With all the Koran says about the mercy and compassion of Allah, the great, overshadowing attribute is power. This was Mohammed's emphasis, and it still rules in the Islamic world. It is power unlimited, unrestrained by any law of holiness or love which would lessen the dignity

217

of Allah and bring him down from the throne of his unapproachable might. It makes no difference to the Muslim to have it suggested that it might be an inner limitation, growing out of the very nature of God, which is essentially holiness and love. It would be a limitation nevertheless, and that is enough for him to spurn the suggestion as entirely untenable. Allah must be able to do as he wills with no let or hindrance. What God wills is right because he wills it, and not because it expresses what is even deeper than will, the very nature of God himself, which is righteousness and love. Sin, then, in man is not a breach of a moral law founded on an eternal ethical cleavage which goes right to the heart of the universe itself, but a violation of an arbitrary command which might be changed according to the whim or caprice of Allah. He thus becomes a typical oriental despot, irresponsible and unrestrained by an undeviating principle of righteousness within.

Another doctrine must be coupled with this to appreciate the kind of God Allah is in relation to his people. It is the doctrine of "difference," which asserts the absolute difference between Allah and man. God is not a Father; that would be to make him like men, for the term "father" suggests to Muslims primarily and almost entirely physical procreation, which they hold would be unworthy of God. So man is in no sense a son partaking of the divine nature; he was not made in the image of God. God must not be brought down to so low a level as that, the Muslim says. Man is carnal and must always remain so. Salvation does not mean the transformation of man's nature so as to fit him for spiritual communion with his Father. It is merely such an obedience to the rules and regulations which have been laid down that man may secure the reward in heaven which Allah has promised. And the heaven is not spiritual, but one suited to the physical desires which man is conscious of in this life and will never outgrow. It is a luscious garden of fruits and running streams with delightful nooks in which are the houris, or damsels, who are the principal reward of the righteous. Such is Islam as it is commonly taught, holding men down to the purely physical level and failing to lift their eyes to a world of spiritual light and beauty where we shall be with God and see him and be like him.

But there were and are Muslims not satisfied with such an outlook. There have been men who felt that God was in their hearts and was speaking to them, who desired communion with him and would be satisfied with nothing else. They are men who desire purity of life, some even going to the extreme of severe asceticism to accomplish their pur-

218

pose. The greatest of these was al-Ghazzali, who died A.D. 1111. He was sure that there was that in man which could come into contact with God. His experience was more than could be explained by the barren formulas of the scholastic theology. Yet he was not unorthodox. He accepted the apostleship of the prophet, the authority of the Koran and the Traditions, and used the methods of the scholastic philosophy. But he was a mystic, seeing the inner light and experiencing the glow of the quiet presence of God in his inner being. He could not deny this reality, and his great work was "to reduce to an orthodox possibility those mystical conceptions and to find a resting place for that possibility in the church of Islam." [10]

Others went far beyond al-Ghazzali and were not so wise as he. They did not stop until they had landed in sheer pantheism, virtually denying all the specific doctrines of their faith and holding that all beliefs and outward practices were meaningless in the presence of the mystic union of the soul and the great All, whom they might still call Allah but whose character as defined by the orthodox theologians they completely denied. The mystical experience was given another vent, however, in the Darwish orders, which are scattered widely over the Islamic world. The meetings of these brotherhoods seek to stimulate the emotional experience by well-worked-out exercises. Though they may be a poor substitute for the communion with God which Christians experience in Jesus Christ, they give abundant testimony to the presence in the heart of the Muslim of a longing after God which only his presence can satisfy.

THE EXPANSION OF ISLAM

The rapid expansion of Islam is one of the marvels of history. When Mohammed died in 632, plans of conquest were said to be already in his mind. During the period of the first four, or orthodox, caliphs (632-661), Persia, Syria, Palestine, and Egypt were subjugated. The homelands of Christianity were swept out of the control of the Christian Church. In the year 711 the Muslim armies entered Spain, having already crossed the entire breadth of North Africa, and by 732 were to be found as far north as central France. Here at Tours they were met by King Charles Martel, or "Hammer," and suffered a decisive defeat, the first check the Muslims had met in their victorious advance. The battle of Tours was one of the decisive battles of the world. The fate of Europe was decided that day, whether it should be Muslim or Christian. The Muslim hordes

[10] Macdonald, op. cit., p. 194.

219

were driven back across the Pyrenees into Spain, where they remained in possession of the greater part of the country for hundreds of years. They were finally driven out in the time of Ferdinand and Isabella in 1492, and Christianity again was triumphant in the Iberian Peninsula.

After the four orthodox caliphs—Abu Bakr, Omar, Othman, and Ali —who ruled from the old seat of authority in Arabia, the center shifted to Damascus, where the Omayyad caliphs ruled from 661 to 750. Then again there was a transfer, and for a brilliant period Bagdad was the center of the Islamic world. Here the Abbasid caliphs held sway in pomp and splendor from 750 to 1258. The last centuries saw degeneracy and the slow but sure decline of Arab prestige. The authority was passing over to the Turks, who had come in from Central Asia and were making themselves masters of the situation in Asia Minor.

How account for the expansion of Islam? Zeal for God was a motive, not unmixed with baser elements, which welded the loosely organized Arab tribesmen into a compact body and drove them out to do battle against the enemies of Allah. To this must be added zeal for plunder and slaves. This made a strong appeal to the Arab. He was to be the soldier of Islam supported by the tribute of the peoples he conquered. Arabia became the breeding place and training ground for army after army which went out to conquer a world. The exhaustion might have come sooner than it did had it not been for the importation of large numbers of concubines and women slaves which were increased greatly by the wars. The countries which were conquered fell by the sword, but after the initial bloodshed there was usually peace. The enormous numbers converted to Islam were not forced into Islam at the edge of the sword, though that happened at times.

With a nation the alternative was Islam or the sword, but with an individual after the new religion had been installed it was Islam or tribute. They might remain Christians on condition of paying tribute, and many did this, as witness the Coptic Church in Egypt, the Armenian, and other Christian churches in the Near East. When people turned Muslims, it was usually the pressure of the whole system. As soon as the Christians paid the tribute, they were under the Muslim protection. The sexual freedom allowed under Islam was a strong inducement to men not strongly under the influence of Christian ideals. The Muslim soldiers and those who followed the armies into any country were free to intermarry with any of the women of the land, and of course the children always became Muslims.

During the last two centuries of the caliphate in Bagdad the real strength of Islam as a political power was Turkish. The Turks had been brought to Bagdad as the bodyguard of the caliphs, with little thought that they would so soon assume the rule. First the Seljukian Turks (from the year 1037) and then the Othmanli, or Ottoman Turks (from 1299 to the present time), took the lead. Islam under the Turk expanded eastward over Afghanistan, Baluchistan, and down into the plains of India. The forays into India began about the year 1000 under Mahmud of Ghazni, who was little better than a freebooter. In course of time Delhi became the capital of a Mohammedan empire, which under the Moghul emperors (1525-1707) was one of the most brilliant epochs of Indian as well as of Islamic history. During these years the faith penetrated more deeply into Central Asia, and going on from there entered China as a powerful force. It had already been known in that country but was relatively small in numbers and weak in influence. In 1507 Islam was carried by peaceful penetration into the southeast and found lodgment in the island world, where it is still spreading and making converts. Java with its population of twenty-five millions is entirely Muslim, the center of the faith among the Malays. The Moros in the Sulu Archipelago of the Philippine Islands are the farthest outreach of the faith of the prophet to the east.

The western area of the medieval advance of Islam was in Africa, in the Sahara and the Sudan. The Sahara fell rapidly to Islam, the inducement to the Arabs being trade in ivory and slaves. They introduced the camel as they advanced, penetrating farther and farther to the south and capturing some of the best people in northern Sudan. Then after a quiescence of three hundred years, during which Islam remained almost stationary, the advance southward has begun again in our own day and threatens to submerge the continent. Why this advance after centuries of inactivity? So long as the slave trade continued to exist, the Arab traders could not desire the conversion of the black men, for by Moslem law they are forbidden from making slaves of fellow Muslims; they all belonged to one great brotherhood. But when the trade in slaves was reduced to a minimum by European intervention, it was then to the advantage of the traders to deal with the blacks as fellow religionists. Their wants would be increased and their desires simulated, as was impossible in their pagan condition. Then, too, when European governments in the last century inaugurated the rule of law and order, wars were brought to an end, and the tribes were compelled to lay down their arms, thus taking

221

away the one effective pagan protection against Islam. When to all this is added the actual patronage of Islam by certain governments for reasons of political expediency and as a means of control, the impression made on the native is likely to be favorable to the religion of the prophet—a strange commentary on the influence of so-called Christian nations.

Thus Islam has advanced until today, with an estimated strength of 250,000,000 scattered all the way from China to the shores of the Atlantic in Africa and from the banks of the Volga in Russia to the waters of the South Seas, the religion of Mohammed is a world religion, the most powerful of all the rivals of Christianity in its attempt to win mankind. It has been said that Islam is a steppingstone toward Christianity. Undoubtedly when a pagan tribe is converted, it is raised to a slightly higher level. But unfortunately it is left there stranded with no possibility of further progress. Islam adds dignity to the savage, clothes him in a certain respectability, and brings him within the bounds of a world-embracing brotherhood. These benefits, together with that of a belief in one great God, Allah, instead of cringing fear in the presence of a thousand spirits and demons, must be acknowledged in spite of the fact that the change in many cases is more seeming than real. But—and this is the final test—when Islam allows even greater sensuality, stimulates divorce and polygamy and, in so far as it dares, slavery; when its presence results in the seclusion and neglect of women, the religion of Islam can be looked upon only as a drawback to the advance which should be looked for in any people. And as for being a steppingstone, the proud and overbearing attitude which is always assumed in the presence of the followers of any other religion—and this is particularly true of Christians—would make Islam appear to be the greatest barrier to the progress of Christianity in the world today.

But Islam has not presented a united front. Deep cleavages began soon to appear and have always been present. The most significant is that between the Sunnis and the Shiites. The Sunnis represent the great body of Muslims, the followers of the Sunna, or Traditions. The Shiites, or "Followers," are the adherents of Ali, who married Mohammed's daughter Fatima and thus continued the prophet's line. The Shiites hold to "the divine right of the descendants of the prophet through the children of Ali and Fatima" [11] to be the rulers of the Islamic world. This claim is repudiated by the Sunnis, who have allowed the choice of the people and political circumstances to determine the leadership of the

[11] Goldziher, Mohammed and Islam, p. 222.

faithful. The Shiites, who are about nine million strong, are found principally in Persia, though like-minded believers in Ali are widely scattered in other Muslim lands. To them Ali was the first Imam, or head of the religion, after the prophet. He is raised to such a level that even Mohammed pales into insignificance before him. An Imam is imperative for every age as the religious authority for the people as well as their political ruler. There have been twelve of these Imams (or seven on a theory accepted by another group), the last of whom is still alive, though he has disappeared and exerts his influence invisibly. In the end a Mahdi, or "guide," is to appear to restore all things and usher in the final consummation. The messianic idea thus has its place in Islam, repudiated for the most part by the Sunnis but forming "the vital nerve of the entire Shiite system." [12]

Out of the Shiite Mohammedanism has come Bahaism (originally Babism), which has significance because of its influence in Persia and because it has been carried into the Western world and has a following in the United States. There is a remarkable temple in process of erection in Wilmette, a suburb of Chicago, well worth investigation. The story is a long one, hard to summarize briefly. This cult arose in 1844 in Persia through the claim of one Ali Mohammed to be the Bab, or "gate," through which contact is established with the Imam, now in a state of "occullation." Because of his claim to the headship of the state he was put to death in 1850, as were a large group of his devoted followers. But the movement did not die; it came to life again in the claims and activity of Bahaullah, a very remarkable thinker and seer, who made his center in Palestine. From there his message of world peace and good will to all has gone out through the world. It does not have a high reputation in Persia, where most of its followers are to be found, and in America it has not won a wide allegiance. Its Islamic background is kept in the background in the West, but its connection with Shiite Islam becomes evident with very little study—and it is an evidence of the expansive power of the faith originally promulgated by Mohammed.[13]

Islam in the World Today

In 1908 Lord Cromer, governor-general of Egypt, declared in his work *Modern Egypt* that "reformed Islam is Islam no longer" [14] No one

---

[12] *Ibid.*, p. 246.
[13] The literature is very extensive, but see especially George Foot Moore, *History of Religions*, II, 509-19.
[14] II, 229.

would make such a statement today who had even a passing acquaintance with the Islamic world. These people are on the march just as all others in Eastern countries, and what the end will be no one can say. This does not mean that there is not strenuous opposition to change. One of the strongest and most significant movements in the Islam of our day was initiated by Mohammed Ibn Abdel-Wahhab, who as early as 1740 started a campaign to rid Islam of the innovations which had begun to show themselves. He was an Arab and saw Islam through Arab eyes. Sacred shrines, richly ornamented tombs, prayers to saints, and luxury penetrating into the life of the people were anathema to him. All these were contrary to primitive Islam, and that was enough; the only thing for him to do was strenuously to resist every such tendency. It was a reform movement to restore the faith to its pristine purity. Wahhab was succeeded by his son Saud, who was even more zealous. He captured the holy cities of Mecca and Medina and for nine years ruled from Mecca. A Turkish army was sent against him. He died during the war and was succeeded by his son, who was captured and publicly executed in Constantinople in 1818. As a political movement the Wahhabis had failed, but the effect of their reactionary, reforming zeal has continued through the decades and came to life again after World War I. Ibn Saud became the leader of the Wahhabi people, the reactionaries to be found throughout the peninsula, and became the ruler of all inland Arabia. And now all opposition has been put down, and the Wahhabis are in complete control of the homeland of Islam.

Not only in Arabia but elsewhere among the Muslims the same tendencies are standing in the way of progress. There is in India a full defense of historic Islam. They justify the prophet in every detail of his life. They want no change whatever. Even polygamy is condoned, being looked upon as "the Muslim solution of the social evil." [15] The seclusion of women is defended as "a protective device to save women from evil." [16] The Koran is just what it purports to be, a direct revelation of divine truth to Mohammed, which is to be received and acted upon as final authority on all questions with which it deals. The real strength of reactionary orthodoxy resides in the Ulama, the doctors of the Law, corresponding to the "scribes" among the Jews in the time of Christ. They

[15] Here and throughout this section indebtedness is acknowledged to four volumes: *The Expansion of Islam*, by W. W. Cash, *Modern Tendencies in World Religions*, by C. S. Braden, *Modern Trends in Islam*, and *Mohammedanism: A Historical Survey*, both by H. A. R. Gibb.

[16] Cash, *op. cit.*, p. 219.

are the repositories of tradition, the expounders of the ancient law, and the defenders of the faith, who stand against innovation and who believe that any modernizing of the primitive beliefs will destroy the precious deposit which has come down from Mohammed.

But Islam does change. Under the leadership of Mustapha Kemal in the years following World War I, Turkey rose from its decrepitude and established itself as a vigorous, forward-looking nation. To the amazement of the Western nations the new state was secularized, and the relation between the state and Islam was severed. In 1924, the caliphate, which for centuries had been the possession of the Sultan of Turkey, was abolished, and since that time Islam has been without a spiritual head, a caliph or successor of the prophet. Several conferences have been held, but no tangible results have materialized. Many Muslims are in deep perplexity as they face such an unheard-of situation. To them the unity of Islam has been broken. Now more than ever the meeting of the pilgrims at Mecca must be the connecting link of the Muslim peoples.

Not only in Turkey but in Egypt, India, and Indonesia the spirit of independent nationalism has swept like a mighty wave through the land with revolutionary results. Egypt is now proudly independent and is resentful of the slightest interference by Great Britain at the Suez Canal and in the Sudan. India not only has won her complete independence, but has been the scene of a most serious religious disruption. Freedom had no sooner been achieved when an agitation began for an independent Islamic state, which, to the surprise of the world, was achieved with the establishment of Pakistan, independent, intensely active, and jealous of any encroachment on the part of India. And Indonesia, particularly in Java, where the population is almost solidly Muslim, is now in process of shedding the last vestiges of Dutch rule in the archipelago.

The changes which have touched the inner life of Muslims have been caused almost entirely by contact with the West. Some of them have been very radical. Attacks have been made on the ancient religious dogmas, the whole social system, and on the prophet himself. This would indicate that irreligion is widespread in Islam as in other parts of the world. It has reached its extreme in Turkey, where the whole trend is secular. It has spread widely, however, and among young Muslims educated in the West or in contact with Western thought there is a turning away from the old faith. It is, of course, not a uniform movement. It embraces all degrees of reaction against the old beliefs and practices. There are those who hold a mediating position and attempt to rationalize what is not to their liking. Religion, so they say, even their Islam, is not to be looked on as static, but is subject to evolution.

As these lines are written, there is definite evidence that in Iran and Turkey, there has been something of a reaction against the secular tide. There is a decided movement to turn again to the time-honored teachings of the Koran.

The center of these newer tendencies has been in North India. Ahmad Khan (1817-1898) promoted education and founded, against great opposition, the Muhammadan Anglo-Oriental College in Aligarh in 1875, which later developed into the Muhammadan University, the center of Indian Islamic culture and scholarship. Ahmad Khan was followed by Amir Ali, who wrote an important book, *The Spirit of Islam,* in which he defended the prophet against Christian attacks. He would have Islam lay aside the whole legalistic structure of Islam if necessary and go back to the pristine beauty of the matchless Book and the matchless Prophet.[17] These leaders were followed by Sir Mahomed Iqbal (1876-1938), "the exponent of the most sweeping modernist reformation of Islamic doctrine." [18] He gave systematic form to his ideas in a volume called *The Reconstruction of Religious Thought in Islam* (1928), which is radical but whose influence has not extended widely. Outside of India there have been few stirrings which give promise of a real breaking away from tradition.

An organized movement, the Ahmadiya, as contrasted with those intellectual tendencies, arose in 1889, founded by Mirza Ghulam Ahmad in North India. This is a reform movement which has not separated itself from Islam but which is considered unorthodox by the great body of Muslims, both conservative and liberal. A vigorous opponent of Christianity, the founder made a claim for himself as the hope of all nations, which alienated many of his own followers. But despite divisions this group has visions of a world-wide expansion of Islam, visions which have produced a missionary movement reaching out to the Western world, where there are a few small groups of believers in the claims of the prophet of Mecca and his book.

[17] See Murray T. Titus, *Indian Islam,* p. 197.
[18] H. A. R. Gibb, *Mohammedanism: A Historical Survey,* p. 185.

Suggestions for Further Study

Andrae, Tor. *Mohammed: The Man and His Faith*. New York: Charles Scribner's Sons, 1936. A translation from the Swedish; valuable, but to be used with caution.

Gibb, H. A. R. *Modern Trends in Islam*. Chicago: University of Chicago Press, 1947.

————. *Mohammedanism: A Historical Survey*. New York: Oxford University Press, 1949. Two volumes of the greatest importance, by a recognized authority.

Jones, L. Bevan. *The People of the Mosque*. London: Student Christian Movement Press, 1932. A complete survey by a missionary to India.

Lammens, Henri. *Islam: Beliefs and Institutions*. New York: E. P. Dutton and Company, 1929. Very valuable, by a Jesuit missionary in Beyrouth, Syria.

Macdonald, D. B. *Aspects of Islam*. New York: The Macmillan Company, 1911. One of the best interpretations, by a master.

Moore, George Foot. *History of Religions*. Vol. II, chs. XVI-XXII.

Rodwell, J. M., tr. *The Koran*. Everyman's Library. A convenient volume, with suras arranged chronologically, and with notes on the text.

Stanton, H. U. W. *The Teaching of the Qur'an*. New York: The Macmillan Company, 1919. A short summary with a full index.

Titus, Murray T. *Indian Islam*. New York: Oxford University Press, 1930. Needs revision, but excellent on the historical development.

CHAPTER XII

CHRISTIANITY

JESUS CHRIST

LITTLE IS KNOWN OF THE EARLY LIFE OF JESUS CHRIST. BORN A FEW years before the year 1 in Bethlehem of Judea, he lived in Nazareth, a city of Galilee, until he was about thirty years of age. We have no reason to doubt the tradition that after the death of Joseph, the head of the family, Jesus became the main support of Mary and the younger children. He worked at his trade, that of a carpenter, and lived the life which would be expected of a religiously-minded young Hebrew. We have only one glimpse into his life and mind during all this period, and that was when Jesus was a boy of twelve. He went up with Joseph and Mary to Jerusalem to the Feast of the Passover. Here he came into touch with the official teachers of the people and amazed them by his questions and his answers. He was not only religiously inclined but showed insight and discrimination beyond his years. He seemed already to show a sense of unique relationship with God, whom it was natural for him to call Father. With this beginning at twelve we may imagine the inner development and preparation for his life task which must have taken place during the subsequent eighteen "silent years" at Nazareth, before he appeared in a new role as a teacher of the people.[1]

At about the age of thirty Jesus suddenly appeared at the Jordan, where John was performing the rite of baptism on those who came professing a desire to amend their ways and live better lives. Jesus also came and, against the scruples of John, who saw that Jesus was in a different case from the others, was baptized. It marked the turning point, for with the outward ritual act came an inner spiritual experience of profound significance for Jesus. A voice assured him that he was in a unique sense his Father's "beloved Son," in whom he was "well pleased." It seems to have been the consummation of his thought and prayer and

---

[1] See T. R. Glover, *The Jesus of History*, for suggestive thoughts on these years.

eager yearning for many years. He had received his revelation; he would proclaim God as a Father and men as his sons. He was filled with a sense of mission, of having a work to do and a message to deliver, which to the end of his life did not leave him for a moment.

Immediately after this new experience Jesus passed through a period of "temptation," in which he decided upon the principles and the methods of his work in bringing in the Kingdom of God. This was his God-given task; how was it to be performed? The Kingdom must be ushered in by a clear emphasis on the spiritual rather than the physical; by a firm reliance on God's goodness and power, which would make spectacular methods seem incongruous; and by such a single-hearted allegiance to God that compromise with evil and subservience to the lower standards represented by the evil one would be repellent. Having passed through the crisis, Jesus went out and for a period, variously estimated from one to three years, proclaimed the message of the new Kingdom.

He went from place to place in Palestine, preaching in the synagogues and out-of-door places wherever the people congregated and talking to individuals and to groups as they came to him with their questions and problems. He began to gather about him a little company of disciples who accompanied him on all of his journeys. He spent much time giving them instruction and on several occasions sent them out to heal and to preach. He spent much of his time in and about Galilee, though on several notable occasions he went to Jerusalem, the religious center of Jewish life, and there came into contact with the leaders of the people. But whether with individuals or larger audiences, whether among friends or bitter opponents, Jesus preserved the same poise and self-control. He was always simple, candid, and sincere, and carried about with him such an atmosphere of quiet assurance that what he said always struck home and caused men and women in spite of themselves to recognize his right to speak and to be heard. His words carried their own authority and did not need the backing of quotations from rabbis and teachers and writings of recognized worth. He was heard with equal eagerness and understanding by the ignorant and learned, so simple and concrete were his words. Yet lurking behind these vivid stories, taken from the life all knew so well, were the most profound and fundamental truths, which the careless were quite likely to miss. Jesus frequently cast his thought into story form, that of the parable, partly for the very purpose of testing his hearers. At other times his thought took

229

the form of epigrams, which among the peoples of the East are so dearly loved, and still again he would use the forms of the apocalyptic writers of his age. Whether all the imagery and all the predictions placed in the mouth of Jesus in the great apocalyptic discourses were given out by him in just this form, or in a few cases at all, is an exceedingly difficult question. What we may feel sure of is that he was not only a preacher of assuring and comforting things but could be as severe as the divine judgment itself in his denunciations of sin and unrighteousness, of hypocrisy and unreality in religion.

Jesus came to establish the Kingdom of God, and this was the burden of his message. But he never forgot that the form of the Kingdom and many things connected with its coming were of lesser significance than the inner meaning and the principles on which it was based. The first of these was man's relationship with God. God is our Father, with all the tender love which the term "Father" has taken on through Jesus' words and example of filial trust. And quite as much did the term take on new meaning through Jesus' example of compassion and solicitude over suffering and sinning men and women. He taught that this Father was ready and anxious to forgive all who came to him without respect to race or position in society or any other outward distinction. The condition of the heart was the only thing which mattered. The seriousness of the issues of life were not minified, and terrible things were spoken with respect to the fate of the obdurate, only it was never to be forgotten that men were always dealing with a Father whose compassion would never fail and who could save to the uttermost.

Jesus was not a social or political reformer. We cannot even tell what he felt and thought about certain questions which were agitating the men of his day, not to speak of all the movements with which his name has been connected from that time to this. Yet he laid down principles of the relations of man to man which have been revolutionary in the history of the world. He recognized none of the arbitrary distinctions which divide men, and on the basis of his attitude a true democracy has been made possible. He did not explicitly condemn slavery, but men have been made free only where his example and his teaching have been made known. He did not inveigh against the forms of government which prevailed in his day, but all tyrannies and autocracies have had reason to fear when oppression and disregard of the rights of man have been seen in the light of his teaching. Jesus was always ready to urge that his Kingdom was spiritual, to be realized within the hearts of men, but the effect

230

of such a conception has been to work its way out into all the relationships in which men find themselves and bring them into harmony with his ideals.

Jesus was constantly dealing with the malady at the root of human life. His analysis of character and his ability to read the inner motives of men give ample evidence of the deepest moral insight and concern. Yet with all this he was not conscious of sin in his own life and was not unwilling to throw out the challenge to anyone to lay his finger on any spot or blemish. That a man should be able to state an unbelievably high ideal is an achievement, but that this teacher should match his ideal with his life and should live it out so that the example is more beautiful than the precept is to raise Jesus to an unapproachable pinnacle of excellence. We must use words which cannot be applied to any other of the sons of men. That was the impression he made then, and it is the same today. A unique event took place. A being trod our earth, of whom it can be said that he did not sin. We are on hallowed ground when we come into the presence of Jesus Christ.

But of all the impressions Jesus made, the strongest was that he was in touch with God his Father and that this was the explanation of all the wonderful things about him. God was to him a personal Being, not some power or indefinite being far off to whom we must send our prayers and who lives in a world so far off that he cannot enter into the meaning of our mundane life. But this above all else is what men want to know: Is there a Being at the center of the universe who cares? How can we be sure? In the presence of Jesus their questions were answered. In some marvelous way the association of his disciples with him carried them farther than they had thought possible. They began to realize that to be with Jesus gave them a sense of nearness to God, and this continued until these Jews, dyed-in-the-wool monotheists as they were, found themselves offering a homage to their Master which was not different from their attitude toward God, and were doing it with no sense of incongruity.

Jesus, however, was not only winning followers and bringing them close to God; he came into collision with the religious authorities of his people, and in the end lost his life at their hands. The opportunity came when Jesus appeared in Jerusalem at the Feast of the Passover. He was seized and, after having had a preliminary hearing before the Jewish high priest and Sanhedrin, was taken before Pontius Pilate, the Roman procurator, and was condemned to death. He was crucified and died at

231

the end of six hours' agony on the cross. His body was taken down by friends in the early evening and laid in a rock-hewn tomb. The hopes of his disciples were dashed to the ground, and undoubtedly the Jewish leaders and the Roman authorities thought they had rid themselves of an exceedingly troublesome creature.

But such was not to be, for a very remarkable thing happened the third day after. To the utter amazement of his disciples, who had not recovered from the paralyzing effect of their grief and disappointment, Jesus appeared to them so unmistakably that they were convinced that death had not been able to hold its victim and that Jesus was alive. Their new enthusiasm, the founding of the Christian Church on the assurance of the presence of the living Christ, the adoption of the first day of the week as a memorial of the day when Jesus reappeared alive— all these historic facts bear witness to the genuineness of the disciples' testimony that the same Jesus who had journeyed with them, who had died and had been laid away in the tomb, was raised from the dead, their living Master forevermore. They immediately went out to preach "the gospel of the resurrection," and with that the history of the Christian Church began.

DEVELOPMENT OF LIFE AND TEACHING

The earliest Christians were Jews. The only difference between them and the non-Christian Jews was that they believed that Jesus was the expected Messiah and the others did not. This little group felt it incumbent on them to observe the regulations and take part in the ceremonies of the Jewish faith. It was hard even for the disciples of Jesus to learn the lesson that it was a spiritual Kingdom which was to be inaugurated and not a political kingdom, whose capital was to be in Jerusalem. These early disciples took it for granted that the way to Christ was through the portals of Judaism. Already the idea of Gentiles becoming fellow religionists had become familiar through the inclusion of proselytes in the Jewish community. All this was well known to the early Christians, and it did not occur to them that Gentiles should come into their ranks in any other way.

This rigid theory did not continue long without challenge. One of the most interesting developments which may be traced in the book of Acts is the movement toward greater liberality. But the really significant move occurred when Paul forced the issue and brought matters to a settlement in the Jerusalem council, described in Acts 15. He had become

232

quite free in admitting Gentiles and had arrived at the conviction that the new religion ought to stand in its own right, not restrained by the trammels of Judaism. Paul brought the matter to the elders at Jerusalem, and after careful deliberation the momentous decision was reached that the Gentiles might be admitted to the Christian churches irrespective of their relation to Judaism. It was the first crisis through which the early Church passed.

The second Christian century is most obscure; we know little of the important changes which were taking place. We do know that the churches came into contact with a movement or tendency called Gnosticism. These "Knowers" had doubtless been influenced by a philosophy of life emanating from Persia or even farther east. These ideas mingled with Greek theories, and a doctrine was developed according to which a fundamental cleavage ran right down through the universe, a cleavage not only between right and wrong, but even more fundamentally between spirit and matter. The two are separated by a chasm so deep and wide that it would seem almost hopeless to bridge it. Matter was looked upon as intrinsically and inevitably evil simply because it was matter. It could not be saved; it must be left behind if the spirit of man were to be emancipated. And it was just there the problem pressed; man was both spirit and matter. He sought to be free yet was held down by an unsupportable burden by the flesh and its desires. The only hope was that, by repudiating the flesh and by giving oneself to ascetic deprivations, the body would have less and less hold and the spirit would be free to rise slowly through degrees of divine attainment to the plane of pure spirituality for which it longed. This movement secured access to the Church itself and formed one or two sects, about which little is known. They wore themselves out in course of time without destroying the central stream of Christian life. The influence of the movement remained, however, in an ascetic attitude which has been far from wholesome in the Church. Continuing to believe that the body was inevitably corrupt and that its desires, particularly the sexual impulse, were evil and should be suppressed, a ban was put on marriage, and celibacy was declared to be a higher state. The tendency maintained itself in the "praise of virginity" and the enforced celibacy of monks and nuns and of the priesthood of the Church.

It was not long before the new faith came into contact with the most powerful intellectual weapon ever forged by the human mind, Greek thought. The origins of Christianity were Hebraic; its forms of thought and the method of presentation were derived from the Old Testament and the habit and mind of the Jewish people. It was inevitable that Christianity would sooner or later be influenced by the powerful instrument of Greek thought and be compelled to think out its doctrines anew. At the very center of the faith was Christ. He had saved men and women from their sins; he had given them the hope of everlasting life; he had furnished a new moral dynamic and had given history a new meaning. In all these respects what Christianity had to present was new and startling. Nothing like it had been known in the world of paganism. But a question began to press itself home among the more thoughtful as to the kind of being this Christ was. The discussion took many forms, but what to make of Christ, related to both God and man, was the burden of every argument. Jesus was a human being; that was quite evident from his life among men. But these Christian thinkers could not be satisfied to leave him there. He was man, but more than man. To them he was the God-man.

How could a being be God and man at the same time? There were no human analogies to which appeal might be made. Two marked tendencies appeared, one to make Jesus Christ the highest of all the creatures God had made, far above any other being known in the universe, and yet a creature below the dignity of God himself. The other was to take the bold step of asserting that Jesus was truly man and at the same time truly God, that he was not a creature, but of the very essence of the Godhead, that he was as much a part of God as the Father himself. This is the meaning of the decision reached at the first general council of the Church held at Nicaea in 325. Arius contended that Jesus was a created being, withal the very highest of God's creation, while Athanasius carried the council with him in asserting that Jesus was of the "same substance" with the Father, and as eternal Being had never been created at all. The Christian Church has gone with Athanasius. The Christian doctrine of the Trinity is not easy to understand, but so long as men are brought into the presence of Christ and see in him their Saviour and Lord, the doctrine will be proclaimed. So long as lives are being made over in the image of Jesus Christ, so long will men insist upon lifting him up to the only level which will satisfy their sense of the eternal fitness of things.

All these discussions took place in the East, which was essentially metaphysical. The day of the West was to come; it was gathering strength during the years, and in the fourth and fifth centuries came the com-

234

manding figure of Augustine (354-430), the greatest theologian of the Western Church. The West was the complete antithesis of the East; it was pre-eminently practical, concerned less about metaphysical distinctions than with problems of organization. Its genius was shown in the formulation of the practical doctrine of salvation, of God's grace in receiving sinners and placing them on a standing as citizens of the heavenly Kingdom. This was the great work of Augustine, who, after a long experience in Italy, had become Bishop of Hippo in North Africa. Together with this unfolding of the doctrine of salvation another movement was in progress, that of building up the Church in theory and in practice as the representative of God on earth. So, when the Church came more and more to stand between God and men and claim possession of the only means—the sacraments—through which men could gain access to God, the power of the Church over the conscience and destiny of men became unbounded. This assertion by the Church of the right to control the life of men, individually and in every relationship even up to the high position of king and emperor, was the dominant note of the Middle Ages. The modern world could be ushered in only by breaking through the authority of the Church and setting free the mind of man from this bondage.

This is what the Reformation did. It gathered into striking power the forces which had been developing for generations and proclaimed that man was free. What the Renaissance of the fifteenth century did for the intellect—and with many unfortunate features withal—that the Reformation in the next century, led by Martin Luther, accomplished for the conscience and the spiritual life. It declared clearly and unhesitatingly that the soul of man stood immediately in the presence of its Maker, and that it could have direct dealing with him without ceremonies or ritual or sacraments or priests. The Church had its place, but not as an essential mediator between men and God. It was as fallible as the men who composed it and had not the right to demand unquestioning obedience to its behests. So much the Reformation settled for all those who have entered into the heritage of its daring leaders. But having overturned the authority of the visible Church, it set up another authority in its place, that of the infallible Bible. Undoubtedly, all Protestants today recognize the right of the Scriptures to command their lives, provided, of course, they be given full right of interpretation. But the danger has been that the Bible should be made the final fact in Christianity. There are those who would not dim the luster of the Book nor diminish its rightful authority, but who at the same time see clearly that the revelation contained in the Book found its culmination in a Person. So Christianity, as its very name indicates, is in its truest sense the religion of a Person. In this it differs from both Judaism and Islam, which are far more truly religions of a book and of obedience to its requirements. Christians *have* a Book, which is necessary to apprehend the Person, but the Person is primary, the climactic and distinguishing point in the religion.

One of the unfortunate results of the Reformation was the emphasis laid on orthodoxy. Men were to be saved by believing, but belief was defined, not in the Pauline sense of trust, but as an act of the intellect, accepting a set of propositions as true. On this basis the important thing is to believe the right doctrines, so doctrine-making became the occupation of a period which lasted for a hundred years and more. The great confessions, which still are the creedal basis in many churches, came into being. But with all this insistence on correctness of belief the churches did not thrive. They were buried under the burden of being compelled to believe exactly and so much in order to be saved. Orthodoxy was the *sine qua non*, and acceptance of doctrines covered a multitude of faults and even sins, which were more or less likely to be winked at provided men accepted the standards which were imposed. The real religious life of these long generations in the seventeenth and eighteenth centuries lay in other directions. The pietistic movement in Germany, beginning under Spener and Francke late in the seventeenth century, and the evangelical revival in England, under the lead of John and Charles Wesley and George Whitefield in the eighteenth brought tens of thousands of the common people into an immediate experience of communion with God, which warmed their hearts and sent them out rejoicing to tell others the good news of God's forgiving love and the victory they were having over sin.

With this religious quickening came a new sense of social and moral obligation. The emancipation of slaves, the reformation of the prison system, the beginnings of the Sunday-school movement, and the founding of the great missionary societies form a fitting sequel to the stirring of a real religious life among the Protestant churches. Slow to appreciate the significance of social service, the churches have in recent years taken upon themselves in a new way the burden of humanity and have made a social creed a part of their working program. The work has only yet begun, but convictions are being born in the hearts of an increasing number each year that the Church can never fufill its duty and be true to its Master without devoting itself to the task of making this world over again in all its relationships, that justice and love, mutual forbearance and respect, and an equal opportunity for all shall be the mark of our civilization.

THE CHURCH AND ITS EXPANSION

That Jesus did not undertake a mission beyond the borders of his own land is quite evident; that he did not contemplate an expansion of his Kingdom into all the world, as some would maintain, is contrary not only to definite sayings which have come down to us but to his general attitude and outlook. He who saw "all the kingdoms of the world, and the glory of them" at the very inception of his ministry, and he who was steeped in the message of the Old Testament prophets, some of whom include distant peoples as objects of God's care—such a one could scarcely fail to envisage a Kingdom which would be as inclusive as the human race. Surely the Gospel of John rightly interprets the inner meaning of Jesus' life and teaching when it shows him with his eyes fixed on the wide world and tearing down Jewish as well as Samaritan pretensions in declaring that neither at Jerusalem nor yet on Mount Gerizim was the place where the Father should be worshiped. God is Spirit, and all that is required is that he shall be worshiped "in spirit and in truth," a condition which can be met by men and women of any race or nation. This declaration has been called the "Charter of Universal Worship."

The disciples in the earliest day failed to realize the outreach of Jesus' heart and mind. It remained for the imperial-minded Paul to catch the vision of the full sweep of his Master's Kingdom. He made Christianity a world religion. In his own person he carried the gospel into the Greek world of Ephesus and Corinth and Athens, and was not satisfied until he had reached Rome. The whole motive of the book of Acts, according to Harnack, is to trace this advance, from a corner of the empire to the imperial capital itself. When once it was domiciled there, the new religion could claim to be in the full tide of the world's life and might be confident that, given time, it would reach the farthest extremities of the imperial domain. It took about three hundred years to accomplish this result. When Constantine made the new religion his own in 212, Christianity had triumphed. For many years paganism lingered on, showing considerable strength where Christianity had not as yet penetrated deeply,

237

but its doom was sealed. Constantine recognized that it was the one solid, dependable unity in his empire, and espoused its cause.

The adoption of the Church by Constantine was a remarkable testimony to the presence of a new force in the Western world with which no other could be compared. What happened in the decades which followed, when the recently persecuted faith not only was released from the dangers which had constantly hung over it but was placed in the position of favor and of authority, is not pleasant reading. In order to win more readily the many pagans who still were to be found and to make itself less forbidding to the elite and the cultured in the cities and at court, the Church lowered its standards and suffered immeasurably in its inner spirit and life. Its opposition to the loose living which prevailed everywhere was not so genuine, and the admission of pagan practices and rites into the Church contaminated the purity of its testimony. Thus saint and image worship took the place of the old polytheism and idolatry, and various rites which were introduced had a most suspicious likeness to old heathen ceremonies. The Church had conquered the world in onward and formal acquiescence, but the world had infected the Church with its pagan spirit. Undoubtedly much of this took place unconsciously and very gradually, but the influence was just as real. The Church had become a great compact organization, under the theory of the monarchial episcopacy, and this meant that it could not help acting in the manner of such an organization. Political expediency overbalanced all other considerations and made of the Church a great worldly power seeking by all means to retain its ascendancy. And when the unity of the Church, particularly in the West, was assured by the rise of the bishop of Rome to a place of commanding power, its future could no longer be in doubt. The Church which centered in Rome was the one immovable rock in the welter of upheaval and change. It held its own until the world settled down again, and, with all our criticism and condemnation of irregularity and abuse, it must be credited with saving the day for Christianity in a time when the very foundations seemed to be crumbling.

Northern Europe was completely won to the Church and to at least nominal acceptance of its Christ during the Middle Ages. Unfortunately it was so frequently only a nominal acceptance that vital religion seems never to have come to its own among large parts of the population. With little training before baptism and with no adequate instruction in the years which followed, the people remained in ignorance of the true meaning of Christianity. Pagan practices were not uprooted, and attend-

238

ance at the services and the performance of the prescribed rites and ceremonies meant little more to a vast majority than the practices they had left behind, except that they were grander and more impressive and carried with them the surer promise of favor with God and of the life beyond. With ignorance almost unchecked and loose living tardily rebuked, especially among the powerful, the conditions left much to be desired. The Church was strong, so strong that the people were held in terror of the penalties which it could inflict, and even emperors were cowed into submission. The Middle Ages present strange contrasts. There was saintly devotion unsurpassed. It was an age of cathedral building, and we visit these buildings and wonder not only at the skill of the builders but the religious devotion of those responsible for their construction. A succession of scholars kept alive the tradition of learning, and there appeared several of the most noted thinkers of the Western world. But in spite of all this the power of the Church was abused, and the bondage in which the minds of men were held must be broken before a new age could be ushered in.

When the great liberation came in the sixteenth century, a new expansion might well be looked for. A new world had been unfolded before the wondering gaze of Europe by the discovery of the Americas and by the finding of the sea route to India and the East. For hundreds of years, particularly since the crusades, Islam had stood as a barrier between West and East. Europe knew little of the teeming populations beyond and had strange ideas of their condition. But now the veil of mystery was removed, and new empires were to be founded by the youthful European nations in far-off seas. The Roman Catholic Church at once took advantage of the splendid opportunity and sent its missionaries east and west. The daring Jesuits, followed by other orders, went through incredible hardships to carry their message to Canada, South America, and to India, China, and Japan. Strange to say, Protestantism did not respond. The lands of the Reformation were not in contact in the early days with the new world being discovered as were the Catholic nations of Spain and Portugal, but there was more than that. Her task was an arduous one, to conserve the results of the upheaval in Europe, and her mind was occupied with the making of creeds and was more or less blinded by impossible methods of interpretation, which led to the conclusion that there was no longer a call to the Church to undertake a mission to the heathen. That had been done by the original apostles, and if the nations were not now Christian, that was their own fault. This was not, of course, the view of all the Protestant leaders, but at best there was very little accomplished in carrying the message of Christ to the pagan world for a hundred years and more.

But the pietistic movement in Germany and the evangelical revival in England stirred the hearts of men and led to earnest questioning concerning the non-Christian world and to the conviction that the gospel must be carried where it was not known. At the end of the eighteenth century, under the leadership of William Carey and his associates in England, action was taken, first by the Baptists, then by other bodies, until on both sides of the Atlantic and on the continent of Europe Protestantism was taking seriously the task of evangelizing the whole world. This has been one of the chief notes of church life in the nineteenth and twentieth centuries, and almost the entire non-Christian world has been occupied.

CHRISTIANITY IN A TIME OF CRISIS

Everything in the world since 1914 must be studied in the shadow of the two world wars. Nothing so sweeping has ever touched the life of mankind as these devastating world-wide conflicts. Like everything else, Christianity has felt their influence to its very core. Movements have arisen within the churches themselves which have made a re-examination of its age-long attitudes inevitable. The outward relations of the churches to the state and to various movements in human society have been not only overhauled but significantly changed.

The Christian churches have been shaken out of their complacency. They realized what had never come home to them before, that in every land, even in those in which the Church is officially established and actually an agency of government, Christians are a minority group. In those countries in which the official census figures show a large nominal body of baptized members of the Church, those who are convinced believers and can be counted on to take a definitely Christian stand are very much fewer in number. Western civilization has been called "Christian," and undoubtedly everything in the life of the Western peoples has been affected by centuries of Christian teaching and example, but the wars and the attitudes of mind which have been produced by them have revealed the sobering fact that the populace as a whole not only is ignorant of the Bible and of the most elementary facts and meaning of Christian teaching but it is not being molded in its conduct and outlook on life by the influences which should have come from Christianity. The greatest enemy of the faith is now clearly seen as secularism, the attitude that human beings individually, in society, and organized as nations are sufficient to themselves, that no force beyond human ability and will power is available, and that relations with God and the supernatural are not only unnecessary but impossible. How could there be when there are no God, no supernatural sanctions, and no immortality? Christian leaders have become aware that one of the greatest "mission" tasks in the world is that of reaching the unchurched, the pagan population at our very doors.

The churches had grown lax during the easy, prosperous, safe days before 1914. An extreme form of liberalism had made its way into the Christian ranks and was proclaiming an attenuated gospel. All the severe aspects in human nature and in the attitude of God toward sin had been toned down, and religion took an optimistic outlook on every feature of human life. It was easy to talk about the fatherhood of God and the brotherhood of man and to believe that the whole tendency of life was "onward and upward forever." The ills in human life were on the way to elimination by what man was able to do. He himself was on the way to inaugurate the Kingdom of God among young men. Of course this attitude was far from being universal, but even when it did not dominate it tinctured the thinking of men and women in the churches very widely.

Then came World War I and shattered the dream. A period of about twenty years followed, filled with chaotic thinking and uncertainty, to be followed by the even greater devastation of World War II. We are not yet over its effects and stand today on the threshold—of what? A great body of the most thoughtful men and women in every nation are increasingly convinced that we are living in a short period of deceiving lull and that we are on the verge of the horrors of World War III. The effect of these disillusioning experiences could not help affecting the interpretation of the Christian faith. There are those who still cling desperately to the old liberalism, but most of the old liberals have a very modified attitude or have gone to the opposite side, some becoming conservative and even reactionary.

The most pronounced movement is that which has been connected with the names of Karl Barth and Emil Brunner on the continent of Europe and Reinhold Niebuhr in our country. This neo-orthodoxy, as it is most frequently called, repudiates the whole attitude of liberalism. The sovereignty of God is the great point of emphasis. He is "high and lifted up," and his awful majesty and holiness separate him by an impassable gulf from man. He has become *Deus Absconditus*, the Unknown God. Over against this God, terrible in his righteous indignation, stands puny man, who was made in the image of God but lost almost every trace of that likeness through "the fall" and is so far gone from original righteousness that, in the view of Barth, there is nothing in him which can respond to the call of God. God must "crash in" and convert those who have been predestined to eternal life. This extreme view is not shared by all representatives of the school, but at best man is helpless; his reason is so impaired that it cannot be depended on to lead aright in his search for God. So thoroughgoing has been this revolt against the old complacent optimism that every doctrine in the Christian system has been subject to review and modification. It has even reached unfortunate limits in its pessimistic attitude toward human nature and the possibilities of Christian growth and victory over sin, and also in its denial of the improvability of the human lot and the ushering in of a better day for humankind.

But with all the obstacles from without and the dreadful lag from nominal Christians within, the Christian movement has made remarkable progress. The "Advance Through Storm," as Professor Kenneth Scott Latourette has called the missionary activity since 1914, has been a real advance. It has registered itself in a series of world conferences, among which the conferences of the International Missionary Council at Jerusalem in 1928, at Madras in 1938, and at Whitby, Canada, in 1947 could report marked increase in accessions to Christianity and remarkable progress in strength of organization and unity of purpose. One of the most outstanding facts which came, as it were, like a new revelation at Madras was the fact of the actual existence of a World Church and the emergence of the churches of the so-called non-Christian world as vigorous and mature members of the great Christian brotherhood. They could no longer be looked on as "mission" churches under the direction and domination of the "home" churches in the sending countries but as members on an equality with those which had given them birth and nursed them through their years of childhood and youth. The only title which could be given them, and which they themselves appreciate, was that of "younger churches" in full fellowship with the older churches, which they might now look upon as comrades and fellow workers in Christ. The meaning of this new realization was summed up in a succinct yet most significant utterance which William Temple

242

included in his address on the occasion of his enthronement as the Archbishop of Canterbury in 1942:

As though in preparation for such a time as this, God has been building up a Christian fellowship which now extends to almost every nation, and binds citizens of them all together in true unity and mutual love. No human agency has planned this. It is the result of the great missionary enterprise of the last hundred and fifty years. Almost incidentally the great World Fellowship has arisen from that enterprise. But it has arisen; it is the great new fact of our time.

The rise and expansion of Communism has come almost as a body blow to Christianity. The only parallel in Christian history is the rise of Mohammedanism in the seventh century and its expansion, which continued to be a menace until the very time of the Reformation. This menace was even more severe than the Communist advance, that is, so far as it has secured control today. But when we see Russia and all Central Europe either completely Communistic or so tightly controlled that all orders must be received from Moscow, and when the whole of Western and Northern Europe is threatened by Communist occupation and domination, and when—what is even more terrible—we realize that the atheistic and secularist Communist state is filled with hatred of Christianity and all it stands for, then we come to know the seriousness of the hour in which we live. Coupled with this, we cannot for a moment forget the engulfing of China by the Communist ideology and the threat to India and all the countries of southeast Asia. What the end will be no one can predict. That the Christian churches can survive has been and is being demonstrated on every hand, but we are able to see with equal clarity that their activities are curtailed and hampered to a degree which in places almost amounts to complete frustration—and what further restrictions will be imposed cannot be foreseen.

The ideal which was in the mind of our Lord and of the apostle Paul was that of one united fellowship of Christians, held together by loyalty to one Lord Jesus Christ. But even in the New Testament we have anticipations of divisions and differences, and in the early centuries the record of heresies and schisms is a sad tale. But the Church held together until the first great division, whch occurred in the eleventh century, when the Western or Latin Church with the Pope in Rome at its head was separated from the Eastern Church, which looked to Constantinople as its capital. This cleavage has never been healed, and the antagonism between the West and the East remains as bitter as it has ever been. The Roman Church continued on its way until the disruption of the Protestant Reformation in the sixteenth century. It then passed through a "counter-reformation," tightened its belt, and with renewed vigor pressed its claims and is now found in great strength in almost every country of the world. Its chief claim is that it is the one and only true church of Jesus Christ, that it contains all the truth in Christianity, and that the only possibility of working together and of any unity worthy the name is in complete submission to the authority of the Pope, the vicegerent of Jesus Christ on earth, and the repository of all authority among men.

By the proclamation of the "priesthood of all believers" and the right of private judgment in interpreting the Bible the Protestant movement opened the door to division and subdivision until in the United States alone the religious census reveals more than two hundred different, independent religious communions. Some are very friendly toward each other, while others are intolerant and antagonistic and refuse to co-operate at any point. But growing out of the great historic Missionary Conference held in Edinburgh in 1910 came the conviction that active steps should be taken to bring the Church into closer harmony and more active co-operation. As a result of this deepening and widely felt conviction the first conference of what was called the Faith and Order Movement was convened in Lausanne, Switzerland, in 1927, and this was followed in 1937 by a similar conference in Edinburgh. Neither of these conferences nor the organization which came out of them had any authority to speak officially for the individual communions, but they exerted a powerful influence as a demonstration of the essential unity of all Christians in their common allegiance to Jesus Christ. It came as a surprise to the delegates in Edinburgh to discover the extent of their agreement in fundamental beliefs. Only on the doctrine of the Church did real differences reveal themselves. These have proved formidable, and no formula has yet been found for intercommunion and the recognition of the validity of clerical ordination by all the churches.

Not only were the churches willing to face together the most difficult causes of cleavage, but from the angle of "life and work" they came together to deal with their contacts with the world outside the churches. A conference was held in Stockholm in 1925 and another in Oxford in 1937, the latter being known as the Conference on Church, Community, and State. By common agreement the Conference on Faith and Order in Edinburgh and that on Church, Community, and State voted to unite in the forming of a World Council of Churches, which came into being officially at a notable gathering held in Amsterdam in 1948.

Parallel with these movements has been another, that toward organic unity of various communions. Significant results have been achieved in the reuniting not only of different members of the same families of churches, but of communions which have come up out of different traditions. This has occurred in the West, but today all eyes are turned toward the movement in the younger churches in Japan, Korea, China, and the Philippines, but especially in India where bold steps have been taken in bringing together episcopal and nonepiscopal churches into a completely united communion. The way is difficult; progress is slow; all sorts of proposals are in the air; many are dubious as to methods of procedure and even as to the feasibility of any of the proposed schemes; but the rising tide of desire and conviction that all who call Jesus Christ Saviour and Lord should be one is clear evidence that slowly but surely the way is being opened for the coming of the day when all will be united in true fellowship and service.

Suggestions for Further Study

The Amsterdam Assembly Series. New York: Harper and Brothers, 1948.

Bevan, Edwyn. *Christianity.* New York: Henry Holt and Company, 1932. Valuable short acount of the entire story of Christian development.

Butterfield, Herbert. *Christianity and History.* New York: Charles Scribner's Sons, 1950. By the professor of modern history in Cambridge University.

Latourette, Kenneth Scott. *Anno Domini.* New York: Harper and Brothers, 1940.

———. *The Christian Outlook.* New York: Harper and Brothers, 1948.

———. *The History of the Expansion of Christianity.* 7 vols. New York: Harper and Brothers, 1937-45. A great authoritative history of the entire expansive movement from the earliest times to 1944. Indispensable for reference.

———. *The Unquenchable Light.* New York: Harper and Brothers, 1941.

Van Dusen, Henry P. *World Christianity.* New York and Nashville: Abingdon-Cokesbury Press, 1947. An authoritative account of the movement toward unity "yesterday, today, tomorrow."

INDEX

Abbasid caliphs, 220
Abu Bakr, 210
Abu Talib, 205
Achaemenides, 135
Acharya, 101
Adigranth, 128-30
Aeschylus, 79
Agni, 93-94
Agreement (Ijma), in Islam, 214
Ahmad Khan, 226
Ahmadiya Movement in India, 226
Ahura Mazda (Mazdah), 133
Ajiva, 122-23
Al-Ashari, 217
Alexander the Great, in India, 150; in Persia, 135
Al-Ghazzali, 219
Algonquian family of Indians, 37
Ali, 208, 222-23
Aligarh University, 226
Al Mohammed, the Bab, 223
All-fathers, in animistic religion, 42
Almsgiving, in Islam, 215
Amaterasu-o-mi-Kami, 178
Ambedkar, B. R., 107
Amen, 56
Amenhotep IV, 60-61
Ameretat, 133
Ames, E. S., definition of religion, 18
Amesha Spenta, 133
Amida, 183-84
Amir Ali, Syed, 226
Amitabha (Amida), 153
Amritsar, 127
Analects, 165
Ancestor worship, as origin of religion, 25; in China, 161-62
Andrae, Tor, on sanity of Mohammed, 208; on inspiration of Mohammed, 209
Angra Mainyu (Ahriman), 133
Animal-worship, in Egypt, 68-69
Animism, in Babylonia, 66; in Greece, 72; in lands of Southern Buddhism, 156; in China, 160
Animistic religion, name of, 32
Annam, 155
Aphrodite, 75
Apollo, 74-75
Aramaiti, 133
Aranyakas, 96
Ares, 75
Arhat (Arahat, Arahant), 147

Aristotle, 79-80
Ark of the Covenant, 193
Arnold, Matthew, definition of religion, 16
Artemis, 74
Arya Samaj, 113
Aryans, in India, 91, 131
Asha, 133
Ashur, 67
Asoka, 150
Asrava, 123
Astrology, in Babylonia, 69
Atargatis, 89
Aten, 60
Athanasius, 234
Athena, 72-73, 75
Attalus, 87
Attis, 87-88
Augustine, 235
Augustus Caesar, 86-87
Avalokitesvara (Avalokita, Padmapani), 157
Avatars, of Vishnu, 108-9
Avesta, 133

Ba (Bai), 64
Baal worship, 194
Bab, 223
Babylon, 66-68
Bagdad, 221
Bahaism (Babism), 223
Bahaullah, 223
Bain, Alexander, on instinct, 21
Bali, 155
Barth, A., on Varuna, 93
Barth, Karl, 241-42
Benares, 142
Benares Hindu University, 116
Besant, Mrs. Annie, 115-16
Bhabha, H. T., on Parsi belief, 137
Bhagavad-Gita (Gita), 110
Bhakti, 110
Bhaktimarga, way of loving devotion, 98
Blavatsky, Madame, 115
Bodhidharma, 173, 182
Bodhisattva, 154; in Tibet, 157
Brahma, Creator, 108
Brahman, the Absolute, 108
Brahmanas, 96
Brahmins, priests, 105-6
Brahmo Samaj, 113
Brown, Lewis, on origin of religion, 21
Brunner, Emil, 241
Buddha, Gautama, life and work, 139-43

247

Budge, Ernest, on Amenhotep IV, 61
Burma, Buddhism in, 156
Bushido, 188

Caliphate, abolished, 225
Caliphs, 220-21
Cambodia, 155
Canaanites, 193-94
Carey, William, 240
Caro, Joseph, 198
Carter, J. B., on Etruscan influence, 85; on Sibylline books, 85
Cash, W. Wilson, on seclusion of women in Islam, 224
Caste, defined, 102-7; origin of, 105; good and evil in, 106
Cave, Sydney, on Siva worship, 109
Celsus, on Egyptian religion, 56, 62
Ceres, 85
Ceylon, Buddhism in, 152, 155
Chamberlain, B. H. 190
Chang Tao-ling, 171
Ch'an tsung school of Buddhism, 173
Charles Martel, 219
Child marriage, in India, 104
Ch'in dynasty, 160
Ching T'su-tsung, school of Buddhism, 193
Chou dynasty, 164
Chthonian gods, 75
Chu Hsi, 169
Cicero, definition of religion, 13
Clarke, W. N., definition of religion, 20
Clodd, Edward, on tree worship, 39
Cochin, China, 155
Codrington, R. H., on mana, 37
Coe, G. A., on religious nature of man, 21
Comte, A., on fetishism, 41
Confucius, life and work, 163-69
Confucianism in Japan, 186-90
Constantine, 237
Council of Jerusalem, 233
Covenant at Sinai, 192-93
Creation, in Bible and in Babylonian myths, 68
Creed of Islam, 214
Cromer, Lord, on Egypt, 223
Cybele, 87

Dai Nichi, 181
Dalai Lama, 157
Darwish orders, 219
Das, Govinda, on transmigration, 97; on Hindu standards of orthodoxy, 102
Davids, Mrs. C. A. Rhys, on life and character of Gautama, 145, 153

Davids, T. W. Rhys, on death of the Buddha, 143-44
Dayananda Sarasvati, 113
Death, in animistic religion, 40
DeGroot, J. J. M., on ancestor worship in China, 162
Deists, English, on definition of religion, 14; on origin of religion, 22
Delhi, 221
Delphi, 74
Demeter, in Greece, 75, 77
Dependent Origination, in Buddhism, 148
Desire, the root of evil in Buddhism, 141-42, 145-46
Devi, 109
Dhalla, M. N., on final victory of Ahura Mazda, 134
Dharmakaya, 155
Diana, 86
Difference, doctrine of, in Islam, 218
Digambara, 120-21
Dionysus, in Greece, 76
Divination, in Babylonia, 68-69
Dokhmas, 136
Dravidians, 93
Dreams, among animistic peoples, 36-37
Dualism, in Zoroastrianism, 135-36
Durga, 109

Ea, 67
Eastern Orthodox Churches, 243-44
Edinburgh Missionary Conference, 244
Egypt, as gift of Nile, 55
Eleusinian Mysteries, 76
Elijah, 194
Eliot, Sir Charles, on Zen Buddhism, 182
Emperor-worship, in Rome, 87; in Japan, 178, 189-90
Enneads, in Egypt, 58
Epicureanism, 80
Etruscans, 84
Euphrates, 66-67
Euripides, 79
Evangelical Revival, in England, 240
Exogamy, 45

Fairbanks, Arthur, on Greek gods, 75
Faith and Order Movement, 245
Farquhar, J. N., on Aryans in India 91-92; on Brahman, 99
Fasting, in Islam, 215
Fatima, 205, 222
Ferdinand and Isabella, 220
Festivals, in Rome, 84
Fetishism, 40-42

248